# SOCIAL WORK IN A
# SUSTAINABLE WORLD

**Also Available from Lyceum Books, Inc.**

Advisory Editors:  Thomas M. Meenaghan, *New York University*
                   Ira C. Colby, *University of Houston*

STRAIGHT TALK ABOUT PROFESSIONAL ETHICS,
by Kim Strom-Gottfried

SECONDARY TRAUMATIC STRESS AND THE
CHILD WELFARE PROFESSIONAL,
by Josephine G. Pryce, Kimberly K. Shackelford, and
David H. Pryce

THE DYNAMICS OF FAMILY POLICY,
by Cynthia J. Rocha and Alice K. Johnson Butterfield

SOCIAL WORK WITH VOLUNTEERS,
by Michael E. Sherr, foreword by John G. McNutt

EMPOWERING VULNERABLE POPULATIONS:
COGNITIVE-BEHAVIORAL INTERVENTIONS,
by Mary Keegan Eamon

SOCIAL WORK PRACTICE WITH FAMILIES:
A RESILIENCY-BASED APPROACH,
by Mary Patricia Van Hook

SCHOOL SOCIAL WORK: PRACTICE, POLICY,
AND RESEARCH, 6E
by Robert Constable, Carol Rippey Massat, Shirley McDonald,
and John P. Flynn

HUMAN BEHAVIOR FOR SOCIAL WORK PRACTICE:
A DEVELOPMENTAL-ECOLOGICAL FRAMEWORK,
by Wendy L. Haight and Edward H. Taylor

# SOCIAL WORK IN A SUSTAINABLE WORLD

Nancy L. Mary
*California State University, San Bernardino*

LYCEUM
BOOKS, INC.

Chicago, Illinois

© Lyceum Books, Inc., 2008

Published by

LYCEUM BOOKS, INC.
5758 S. Blackstone Ave.
Chicago, Illinois 60637
773+643-1903 (Fax)
773+643-1902 (Phone)
lyceum@lyceumbooks.com
http://www.lyceumbooks.com

6  5  4  3  2     08  09  10  11

ISBN 978-1-933478-19-7

Library of Congress Cataloging-in-Publication Data

Mary, Nancy L.
   Social work in a sustainable world / Nancy L. Mary.
      p. cm.
   Includes bibliographical references and index.
   ISBN 978-1-933478-19-7
   1. Social service—Philosophy. 2. Public welfare. 3. Human
services. 4. Social ecology. 5. Sustainable living. 6. Sustainable
development. I. Title.
   HV40.M428   2008
   361.301—dc22

                                                    2007042994

To Dr. Teresa Morris, colleague and friend. May you continue to be a source of nurturance for my mind and my soul.

# Contents

# Preface

This book is about new thinking in science. It is also about faith and hope.

I have been a social worker for thirty years. For the first five, I didn't think much about issues beyond those affecting people with developmental disabilities, for that was my field of practice. Then I became a parent and everything changed. I walked around scrutinizing the face of every adult and thought, "I wonder what they looked like as an infant? Someone's son or daughter. The love of their life! Perfect. Innocent. The future." I was in love with everyone in the world. In short, I had a paradigm shift—big time.

After reading a book called *The Fate of the Earth*, I joined an organization called Beyond War. My focus now extended to the future beyond my own life span to my child's. My worldview had expanded, and I concluded that if we did not change our course of action, as a species, we might not be around too long—nor would my children's children.

So, as I entered my current profession, I carried this concern with me: What is the responsibility of social work in ensuring that we have a future? What is our role in influencing decisions that will help sustain families, communities, nations, and even the planet? Thus, I have written this book. It is intended to be an exploration for social workers at any level in training. Because the book expands the person-in-environment paradigm, it could be easily used in the study of human behavior and the social environment. With a new paradigm of social work practice and suggestions for new practice roles, the book can be used in both micro and macro practice classes, as well as in policy advocacy.

My task as an individual is to figure out my place on this magnificent planet. I believe that my job as a social worker is to help others do so but in a way that connects them to others and to an understanding that the world, just like people, is fragile. So, part of my calling is to help maintain our home for those that follow after us. It is in this spirit that I offer you this book.

# Acknowledgments

My mentor, Dr. Alex Norman, always told me in class that context is everything. He is right. I want to thank him for his insights, humor, and patience with my "hotshot" questions.

My mother sacrificed a lot to put me through school. I am grateful to her for her faith. She had trust that I would not go away to school to be closer to my boyfriend and become pregnant and waste her money on a very expensive, private liberal arts education. She was right.

My students are the reason I go to work. What other job affords one the pleasure of dialogue, tutelage, and discovery, with no heavy lifting, and pays one to do so! Everyone should be so fortunate.

My husband, Ed, and my children, Lane and Seth, have been a source of strength, laughter, and pride for me. I want to thank them for their accomplishments, their antics, and their wisdom. I am grateful they saw the soundness of my priority of reading wall-to-wall books rather than cleaning the floor underneath them.

My helper, Tom Meenaghan, was extremely astute in the clarification of my thinking about this material. Thank you, Tom.

My publisher, David Follmer, and my editor, Katherine Faydash, at Lyceum, are to be thanked for their patience and skills. I thought I could write, till I ran in to Katherine!

# CHAPTER 1

# Social Work's Role in a Sustainable Future

We are now experiencing a moment of significance beyond what any of us can imagine. . . . The distorted dream of an industrial technological paradise is being replaced by the more viable dream of a mutually enhancing human presence within an ever-renewing organic-based Earth community.

—Thomas Berry, *The Great Work*

The world is changing. Our human activities are clearly becoming global in nature. Our understanding of nature—the infrastructure upon which all humankind rests—is changing as well. Yet social work continues to hold a limited view of its role in what we now know are globally interconnected social problems. These problems cannot be solved through a casework or therapeutic approach alone. We have reached a point in our understanding of systems at which social welfare must be considered part of a larger global imperative of planetary survival. There is a profound connection between the micro problems that individuals and families manifest (e.g., environmental pollution, the lack of sustaining and meaningful work, addiction, domestic violence) and the macro problems that local and global communities experience. It takes a major shift in the ways we think about our work, our world, and our mission to make change in the lives of people and their environment.

A big part of this connection is a better understanding of Mother Earth and of our impact on and relationship to her in the many roles we play. As inhabitants of the planet, we may need to shift our relationship with nature from one of exploitation to one of respect, in order to preserve its diversity and figure out ways to coexist with all its species. We are consumers, producers, and laborers. But the market's mantra of growth has driven our

1

economic activities, with only secondary attention to the externalities of such growth in environmental devastation and global
poverty. As the role model of this mantra, China has now sur-
passed the United States in its use of all natural resources, save oil.
This global race to keep up with the Joneses may be unsustainable.
As citizens of the most powerful democratic nation, our behavior
may need to broaden from passive voter to involved public citizen
in the creation of and participation in decision-making structures
and agendas that go beyond interest-group politics and a dominator model of society. Our role on the global stage is critical as well.
Through the influence of nongovernmental organizations, citizen
action groups, government efforts, and other mechanisms we
have yet to invent, we can collaborate in efforts to save and to sustain our life on this planet. As social workers, we are members of
a profession with a knowledge base of social science that we draw
upon to understand the world, but we also are called to be change
agents. Thus, our use of science is tied to a belief system, a set of
values, a purposefulness. Given what we are coming to understand
about the interconnectedness and vulnerability of our natural and
social systems, some shifts in thinking about how we perceive and
practice our calling may well be necessary.

The purpose of this book is to reexamine the profession of social work in light of new literature about systems, the material and
spiritual worlds, and the social institutions we have created to sustain our world. The scope of this reexamination focuses on social
work as it is practiced in the United States—the country I know
best, wherein I have spent my life as a social work practitioner and
educator. The United States is also the country with the greatest
wealth and resources to influence change in thinking about global
sustainability, should we choose to do so. However, this book also
employs a global perspective on social welfare and social work
practice. This is not to be confused with an international approach, which usually refers to social work activities in many countries, often in a comparative way. Rather, the approach of this
book is that human activities and the institutions we create cannot
be contained within any one country or system, but they affect the
world as a community, the natural environment, and the planet as
a whole.

Let us first examine the current paradigm of social work: how
we understand the world, how we perceive society and social problems, and how we approach social work practice. I will discuss the

shortcomings of this paradigm in light of the challenges facing us today. As the book progresses, I will examine the overarching concepts of sustainability and its application to major systems (e.g., the natural environment), the idea of all systems as an interconnected web of life, the economy, and the polity. Finally, to meet these challenges, I propose a new sustainable model of social work that involves an expanded ideology and mission, and I discuss how these translate into social work policies and practice strategies in a sustainable world.

## THE PARADIGM: HOW DO SOCIAL WORKERS UNDERSTAND THE WORLD TODAY?

Social workers frame the world as a social construction. How we frame it determines our focus, the knowledge we bring to bear, and the directions we take in policy and practice. The selection and focus on a social unit—be it the individual, the family, the organization, or the economic system—is an act that then translates into professional methods of intervention in social service organizations. The concepts and theories related to these social units are the ones that schools of social work education emphasize. They influence how we conceive of social problems and social change in our ultimate pursuit of functioning and sustainable societies.

In science and social work, the current movement to understand the world is from the reductionist perspective. We employ a narrow lens in an attempt to control the elements of interest for an eventual intervention. Sometimes we use a microscope and find the locus of the problem within the organism. Sometimes we use a telescope to frame the unit of analysis—the individual or the family—within the system that immediately surrounds it, which screens out other systems that interact with the unit under focus.

This reductionist perspective is most apparent in the fields of mental illness and substance abuse, two of the most rapidly growing fields of social work practice in the United States. For people with mental heath problems, social work currently focuses on an individual's presenting problems and a diagnosis. Genes, abnormal brain functioning, metabolism, nutrition, and other biochemical processes are of great interest to scientists at the National Institute of Mental Health, social workers, and agencies providing mental health services. Unlike the array of comprehensive mental health services offered in the field thirty-five years ago, the mandate of these agencies has been curtailed, and they now offer most of their services to people with severe mental illness, who often have a dual diagnosis of substance abuse and mental illness. The disease model prevails in both the substance abuse and mental illness fields of practice, and pays little attention to the host of contributing societal factors, such as lack of affordable housing, life in violent households and neighborhoods, poverty, unemployment and/or the lack of jobs with livable wages, and the increased exposure to illegal enterprises and criminal behavior that often accompanies these factors.

Thus, the most common unit of analysis in the assessment and intervention in social problems related to mental health, substance abuse, and many other fields has become the individual. For example, the focus of study and the intervention in problems of aging people is biological decline and disability, not limited income, lack of long-term-care options, and ageism. As gerontology becomes a bigger part of the field of medicine, the concern of social workers is on the assessment and treatment of organic pathology and less on the social and economic forces that limit older people's opportunities to maintain quality of life. The reductionist perspective abounds. The problem is not a lack of affordable housing but homelessness. Welfare reform addresses not poverty but a lack of personal responsibility and job skills. The problem of alcohol abuse has been stripped of its social context completely; alcoholism is a disease (Meenaghan, Kilty, & McNutt, 2004). Individual problems are pervasive; social problems are less manifest. Even the media support this perspective. For example, the movie *Crash* dwells not on institutional racism but on misunderstandings due to individuals' poor communication patterns. Such scenarios are all about reductionism.

Why such a narrow field of vision? Because the sociopolitical environments that surround and interact with science and social work support the use of a microscope to identify the problem. Three trends exemplify how the individual has become the unit of analysis for pinpointing and intervening in social problems: (1) the continuation of a residual perspective on the role of social welfare, (2) the accompanying accountability movement of the 1980s, and (3) the emphasis on the study of the individual over the study of social behavior in schools of social work.

Many social work historians have documented the waxing and waning of the residual perspective versus the institutional perspective on social welfare in the United States (e.g., Day, 2000; Popple & Leighninger, 2005). Exceptions to the country's historically dominant residual perspective in the role of social welfare are the Great Depression, the civil rights movement, and the War on Poverty of the 1960s and 1970s. However, since the oil crisis and burgeoning social welfare expenditures of the mid-1970s, governments and society as a whole have shifted their attention from society's ills to individuals' ills. The current belief system, intact since it emerged in the mid-1970s, holds that the economy and the job market are healthy, and people who are suffering are the unhealthy ones.

For example, an estimated 12 million households pay more than 50% of their yearly income for housing, either in rent or in mortgage payments. A family with one full-time minimum-wage earner cannot find an affordable two-bedroom apartment anywhere in the United States (Bodaken, 2000). Yet throughout the 1980s and 1990s, we continued to build shelters and special segregated schools for children of the homeless, the "unfortunate few" who need to get back on their feet. The result: the victims get blamed.

This residual perspective has not always been the case. Today, at the federal level, many government consultants have backgrounds in business. However, in the 1930s, administrator Harry Hopkins and social worker Frances Perkins, who later became secretary of labor, advised the president on responses to poverty and unemployment. Interest grew in program evaluation and cost-benefit analysis as it applied to social service interventions. Later, as a result of the War on Poverty in the 1960s, opportunities opened up for social workers to head social service agencies. Schools of social work began to shift their focus from community organization to administration in order to teach social workers how to manage social service organizations.

But in the 1980s, the accountability or managerial movement emerged and today it reinforces the residual perspective of social welfare by blaming victims for their failures (McDonald, 2003). As welfare expenditures began to increase in the mid-1970s, the concern for accountability, effectiveness, and efficiency in social service agencies grew. Increased contracting for services promoted greater monitoring of costs and services. In the past twenty-five years, the managerial model has pervaded social service organizations with its models of managed care and managed behavioral health care. Concurrently, there has been an increase in nonprofit management specializations in masters programs in business administration and public administration, which stress the administrative control of resources. However, social work frames the administrative curriculum in social work values and ethics. Recent research has shown that of the models of nonprofit management, master of social work curricula tend to emphasize advocacy, public policy, and community organizing over the financial management, strategic planning, and legal issues that masters programs in business administration and public administration emphasize (Mirabella & Wish, 2000). Clearly, different professions teach social service administration differently.

Nevertheless, the reality of the managerial movement is that the role of the social service manager has become one of trying to manage the status quo. Faced with shrinking resources and the call for efficiency, social work managers have turned their attention from the interests of clients to the select constituent interests of funders and regulators in their concern for accountability.

Accountability is not a bad thing. The question is, accountability to whom and for what purpose? Of course social service administrators have to be accountable for how they spend money; however, the goal of social work in social service organizations is to add to the social health of community members. In addition, the code of ethics of the National Association of Social Workers (NASW) supports the goal to create organizations that empower clients and to fight against the impersonality, dehumanization, uniformity, dependency, and disempowerment that modern organizations often impose on the individuals and families they serve. Thus, accountability in terms of evaluating social service programs should involve both indicators that capture the degree to which programs add to the social health of clientele and the clientele themselves.

But here again, the unit of analysis for determining program effectiveness is the individual. Over the past twenty-five years, accountability and program effectiveness have translated into an emphasis on measuring individual outcomes, whereas "outcome goals might have focused on reducing the disparity between the rich and the poor; increasing supports for women and racial and ethnic minorities so that they have full and fair access to major social institutions; and reducing the need and risk associated with gender, race and ethnic origin" (Meenaghan, Kilty, & McNutt, 2004, pp. 17–18).

The focus has been on the individual and the family because they are the units of analysis and intervention. The focus of accountability in terms of outcomes in social services today is not the number of consumer-owned economic enterprises in the community, the number of consumers earning a livable wage, or even the number of jobs created, but job readiness and the number of new job skills that clients learn. Program evaluation, then, focuses on the assessment of client growth in treatment, education, rehabilitation, or other aspects of individual change and not on social goals, such as increasing social networks and the power of groups and neighborhoods to help themselves and build their own capabilities and resources; organizational goals, such as creating participatory work environments and empowering staff and clients to contribute to these environments; or client input and assessments, such as the methods and quality of staff-client interactions and outcomes of services.

This narrow field of vision in defining the locus of problems in the individual rather than in the organization or the larger social system leads us to the knowledge we bring to bear on the problems we face.

## WHAT KNOWLEDGE DO WE TURN TO?

The mandates of the accrediting body of social work, the Council on Social Work Education (CSWE), indirectly guide the initial knowledge base of the social work profession in the United States. The CSWE mandates foundation year curriculum in the following areas: at-risk populations, social and economic justice, human behavior and the social environment (HBSE), social welfare policy and services, social work practice, and research, as well as "theories and knowledge of biological, sociological, cultural, psychological, and spiritual development across the life span; the range of social systems in which people live (individual, family, group, organizational, and community) and the ways social systems promote or deter people in maintaining or achieving health and well-being" (CSWE, 2004). However, each individual program can determine how it packages this content.

Current research on HBSE course content and textbooks suggests that the content related to the social context of behavior may not be presented comprehensively or very coherently across courses (Stone, 2004). Other findings suggest that "increased attention to content related to the macro social environment and to the inter-relationships of macro, meso, and micro forces would strengthen HBSE texts" (Taylor, Mulroy, & Austin, 2004, p. 92).

The dominant paradigm of HBSE as it is taught within schools of social work is that the social environment is an important context for human development and adaptation. Ecological systems theory focuses on the interface between individuals and their environment. Attention is paid to understanding the impact of family, culture, and society on the individual, and societal institutions provide context. Though the attention spent on social theories varies from program to program, the focus is most often on psychological and psychosocial theories of human development (e.g., Ashford, LeCroy, & Lortie, 2001).

Consider the individual focus in terms of social workers who study and work with families in the United States. We claim to have distinguished between family therapy and family-centered practice. Acknowledging that family practitioners have often neglected the larger social context within which families function, we claim greater responsibility, as social workers, for macro interventions such as advocacy, legislative action, boycotts, or protests. But we often frame practice with families as family treatment and target the family as the system for change.

Even international studies of families that purport to examine a wide range of factors contributing to child and family welfare end up with a focus on family dynamics and structural characteristics of families, with very little attention to the need for intervention and change in the social systems that create poverty, unemployment, and family difficulties (Zeitlin et al., 1995). In a study by Zeitlin and colleagues (1995), the variables that determine child welfare and development and family social wellness are such constructs as family dynamics, family management, family carrying capacity, family beliefs, and family boundary maintenance, with the family as the unit of focus. It is interesting that the final chapter of the study consists of policy recommendations (e.g., employment intervention, changes in male-dominant inheritance laws), which have little relevance to the study's narrow unit of analysis.

In contrast, if we make connections among individual and social problems and the social, economic, and political structures that contribute to these problems, we can integrate the knowledge base of theories of individual development with those of social structure and social change. Indeed, our profession is committed to change across social systems and to social justice, as the CSWE code of ethics articulates. This requires that we understand theories of social structure, social institutions of the economy and the polity, and social change.

Recent encouraging efforts to break the micro-macro divide between understanding individuals and understanding the systems with which they interact and cocreate should be acknowledged. Katherine van Wormer (2006) has made the connection across systems in her approach to social work and social welfare. In collaboration with Fred Besthorn and Thomas Keefe, she offers a broader approach to the person-in-environment framework in her latest two volumes on HBSE (2007a, 2007b). The authors also pay long-awaited attention to the natural environment and consider ecology part of the social environment.

Joe Schriver's *Human Behavior and the Social Environment: Shifting Paradigms in Essential Knowledge for Social Work Practice* (2004) opens up our thinking about all levels of systems, from the individual to the international arena. This book stimulates critical thinking by exploring each system from both the traditional worldview, or scientific, empirical modern paradigm, and alternative worldviews that are more humanistic, subjective, and interpretive in nature. For example, Schriver examines development using Piaget's (1952) theory and the perspectives of other groups, such as Cass's (1984) model of homosexual identity formation or Cross's (1971) model of African American identity development. This emphasis on multiple ways of knowing through multiple lenses, however, is still rare in the mainstream, narrow-lens approach that dominates today's study of HBSE and the practice environment.

## THE CURRENT APPROACH TO PRACTICE: THE NARROW LENS

Certainly, since its inception, the social work profession has played an important role in helping vulnerable and less privileged people cope with the ill effects of social disorganization and poverty that have resulted from a growing industrial society. Having said that, I submit that in the United States today, social work is, for the most part, irrelevant to the goals of a sustainable future—not bad, just irrelevant.

A 2006 study on the workforce by the NASW and the Center for Workforce Studies supports my view. A random sample of 10,000 social workers was drawn from the social work licensure lists of forty-eight states and the District of Columbia. Here are some of the findings of that study:

- The respondents spent most of their time providing direct service (96%). Relatively few social workers spend as many as twenty hours per week in a role other than direct practice (61%) or management (20%).

- The most commonly reported practice area of the respondents was mental health (37%), followed by child welfare/family (13%) and health (13%).

- Survey respondents treated clients with various problems that are physical, psychological, or social in nature, ranging from psychological stressors and mental illness to neurological conditions, developmental disabilities, and substance abuse.

The study's sample does not include unlicensed social workers, which may skew the results toward a more clinical profile of social work, as settings such as mental health, hospitals, and even public child welfare in many states require licensure for social workers to retain their job or to be promoted within the organization. However, the emphasis of social work on treating clients who have multiple "maladies" and the pursuit of private practice are trends that have grown significantly over the past quarter century.

Social workers are the primary providers of mental health services in the United States—and our profession is under attack. With the optimism of the twentieth century and the development of the welfare state and the social work profession, social work was, at its best, a force for collective activity to improve social conditions and to help people live their lives to the fullest. But the winds have shifted. Many of us feel that if we attempt to target the larger social problems and fight social injustice or to work with the poor and advocate for their empowerment, we become members of a profession at risk of occupational ostracism.

Catherine McDonald (2003), an Australian social worker, points out that there has been a global marginalization of the role of social work since World War II. In the United States, we have also experienced this marginalization over the past thirty years. As the support for human services at the state and federal levels has waned, social work has been one of many professions struggling with the cutbacks in social and health services and with managed care. In responding to these trends, social workers have followed an aspirant model of professionalism (Jones, 2000), pursuing occupational status and security by adopting strategies of the established professions of medicine and law.

Thus, there has been increased attention to title protection, clinical licensing, and continuing education in clinical social work at state and national conferences. The insiders of this professional group are the licensed clinicians, who are afforded status and a degree of respect; they are those whom local communities, the state, and broader society regard as "real" professionals. Outsiders are those who are not licensed and who work with the poor on projects in domestic violence, homelessness, HIV/AIDS prevention, registering citizens to vote, and even "taking back the streets," but they do not do so on company time.

As social workers, we are not victims in this process; we are co-conspirators. Over the past twenty-five to thirty years, social workers have been members of a destabilized occupational group in an environment that has made difficult the macro roles of social development, community development, and political advocacy for all interest groups. As professionals, this has created much anxiety for us. What do we have control over? Can we protect our own boundaries from nurses or case managers, or from marriage and family therapists? Can we assert ourselves in the same management arenas where MBAs are flexing their muscles of efficiency and cost-benefit analysis? Do we know what we are doing, and can we prove it to other occupational interest groups that are vying for our business and to a society that hammers at us daily about accountability for precious tax dollars spent on social services?

In response to these pressures, social workers have opted to turn our attention to that which we think we can control: individual diagnosis, treatment planning, and measurement of individual outcomes. But we have other options. This environment of outcome-focused managerialism has whittled away professional autonomy and privilege and has tightened the grip on managers' accountability, and McDonald (2003) suggests that we consider some other routes to the future. For example, we could reposition ourselves in the workforce by rearticulating what we do along a continuum of work from paraprofessional to professional, or we could turn our attention to global and international social work arenas. We could take a critical theory approach to social work, and in recognition of the need to empower our constituents at every level, we could develop interventions aimed at greater citizen participation and democratic environments in the organization, the municipality, and state and federal arenas. Or we could turn to evidence-based practice (EBP).

Social workers in the United States and the United Kingdom have clearly chosen the fourth option. In fact, a 2002 NASW policy statement called for 25% of all dollars spent on health, mental health, and substance abuse to be spent on research-based intervention and prevention strategies (Proctor, 2002). What is EBP and why are we gravitating toward it as a way to validate our professional practice?

## THE LURE OF EVIDENCE-BASED PRACTICE

Paradigms of EBP essentially stress the role of the practitioner as a clinician and a user of scientific findings. Interventions are tested through randomized, controlled trials, and those that are effective are then deemed useful to service programs (Gellis & Reid, 2004). Developed in the field of medicine, EBP found its way into mental health via controlled experiments conducted during the 1990s that grew out of the experiments of psychologists and psychiatrists (Reid & Fortune, 2003). Social workers' move into prominence in clinical mental health services validates our expertise as scientists and clinicians. Evidence-based practice, then, positions social work alongside more prestigious professions.

However, EBP has not been embraced without criticism (Mullen & Streiner, 2004; Parton, 2000; Witkin & Harrison, 2001), and a major limitation to the approach in the twenty-first century is that it focuses a narrow lens on the problem and the solution. Specifically, EBP narrowly defines the problem, the relevant evidence, from a positivist worldview. Within EBP there is an accepted hierarchy of evidence (Lang, 2005) in which randomized, controlled trials are at the top, and practice wisdom, values, and other ways of knowing the world either are lower on the hierarchy or are screened out completely. The aim of EBP is not so much to understand the phenomenon at hand as it is to control and predict it. The focus is on diagnosing and treating people who are experiencing society's problems or coping with their complex human conditions. Thus, that brings us back to the locus of the problem and the solution in the individual.

The result of this narrow focus screens out the divergent knowledge that is brought into play in the social work context of problem solving with the person and the environment. Any rigid attempt to apply a narrow template of empirical methodology devalues the ever-changing sociopolitical, value-laden context of practice (e.g., the culture of both client and organization, the demands of competing constituents of the agency-rendered technology, different definitions among client and worker of the desirable outcome). Thus, client and worker are assumed to have compatible worldviews and interests, and the process of intervention follows a rational problem-solving model. Client and clinician quickly agree on the client's problem, and the expert clinician follows the prescribed regime; the client, who is the receiver of services, is conditioned to comply with the program.

The process of social work, then, becomes an exercise in technical rationality, with replicable techniques derived from positivist scientific research and applied in the same way as, say, engineering becomes the application of engineering science (Parton, 2000). This process perpetuates modern linear thinking. The interconnectedness of mind, body, spirit, and the social and political environments that are ever present in any practice situation—which both influence and are influenced by the individual—are not seen through a narrow lens and thus are of little concern. The appeal of using a narrow lens is understandable, given our professional anxiety when we are faced with the complexity of the world and the pressure for social workers to carve out a place in which we can control and predict the results of our efforts. If we can select a small-enough unit of analysis, we can diagnose problem behaviors, apply a strict set of interventions, and prove our effectiveness, all while greatly reducing our anxiety. We are technicians; clients are the raw material. We can measure the results on the basis of the evidence of individual outcomes that we expect as a direct result of our application.

But the world of human behavior and the environment is complex and interconnected. The world of clients is complex.

The work of social workers is interactive and reflexive. It influences and is influenced by the client's worldview, and by his or her natural and sociopolitical settings. Thus, we must use "multiple lenses to focus on the actual experience of persons in interaction with groups and communities" (Schriver, 2004, p. 16), because culture and myriad other factors mold their realities or worldviews. We use our methods, then, to negotiate solutions to problems rather than to impose solutions (Parton, 2000). The context of the practice world is not just a backdrop to be screened out of the action—and it is not subject to prediction or calculation. A postmodern or transformational view of the world accepts human difference, diversity, ambiguity, chaos, and uncertainty as the stuff of the real world. Nor is practice rational and value free. It is driven by our own values, by the ethics of the profession, by the exigencies of organization and society, and by the hopes and dreams of our clients.

In summary, if we use a narrow lens to focus on the individual as the unit of analysis, and if intervention is the application of empirical evidence of positivist research designs, there is no place in our work for alternative worldviews. Practice wisdom, intuition, belief systems, culture, faith, and other nonrational aspects of human behavior found in clients, organizations, and policy arenas are, at best, secondary evidence. But these things comprise the very stuff of global social problems that threaten our future welfare and that of the planet. We may be able to agree on some of the evidence that helps us describe circumstances around us or on what we should do to help, for example, malnourished children. But when the context is a war-torn community, whether South Los Angeles or Darfur, Sudan, the solutions are many and complex, and they change as the context changes. The response depends on what country we are in, that country's status in the world community, the stability of the political system, the position of the United Nations (UN), and the ultimate ability of the community to pull together resources for now and for the future. Such a lens is a broad, multifaceted one. The process is messy, interactive, and political. It is the work of a social worker.

Thus, if we intend to play a viable role in changing systems that affect us all, we must broaden our lens. We must shift our paradigm of thinking about the world and about our practice within it. To make such a shift, we first must examine what a paradigm is.

What is the modern paradigm within which social work evolved? What is new-paradigm thinking? Finally, where will a new paradigm of social work take us?

## WHAT IS A PARADIGM?

Thomas Kuhn, in his 1996 book *The Structure of Scientific Revolutions*, explains that modern scientific paradigms are coherent traditions of scientific research. These traditions rest on the commitment of a scientific community to the same rules and standards of scientific practice, which include laws, theories, application, and instrumentation. *Merriam-Webster Collegiate Dictionary*, tenth edition, defines a paradigm, broader than a scientific theory, as a "philosophical and theoretical framework of a scientific school or discipline, within which theories, laws, and generalizations, and the experiments performed in support of them are formulated."

Fritjof Capra, a philosopher and physicist, has taken Kuhn's definition and expanded it to that of a social paradigm, "a constellation of concepts, values, perceptions and practices shared by a community that forms a particular vision of reality that is the basis of the way the community organizes itself" (Capra & Steindl-Rast, 1991, p. 34).

So, a paradigm is larger than a theory. It is a way of looking at the world. Kuhn has written extensively about when and how the paradigms of so-called normal science shift, when a field or discipline can no longer solve the various problems it addresses within the framework of the existing worldview (e.g., Newtonian science's inability to explain the atom). Capra and a growing number of new systems thinkers posit that we are in a situation today where the old social paradigms have reached their limits. We may not be able to solve threats such as nuclear war, environmental degradation, and persistent world poverty through the modern worldview paradigm.

## WHAT IS THE MODERN PARADIGM?

Before 1500, the predominant paradigm of the medieval world was organic. People lived in small communities that were close to nature, and they experienced the material and spiritual worlds as interdependent. The scientific framework rested on two sources of information: Aristotle and the church. In the thirteenth century, Thomas Aquinas combined Christian theology and Aristotle's view of nature, which led to the medieval worldview that featured both reason and faith. The goal was to understand the meaning of this world and humankind's place within it, not to control or predict it (Capra, 1982).

With the Enlightenment and the scientific revolution, this worldview changed. The new modernist paradigm and social order that emerged and has dominated ever since is characterized by achievements in science, technology, political democracy, capitalism and the market economy, and the questioning of the place of both humans and God in the universe.

Lyon (1994) identifies several elements that summarize the essence of this paradigm or worldview. Primary among them is the rise of science, especially the shift from the medieval worldview of Galileo and Copernicus to the materialistic mechanistic worldview of Newton, Bacon, and Descartes in the eighteenth and nineteenth centuries. With such a shift, nature and the social order are huge machines, with identifiable parts that are separate from the scientific observer, who can measure and calculate them. The machine in turn calls for differentiation or specialization in science and in one's social life. Life, then, becomes differentiated, laborer from capitalist, work from home, public from private, leisure from work. Rationalization assists men and women in escaping from traditional culture and in making sense of the world around them. Humans can then contain complexity and confusion, and tame nature, all toward the goal of progress and efficiency in the rapidly growing industrial, secular world. Jeremy Rifkin (2004a) summarizes the rise to modernity as follows:

> Spiritual values have been largely replaced by material values. Theology gave way to ideology, and faith was dethroned and replaced by reason. Salvation became less important than progress. Tasks and daily rounds were replaced by jobs, and generativity became less important than productivity. . . . Personal relationships were no longer bound by fealty, but rather by contracts. . . . The sacred lost ground to the utilitarian. Market price replaced just price. Deliverance became less important than destiny. Wisdom was narrowed to knowledge. . . . Love of Christ was challenged by love of self. Caste was eclipsed by caste, revelation by discovery, and prophesy by the scientific method. (p. 120)

The modern paradigm, then, which continues to this day, is grounded in reliance on science and rational thinking, specialization of scientific knowledge, reliance on mankind instead of mystery and fate or faith to provide needed direction for the future, and the belief in human ingenuity and technology to harness the natural resources toward human progress.

## IS MODERNISM FAILING US?

As the United States moves into the twenty-first century we are faced with global threats to social welfare and to our very survival. Brian McCartan (2005), director of the Global Trends Project, reports some good news. Worldwide incomes are at their highest in history, and more than 1 billion people have pulled themselves out of poverty since 1960. Childhood mortality rates have declined worldwide. About half of the world's population now lives in countries that have multiparty election systems. The number of armed conflicts has declined steadily from about fifty in 1990 to fewer than thirty today. These are valid indicators of progress. So, what is the problem with the modern paradigm?

Social movements of the 1960s evidenced some of the first signs that the modern paradigms had reached their limits when they questioned power relations, expressed disenchantment with materialism, and felt a growing sense of alienation in modern organizational life. Moving into the 1970s and 1980s, from the industrial age to the information age, we also began to question the congruence of the goal of unlimited progress with the carrying capacity of the planet. How much longer can we go on poisoning the air and water supplies? Why is the disparity increasing between the haves and the have-nots? Is warfare an obsolete concept since we are already able to destroy the planet? The institutions we have developed that have made us the richest country on earth may, at their roots, rely on paradigms that have outlived their usefulness and sustainability in the future. Today we still face multiple global problems, including homelessness, poverty, illiteracy, unemployment, physical dependency and isolation, and environmental degradation, to name a few (Wilson, 1987).

In response to this old paradigm, in 1992 more than 1,600 scientists, including many Nobel laureates in the sciences, endorsed and made available the report *World Scientists' Warning to Humanity*, in which they stated, "Human beings and the natural world are on a collision course . . . [that] may so alter the living world that it will be unable to sustain life in the manner that we know" (Union of Concerned Scientists, 1992). The scientists asserted that we must step back and gain a whole-systems perspective on the physical, ecological, spiritual, and social challenges that we face.

What is a whole-systems perspective? New systems thinkers suggest that such a perspective calls for conceptualizing problems as interconnected and within a framework of international trends. For example, massive weapons and consumption patterns threaten the planet as a life system (World Commission on Environment and Development, 1987). The internationalization of (1) technology and production, (2) work and migration, (3) finance, information, and debt, (4) military weapons and the arms race, (5) the human impact on the biosphere, and (6) culture and consumption patterns are driving world social change (Henderson, 1989). And these trends are directly connected to major threats to global social welfare: poverty, environmental degradation, terrorism and increased military-based problem solving, and unequal distribution of basic needs such as food, health care, and employment. But is the problem our inability to see the big picture, or do we need to think differently about the future?

## SOCIAL WORKERS AND A DIFFERENT WAY OF THINKING ABOUT THE FUTURE

As a profession, social workers have not been involved in much futurist thinking. Before the mid-1990s, our literature on the future focused primarily on demographic changes and the implications for social welfare and social work (Macarov, 1991; Raffoul & McNeece, 1996). With the approach of the new millennium, however, we began to look at the future from a more global perspective (Ramanathan & Link, 1999; Reisch & Gambrill, 1997).

A report from the 1980 NASW Commission on the Future, developed by Bertram Beck (1980), poses two perspectives of postindustrialism and transformationalism, which offer us some descriptions of plausible outcomes given certain discernable trends. In "Conservers battle achievers" (1979), Kahn's (1976) and Bell's (1973) postindustrial scenarios assume that knowledge, science, and technology are the key forces of social change. In contrast, the transformational worldview, derived from work at the Stanford University Center for the Study of Social Policy, is based on a social and cultural shift predicated on values of conservation and ecological ethics. The importance of transformationalism is its challenge to modern thinking about progress and the reliance on technology to ensure our future survival.

The two perspectives envision a

> struggle between the achievers or "traditionalists" and the "conservers" or non-traditionalists, in a world torn by waning energy resources. The achievers espouse the benefits of rational, scientifically based decision-making, and extol the virtues of individualism, competition, and materialism as the qualities. . . . The conservers recognize the finite nature of our fuel and mineral resources and hence, the need to reduce demand on these resources by curbing unnecessary consumption. "The notion of voluntary simplicity thus [is] translated into an ecological ethic by which humankind [is] viewed as part of the natural system rather than manipulator of it." (NASW News, 1979, p. 6)

Social workers did not take up this challenge to modernism for another twenty years. But it was beginning to bubble and is now fermenting in other areas of both popular and scholarly literature. It is commonly called new-paradigm thinking. Let's explore a bit what is going on.

## WHAT IS NEW-PARADIGM THINKING?

Since the 1980s, a growing body of literature published by scientists, futurists, and social thinkers suggests that we are at the turning point of a new period in human evolutionary history. They "share a planetary perspective, a tempered optimism about technology, a long range view of the continuing evolution of humanity, and a hope for an emerging integral culture of . . . connectivity, between humans and nature, humans and the spirit (variously defined) and humans and humans all over the globe" (Spayde, 1998, p. 43). In 1996, Duane Elgin and Coleen LeDrew (1997) published *Global Consciousness Change: Indicators of an Emerging Paradigm*, a review of existing new-paradigm literature. Two primary features of the paradigm that the authors found are (1) humans' growing capacity for self-reflection as well as observation of the world and ourselves and the ability to be self-directing agents of our own evolution and (2) a whole-systems or living-systems consciousness wherein the cosmos is seen as a living unified system and people, animals, and all creatures are interconnected in a web of life. In addition, their study of global patterns identified five thematic areas in which changes in consciousness and culture are taking place:

1. Global communications patterns and global consciousness
2. Global ecological awareness
3. Postmodern social values (e.g., a shift from competition to partnership, grater tolerance of diversity)
4. Increased lay or personal "experiential" spirituality
5. Shift toward sustainable ways of living

At about the same time, Paul Ray, a sociologist and marketing researcher, published *The Integral Culture Survey: A Study of the Emergence of Transformational Values in America* (1996). Sponsored by the Institute of Noetic Sciences and the Fetzer Institute, and using Family Opinion Inc. and a methodology based on eight years of consumer and opinion research, Ray found three significant values subcultures in the United States: modernists, traditionalists (or heartlanders), and transmoderns (or cultural creatives). Cultural creatives share the following five core values: (1) globalism (concern for planetary ecology and stewardship), (2) ecological sustainability, (3) feminism, relationship, and family, (4) spirituality, mind-body health connection, and personal growth psychology, and (5) social optimism and well-developed social conscience. Cultural creatives reject intolerance of the religious right, hedonism, materialism, and the consumer and business culture. You may want to take a look at the exercise when you reach the end of this chapter to see whether you are a cultural creative.

Futurist Barbara Hubbard considers such efforts part of the "social-potential movement . . . the echo of the human potential movement of the [1970s]" (Spayde, 1998, p. 44). Though this scholarship is provocative and consistent in its recurring themes, it is tempting for newcomers to this literature to label such thinking as new age and thus minimize its legitimacy and importance. Within the past twenty-five years, however, scholars across disciplines have continued to research these ideas and have described what appears to be a new paradigm of thinking. Who are some of these people whose work they have explored? Some of the best known are physicist Fritjof Capra, feminist Riane Eisler, author and philosopher Ken Wilber, economist Hazel Henderson, organizational scholar David Korten, and social scientist Duane Elgin. We will explore them in much more detail in the following chapters. But let us take a peak at the disciplinary scope of this thinking.

In 1987, at the annual American Political Science Association meeting, the Ecological and Transformational Politics Section of this organization was born. In 1998, Stephen Woolpert and colleagues published *Transformational Politics*, a compilation of articles discussing a new paradigm of politics that places major change at its core. Among the themes discussed are ecology and systems thinking, interdependence, partnership, flexibility (adapting to a changing environment), diversity, the linkage of the personal and the political, and the inclusion of the spiritual and the sacred. More popular in appeal but equally important are works such as McLaughlin and Davidson's *Spiritual Politics* (1994), Lerner's *The Politics of Meaning* (1997), and Harris's *Reclaiming Democracy* (1994), all of which explore new connections between morality and politics, and between citizens and their government and illustrate, in part, new-paradigm thinking.

Riane Eisler, whose cultural transformation theory we will explore later, has written a blueprint for partnership education in *Tomorrow's Children* (2000); her partnership model includes a number of the previously mentioned themes. She is also on the editorial board, along with Jonathan Kozol, of *Encounter: Education for Meaning and Social Justice*, a quarterly education journal for teachers that focuses on a holistic perspective, with articles on many themes such as the global village and multicultural education.

Jeremy Rifkin, perhaps one of the most comprehensive social thinkers of our time, discusses the global trends that are driving a new way of thinking about time and space, work, the economy, energy resources, and the commoditization of our biological, physical, and social goods. In his latest work, *The European Dream* (2004a), Rifkin asserts that we human beings may be entering a new stage of consciousness where global connectedness is imperative for our ultimate survival. Particularly interesting is that Rifkin views social work as a profession that can bridge the gap between families and these challenging chaotic changes.

To summarize, then, what is new-paradigm thinking? Coates, a social work scholar, defines the new paradigm as the move from modernism to sustainability. In his book *Ecology and Social Work*

(2000), he summarizes four principles of the new story of the unfolding of nature: (1) everything is one, (2) a new understanding of the importance of subjectivity, (3) complexity, and (4) boundaries of the earth as a closed system.

Others, such as futurist Barbara Hubbard (1998), have called new-paradigm thinking transformational thinking, with the implication that as a species and a planet we may be on the verge of transforming ourselves in terms of our understanding of who we are and how we can survive. In a nutshell, this thinking is evolving from the need to move beyond modernity to consider theories and approaches in natural and social sciences that embrace the following ideas: (1) the interdependence of all life forms, (2) holism, or an integration of physical, mental, and spiritual worlds, rather than reductionism, (3) collectivity and cooperation rather than individualism and competition, (4) diversity of species, cultures, and worldviews, and (5) ecological sustainability.

If this thinking is becoming more popular, and if the profession of social work is going to play a viable role in responding to social problems, should we not avail ourselves of these ideas? We are unique as a helping profession in that we can target changes in the environment and changes in individuals and families. However, "social welfare ultimately depends upon how well underlying economic, political, and intellectual models correspond with realities of the environment" (Garbarino, 1992, p. 21). Perhaps it is time to take a new look at what we now know about ourselves, our connections with the natural and spiritual worlds, our long-term viability as a species and a planet, our models of human interaction, and our institutions. This will, no doubt, expand our thinking and help us revisit roles we can play in the furtherance of global and local social welfare.

## A NEW PARADIGM OF SOCIAL WORK

Let us consider, for a moment, a river as a metaphor for life's journey. Families travel the river in their lifeboats. Many find themselves hurling toward a waterfall. Our job, as social workers, is to catch them as they fall and help them find their way back to the top of the waterfall and onto the river. If we view their problems as rooted in the individual, then we may work with them regarding their chemical dependency or mental illness, or a host of other deficits that impede their ability to steer their own boat away from the waterfall.

However, if we spend any time at the top of the waterfall, we begin to see the structural nature of the problems. There are a few huge boats that simply take another route or manage to find another tributary and avoid the fall. Most of the smaller boats cannot divert themselves to another branch of the river. The sailors are weak, ill fed, illiterate, and unable to read the signs along the river. But our job seldom helps them build bigger and better boats, change the routes, or build a dam. Our job is just to catch them after they fall and try to get them to the top again, back on the river somewhere upstream.

But more and more boats are falling. The waterways are becoming polluted, the riverbanks no longer grow needed food or supply adequate resting places. Furthermore (bear with me here!), it is predicted that within the next twenty years the river will dry up as a result of changing weather patterns and lack of rainfall. There will be a stark lumber shortage for boatbuilding, and there are no plans for new routes, food sources, or better lifeboats.

Still, if we stay at the bottom of the waterfall, our primary role remains one of helping and, more often, of treating those who fall over. We assess their presenting problems as abusers, victims, perpetrators, or patients and get paid to intervene in their anger (or money) management, rehabilitation, and coping. Then we hoist them back up in hopes that their new sailing skills will help them prevent the fall.

How are our actions with patients and clients in mental health clinics, hospitals and hospice, and child protective services related to a sustainable future for us all? They are not; most of it is irrelevant. But when did our goal become curing mental illness? Do we not have more than enough psychologists, psychiatrists, and marriage and family therapists who specialize in behavioral health and mental illness? If our goal is systems change, then we need to let these clinicians do their thing. We can certainly work with them, but there are other things we can do in line with our mission, our vision, our knowledge, and our skills that are critical to ensuring a sustainable future. We can empower citizens and create new initiatives, processes, institutional arrangements, and social policies to meet human needs and prevent a great deal of today's mental illness.

Today we work and live within large systems that create the problems of under- and unemployment, homelessness, poverty, despair, and ill health. As social workers, we try to help people in trouble as a result of the economics of jobs with inadequate wages and unhealthful conditions, and as a result of political systems that provide unjust solutions to social problems and little meaningful contact with or representation of the people they serve. We do this with insufficient social welfare programs that attempt to fill the gaps. We do not often succeed because, for the most part, these institutions are set up to provide not for human well-being, social justice, and human rights, but rather for power and profit for a few at the expense of most of us. Attention needs to shift from the bottom of the waterfall and the sailors' deficiencies to changing the course of the river, the craft, and the relationship between the families and the natural environment that supports their journey. Only then will their journey lead them in a direction that will sustain them. Such a shift is not a minor one; it is transformational, and it will change them and us in the process.

## FOUR THEMES OF SUSTAINABLE SOCIAL WORK

In looking at the new-paradigm literature, I have found many ways to categorize the strains of the so-called transformational thinking. Here I highlight what I consider four crosscutting themes that are closely connected to the core threats to our long-term survival; thus, these themes mark a shift toward sustainable social welfare and social work.

The first theme is long-term sustainability, which pervades new-paradigm thinking and has become an imperative. Since the publication of Rachel Carson's *Silent Spring* in 1962, there is a growing awareness of the effects of human activity on our natural environment, across countries, disciplines, and even faiths. No longer do we reject the notion that our resources are limited. Even the U.S. Senate acknowledged at a recent hearing on Peak Oil that we may be at a crossroads: "The challenge we face is to move beyond slogans, blame, and false promise of 'quick fixes' and seize upon this moment of collective focus to develop long term policy responses that will meaningfully protect our economy while strengthening our national security" (Grumet, 2006, p. 1). Our mode of reaction is often one of crisis, not prevention. It is the tinkering of air standards or the quick fix of energy credits, not long-term, seven-generation thinking.

Because of an outdated measure of economic success, the threat to sustainability cuts across institutions to political systems with outmoded definitions of national security and continued social and economic injustice, to agricultural, industrial, and consumption patterns that fail to preserve or recycle our natural resources. One-sixth of the world's families live in hunger, eking out a living off the land, while one-sixth of families in developed countries have high standards of living. Yet many of the more privileged are alienated from their natural environment, so caught up in the Internet and virtual reality that they spend little time in one another's company. What are the trade-offs? Is this technology available to everyone? Is it helping nurture sustainable family and community life? Many of us are connected to the information highway, but we haven't a clue as to why we are on it or where we are headed.

Sustainability is the notion that humans must live in harmony with the planet and their cohabitants. It recognizes that the natural environment is an integral part and the foundation of our world and must be sustained as a living and sacred part of our global social welfare. Therefore, we will examine the extent to which the institutions of economy and technology, the polity, and social welfare embrace and reflect this reality.

Long-term sustainability also challenges the notion that violence, in the form of warfare and the destruction of both natural and social worlds, is still a viable mode of problem solving. Furthermore, violence as a form of conflict resolution connects at every level: domestic violence is connected to violence in communities and to acceptance of violence at the national level. By the same token, sustainable economics, politics, and environmental policies at macro levels of the community influence and interact with sustainable family practices, such as recycling and taking care of the natural environment.

The second theme is the interactive, interconnected web of life, which makes connections between the physical and social worlds, and local and global connections among social problems such as poverty, environmental resource depletion, social injustice, global violence, and consumption patterns. When the winds shifted over Europe following the Chernobyl nuclear power plant eruption in the Ukraine in 1986, the fallout seemed to be heading west. Our consciousness in the United States was raised. Many of us had a realization, similar to the new perspective gained by the *Apollo* spacewalkers upon eyeing the earth from space, that we are all connected. The air has no boundaries; the earth and its inhabitants are fragile.

When we explore how small landowners in developing countries are pushed off their land to make room for, for example, four-legged competitors (the cattle raised to meet U.S. demands), we make the connection among consumption, world economies, and environmental decline (World Commission on Environment and Development, 1987). When we examine political unrest in the Middle East, it is impossible to point to any one cause. We cannot separate geopolitical history from different religious worldviews or from the coveted resource of oil, which developed countries continue to pursue for energy and commerce. We cannot carry out our wars against poverty or our attempts to remediate environmental destruction from a specialized, one-discipline perspective. We must tackle them with a whole-systems, multidisciplinary perspective.

Systems theories that help us understand these interconnected phenomena are expanding. One view of systems (Capra, 1982) poses a new metaphor of a web for understanding the natural and social world. What is important is to understand the constantly changing interconnectedness—the relationships between the parts of the web and the interactive process (rather than static structure) of living organisms, whether individuals, social groups and nations, or the planet itself.

Other systems theories, such as structuration theory (Kondrat, 2002) and self-organization theory (Hudson, 2000), are important because they are rewriting the role that humans play in the construction of systems. These theories challenge the notion that we are influenced by and react to the environment and have only a limited ability to create a different one. Thus, the examination of linkages among and across systems is important if we are to understand how problems and solutions are interconnected. Perhaps the fate of the individual is linked to the fate of the collective, in the family, in the community, and across the globe.

The third theme is the link between science and spirituality or religion. Recent events such as the Society of Neuroscience's November 2005 invitation for the Dalai Lama to address its national meeting indicate an interest in bridging our understanding of the metaphysical and the material world. But the duality and separation of science and spirit is challenged every day as social workers consider human affairs and social intervention. We know, in part, how people perceive the material world and that its relationship to their spiritual world of beliefs, values, and ethics drives human behavior. In understanding communities and countries and their diverse ethnic and religious groups, we cannot overlook the role of faith, mystery, and the meaning of metaphysical worlds. Wars are fought not only over resources but also over different worldviews in the social construction of evil empires.

The challenge of connecting the material world to that of the spiritual world is twofold: the first is an epistemological challenge. If we acknowledge the spiritual and/or religious aspect of human beings and cultures, then we must also acknowledge the subjective, emotional, and metaphysical realities experienced by diverse peoples. We must reject the notion of an absolute reality. The second challenge is more of a values question. From the perspective of our own professional value base, are there any universal definitions of what is good, strong, and life affirming across various spiritual worldviews? How can we help individuals and groups use these values and beliefs to build better, more just lives? Can we, for example, find a balance advocating social justice for women in a society that relegates women a lesser social position in part because of religious doctrine?

Well, we really must. If we are committed to living life side by side on a planet with people of different worldviews, can we just vote them off the island, as they do on the popular reality show *Survivor*? As I was writing this, I heard the latest rumor that new seasons of the *Survivor* show may involve ethnic groups competing against one another in teams. Is this not a sad metaphor for the mainstream mind-set about how we decide who should prevail? I submit that we must find the balance. I believe that we have knowledge of history and experience to tell us that it is possible, and faith to tell us that it must be so.

The fourth theme is a partnership model of human relationships and society, based on Eisler's (1995) theory of cultural transformation. For centuries the predominant model of human societies has ranked one gender of humankind over another, and the result is a dominator model of society. A sustainable natural and social world implies the need for movement toward a partnership model of social and cultural evolution, wherein relationships among genders, cultures, and with nature are more egalitarian, result in increased social justice, shared power, do not feature coercive hierarchies, and introduce technology that is life enhancing and supportive of a healthful quality of life—all with the goal of improving global social and environmental welfare (Eisler, 1995). Social work practice models congruent with the partnership model are many, such as feminist practice, the empowerment approach, participatory community development and research, and more recent research on collaboration.

## THE PLAN FOR THIS BOOK

The preceding sections have provided a glimpse at the four themes of new-paradigm or transformational thinking, each of which contributes to a different way of conceptualizing our world, our problems, and our solutions. Subsequent chapters will explore each of these four themes. We will begin with a look at sustainability, with a primary focus on the environment, upon which other institutions are built. An exploration of systems thinking about the world as a web of life that connects all systems follows. Then, we will attempt to span the controversial bridge between the material and the spiritual worlds, which lies at the base of so much local and global conflict. We will then turn to the institutions of economics and politics in an effort to redefine them in light of our new knowledge of sustainability and systems. We will explore the fourth theme of partnership in the context of the polity. Finally, I will offer a new approach to social work that integrates each theme in a new model of professional practice.

In each chapter, I will discuss the strengths and criticisms of a modernist worldview, as well as new-paradigm thinking that challenges mainstream modernist thought. I will present questions to stimulate further discussion of the theme and its application in examining behavior in small and large systems as well as practice. I will also provide suggestions for additional reading.

So, where to from here? In the next chapter we will begin to look at the first theme of sustainability. But before we do that, do you want to see if you are a cultural creative?

## CULTURAL CREATIVE QUICKIE QUIZ

1. People should have simpler lifestyles with fewer possessions.
                                     ___ Agree ___ Disagree

2. I believe in the paranormal, the metaphysical, mysteries we cannot explain, the power of meditation and divine love.
                                     ___ Agree ___ Disagree

3. I am concerned about the sustainability of the planet and related issues like pollution, overpopulation, and species extinction.             ___ Agree ___ Disagree

4. I have a sense of nature as sacred (e.g., redwood groves, Gaia, planetary stewardship).        ___ Agree ___ Disagree

5. I think we are all connected in this world, people with nature, and spirit with all.            ___ Agree ___ Disagree

6. We need a more meaning oriented politics toward a new social contract that creates caring communities.
                                     ___ Agree ___ Disagree

7. Technology alone will not solve the problems threatening the sustainability of the planet.     ___ Agree ___ Disagree

8. Standard measures of economic progress do not necessarily mean that society is healthy.       ___ Agree ___ Disagree

9. Overemphasis on materialism and consumption is threatening the quality of life in American families.
                                     ___ Agree ___ Disagree

10. Warfare and violence are obsolete problem-solving strategies in a sustainable future.      ___ Agree ___ Disagree

If you answer yes to many of these questions, you may be evolving into a cultural creative!

## MAIN POINTS

1. Paradigms or worldviews, larger than theories, are ways of viewing the natural or social worlds that encompass science and philosophy, values, and perceptions.

2. The modernist paradigm, based on science and rational thinking, technology, and materialism, may not be adequate for a sustainable future.

3. We arrive at our current understanding of the world via a narrow lens, a focus on the individual, and emphasis on biological and psychological theories of individual behavior, with the environment as only a backdrop.

4. Today's global threats to survival may call for a whole-systems paradigm that embraces the interdependence of all life forms, the integration of the material and spiritual worlds, ecological sustainability, and collectivity and cooperation rather than individualism and competition.

## For Further Reading

Hubbard, B. (1998). *Conscious evolution: Awakening the power of our social potential.* Novato, CA: New World Library.

Ornstein, P., & Ehrlich, P. (1989). *New world new mind: Moving toward conscious evolution.* New York: Simon and Schuster.

Ray, P. (1996). *The Integral Culture Survey: A study of the emergence of transformational values in America.* Sausalito, CA: Institute of Noetic Sciences.

Sagan, C. (1997). *Billions and billions: Thoughts on life and death at the brink of the millennium.* New York: Random House.

World Commission on Environment and Development (1987). *Our common future.* New York: Oxford University Press.

# CHAPTER 2

# Long-Term Sustainability and the Environment

"The slogan in the beginning of the twentieth century was progress. The cry at the end of the twentieth century is survival."
—Muto Ichiyo, *"For an Alliance of Hope"*

Let me begin with my personal perspective of the past sixty or so years. I grew up in Southern California, in a time of the rotary telephone and the radio. There was a refrigerator in our kitchen, but us scantily clad kids still hung out in front of a fan and a block of ice during the summer heat spells. Fewer than fifty years later, I now live in a world that communicates by satellite and e-mail. My relatives all lost their family farms to development and soybeans. I no longer sew my own clothes. My children, when younger, could not believe it when I told them that I was eight years old before we got a television. I came of age in a time of optimism—Kennedy and Camelot; women's rights; and the magic of plastics, petroleum, and petrochemicals. Anything was possible, as we applied our new knowledge to technology. I inherited the benefits of an enhanced quality of life from these postwar technologies; I also inherited the costs. Atomic energy led to the atom bomb and atomic waste. An abundance of new land and sea farming technologies for food and oil led to the destruction of coral reefs and topsoil, as well as ocean oil spills. Transportation that connects people and products all over the world has contributed to the loss of ozone and glaciers and has increased global warming.

I am now a member of the top 2% of my country that holds a doctorate degree; my graduating students belong to the top 10% of the country's population with masters' degrees. We are members of the world's minority: we have regular and easy access to safe drinking water, a real possibility of owning our own home, and jobs that give us access to health care and retirement programs.

We have the luxury to seriously consider and affect the future of our children and of our children's children—and of our homeland, the planet Earth. And we must do so. Moreover, we baby boomers may be the last generation of Americans to share "an intimate, familial attachment to the land and water" as we grew up knowing farmland and forests at the edge of our suburban lives (Louv, 2005, p. 19). Research has led me to believe that we are at a fork in the road where to ensure such a future we must commit to creative thinking and take bold action. Crucial to this commitment is a deeper understanding of our interconnectedness with all systems, the finding of common ground between the physical world (science) and the spiritual one, and a shift toward sustainability in thinking about our institutions.

## WHAT DOES IT MEAN TO BE SUSTAINABLE?

There is no universal definition of sustainability but many different views on what it is and how we can achieve it. The natural environment has framed the idea, and the concept of sustainable development became a common term after the world's first Earth Summit in Rio de Janeiro in 1992. In general, it refers to development that meets the current needs of the present generations without jeopardizing the ability of future generations to meet their needs (World Commission on Environment and Development, 1987). In 1972, the UN Conference on the Human Environment brought both developing and developed countries together to define the rights of people to a healthy environment. However, in the ensuing years, major threats to the environment became more apparent as information emerged on the ozone layer, global warming, desertification in agricultural areas, and the Chernobyl disaster.

In 1983, the World Commission on Environment and Development convened to focus only on environmental issues. After three years of hearings in countries all over the globe, the commission issued the Brundtland Report, which considered threats to global survival from a new perspective and indicated that a clear shift in thinking had occurred. The report discussed as interconnected problems of poverty; the global status of women; the degradation of the environment; political unrest caused by unequal economic development; repression of human rights; and the use of violence, terrorism, warfare, and nuclear threat. Recommendations for solutions could not be isolated but needed to be a panoply of integrated responses across major institutions. The 1993 Rio Earth Summit reaffirmed this interconnectedness. Recommendations from the summit also touched on changes in environmental policy and in economic, social, and political institutions.

Current thinking about sustainability clearly frames the definition more broadly than as a sole concern for the environment. Prugh and Assadourian (2003), two Worldwatch Institute associates, suggest four dimensions of sustainability, all of which are conditions that must be attained to ensure the continuation of all life on the planet: human survival, biodiversity, equity, and life quality. These dimensions are interconnected and imply that sustainability means living in harmony with fellow humankind, bird, beast, air, land, sky, and sea.

From all the definitions of sustainability, I believe that there are key principles or values of sustainability that apply to all institutions: an increasing value of human life and the lives of all species, fairness and equality or economic and social justice, decision making that involves participation and partnership, and respect for the ecological constraints of the environment. These principles that I have culled from the many recommendations of UN reports are congruent with the foundation principles of social work that are found in our code of ethics and our policy statements. They are also at the root of most major religions, and they are supported by decades of literature in social welfare on how to combat poverty and social ills. What follows in this chapter, then, is a discussion of the environment and the relevance of these principles to a sustainable perspective of our natural world. So, now on to Mother Earth.

## SUSTAINABILITY AND THE ENVIRONMENT: FAIRNESS AND EQUALITY

Until recently, the world was large and human activity and its effects on the health of countries were neatly compartmentalized within countries and within their various sectors (e.g., energy, trade, agriculture; World Commission on Environment and Development, 1987). But our knowledge and conception of the world has shifted. Nowhere is the need more evident for a change in thinking than in our relationship with our natural environment.

We are bombarded daily with evidence of the effects of humans on our planet's ecosystem. Commenting on current studies on the connection between ocean and air currents and an increase in pathogens, the world-renowned biologist David Suzuki (2006, p. 1) suggests the following: "Climate change is not a simple process. Our atmosphere, our oceans, and all life on the planet are interconnected. Seemingly small alterations in one area can reverberate through the entire system, affecting the health of a tremendous variety of species—including us." But we do not respond as well to processes as we do to events. Consider the boiled-frog syndrome: "It takes an eruption or an earthquake or a weird belch from a poisonous lake . . . or the collapse of an ice sheet to rivet our attention. I once read of a teacher who illustrated this point with a frog. First, the teacher dropped the frog into a beaker of hot water. The frog jumped right out. Then the teacher put the frog in a beaker of cool water, and turned on a Bunsen burner. The frog kept swimming in the beaker and it boiled to death" (Weiner, 1990, p. 80).

We are, however, beginning to see the consequences of long-term processes. We are also beginning to realize that it is impossible to separate environmental threats from poverty and global inequality. Poverty drives ecological deterioration when desperate people compete for resources or exploit them, sacrificing their future to salvage the present. Immediate needs cause landless families to migrate or to stay and raze plots in the rain forest, plow steep slopes, and shorten fallow seasons. Poor women and children carry out most of this work of daily survival. Families grow larger to ensure the survival of the family unit, which contributes to population growth that a poor country cannot sustain (Mary & Morris, 1994).

Most economic aid has not helped in alternative local sustainable-development projects. In fact, paramount privatization, reduced social safety nets, and reliance on market-based strategies characterize the typical Western development strategy (UN Environment Programme [UNEP], 2002). Consumption patterns of developed countries, with the United States in the lead, have further fueled the poverty cycle. The richest 20% of the world's population, most of which lives in industrial countries, accounts for 86% of total private consumption expenditures and 58% of the world's energy use. And these consumption patterns are growing by leaps and bounds, as newly industrialized countries move forward on the road to a higher standard of living and economic success, as defined by the example of the United States. China has now eclipsed the United States in the consumption of food, energy, and industrial commodities—meat, grain, coal, and steel. The United States still is ahead in the consumption of oil, but that is only a matter of time. The bottom line for Lester Brown (2006), world-renowned environmental scholar and cofounder of the Worldwatch Institute, is that in an economically integrated economy in which all countries compete for the same resources, the existing U.S. economic model is not globally sustainable.

These economic patterns create great global inequality. Peasants, the poor, and women disproportionately feel the ill effects of consumption gaps. Small landowners have been pushed off their land (World Commission on Economic Development, 1987). Where poverty is not a direct cause of environmental decline, it is a ticket to suffer the environmental abuses that others cause. Three-fourths of hazardous-waste landfills in the American Southwest are in low-income African American neighborhoods. In both the United States and developing countries, the rich get richer and the poor get poisoned (Durning, 1990). Thus, an essential characteristic of the current global environmental crisis is a lack of fairness and equity with respect to the production and consumption of the world's resources.

## EVOLUTION OF RESPECT FOR THE ENVIRONMENT

How, then, have we arrived at a place where a significant number of interest groups and governments embrace an ecological perspective that acknowledges respect for the environment and the need to live in harmony with it? Several publications have well documented the place at which we have arrived—from Rachel Carson's *Silent Spring* (1962), a public pronouncement regarding the effects of chemical toxins on the environment, to Ehrlich's concern for population trends, *Population Bomb* (1968), to the publication in 1975 of the first Worldwatch Institute report and the birth of environmentalism. Scientists have traced the forces of globalism, industrialism, and science and technology that have contributed to the multidisciplinary study of ecology, which is the relationship between living organisms and the environment (Sheldrake, 1994). We have become more enlightened in our connection to the universe. Moreover, we saw for the first time the earth from space. Some say this alone created a paradigm shift, as we gazed at a small blue ball from the beyond.

But why did humans consider themselves separate from their world for so many centuries? If we revisit the history of the relationship between humans and the environment, we can see an enormous split in Western consciousness between spirit and nature that occurred in the Middle Ages and persists to this day. We can point a finger at both religion and science for maintaining worldviews that sustain this split and thereby fueled environmental degradation.

Religion and science, until very recently, have sustained that as a species we are superior to other life forms, and therefore have a right to dominate and use nature to our own ends, which is also referred to as human chauvinism (Metzner, 1993). In the sixteenth century, Renaissance humanism, the Protestant Reformation, and the explorations of the Americas were contributing forces to this dominance paradigm. Pre-Christian European paganism and worship of the goddess, which had embraced the spiritual nature of the natural world, were eliminated. Exploration and Manifest Destiny further contributed to the devaluation of the material world through the extraction of natural resources and the subjugation and destruction of indigenous populations, whose relationship to the material world was worship in the form of animism, shamanism, or pantheism.

But in the age of connectedness, there is evidence of our new understanding of the interdependency with nature. But hey! Aren't we still the dominant, supreme species? Why should we care if species are extinct? This is part of natural selection, right? We respect human diversity. But is the diversity of all species so important? Edward Wilson, a world-renowned biologist says, "Yes, indeed."

First, we are far from knowing about all the species on our planet. Although 1.4 million species of life have been discovered thus far, Wilson (1992) estimates that the total number is somewhere between 10 million and 100 million. Second, it may be reckless to believe that biodiversity can diminish without threatening our own survival as a species:

> It is fashionable, in some quarters, to wave aside the small and obscure, the bugs and weeds, forgetting that an obscure moth from Latin America saved Australia's pastureland from overgrowth by cactus, that the rosy periwinkle provided the cure for Hodgkin's disease and childhood lymphocytic leukemia, that the bark of the Pacific yew

offers hope for victims of ovarian and breast cancer, that a chemical from the saliva of leeches dissolves blood clots during surgery . . . and so on down the roster. . . . Ecosystems enrich the soil and create the very air we breathe. . . . The life sustaining matrix is built with green plants with legions of microorganisms and mostly small obscure . . . weeds and bugs. . . . [But] without these the remaining tenure of the human race would be nasty and brief. (Wilson, 1992, p. 347)

Wilson asserts that the advances in evolutionary biology involve genetics and ecology. We evolved, with the rest of this life, on this planet; other planets are not in our genes. We must seek a balance. If we experiment in genetics with human stem cells, we cannot disregard the rest of life's web. It is quite likely that an organism that thinks only in terms of its own survival will inevitably destroy its environment and, thus, itself (Capra, 1982).

To summarize, the earth's social, ecological, and resource problems are interconnected. Increasing population growth and widening disparities between the rich and poor contribute to environmental degradation. The Western history of consciousness, which includes religion and the scientific revolution, has contributed to a view of nature and humankind wherein the role of humans is to dominate, procreate, and use nature to their own design. But a new respect for the symbiosis of humans and the natural world may be emerging.

So, where do we go from here with this awareness? Are there more sustainable approaches to living in harmony with the earth? New thinking may help us develop a personal identity with nature and a larger action plan for the global commons. Let's first look at the theory of Gaia and that of deep ecology, or voluntary simplicity, which leads us to live more simply on the earth.

## VALUING ALL LIFE: OUR IDENTITY IN PARTNERSHIP WITH MOTHER EARTH

How can you buy or sell the sky, the warmth of the land, the freshness of the air and sparkle of the water? How can you buy them?

—Chief Seattle,
*"Reply to the President upon an Offer of a Large Area of Land"*

Studies of ecosystems over the past decades have shown that most relationships between living organisms are cooperative, characterized by interdependence and coexistence, so that the larger system is kept in balance. Congruent with new knowledge about the interconnectedness of systems, studies of the way in which the biosphere appears to regulate the chemical makeup of the air, surface temperature, and other aspects of the environment have led to the notion that we can understand these phenomena only if we regard the planet as a whole as a single living organism (Capra, 1982). This notion is referred to as the Gaia hypothesis, after the Greek goddess of the earth (Lovelock, 1979).

This systems view of the earth as a living organism sets forth two processes that keep the planet alive. One is self-maintenance, which includes self-renewal, healing, homeostasis, and adaptation. The other is that of self-transformation and self-transcendence; that is, the creation of new structures and new patterns of behavior. Sound familiar? This view is based on the work of scientists from various disciplines, among them the chemists Ilya Prigogine and Manfred Eigen, the biologists Paul Weiss and Conrad Waddington, the anthropologist Gregory Bateson, and the systems theorists Eric Jantsch and Ervin Laszlo (Capra, 1982).

A similar vein of thinking, deep ecology is a school of environmental thought that emerged during the 1970s. Its major premise is that there is no absolute separation between humanity and everything else. It seeks to "de-anthropomorphize our view of nature" (Bache, 2000, p. 16) and our view that we are the central point of reference of life on the earth, especially in discussions of the environment. Deep ecology views human beings not as independent of other life forms but in a web of relationships of all life forms. What are the implications for human behavior that arise from this shift in viewing the earth as a machine to viewing it as a living organism? Does it change how we see our behavior with respect to living in harmony with the environment?

Duane Elgin (2000), a social scientist, has studied the evolution of humans and their relationship with their world. He asserts that humans are evolving to a point at which we can accept a life plan of voluntary simplicity. The shift has occurred in four transformations in the evolution of our reality and our identity. The first was approximately 35,000 years ago when we awakened, or realized our consciousness, as evidenced in cave art, stone tools, and burial sites. The second shift was about 10,000 years ago, when we moved from nomadic to agrarian life. The third transformation was the scientific and industrial area, which affected all aspects of our paradigm, including our work, our relationships with others, and our perception of our role in society and our place in the universe. We are now entering a new paradigm, at the heart of which is the idea that the universe is a living organism that encompasses all living creatures. A convergence of the knowledge about the material world and the world's spiritual traditions is informing this understanding (Elgin, 2000).

The basis of Elgin's idea of voluntary simplicity is that humans have a cosmic identity, as Russell Schweickart experienced from space. We are connected to the universe and interconnected to other species and life forms. In a dead universe, materialism makes sense. We can exploit that which is not alive because a lifeless object has no larger purpose or meaning, nor do we. However, with live objects, our every action and decision has consequences, for we are a part of an entire community that comprises past, present, and future generations.

Thus, we need to live lightly on the planet. Voluntary simplicity means "living in such a way that we consciously bring our most authentic and alive self into direct connection with life . . . in an ever changing balance" (Elgin, 2000, p. 76). Henry David Thoreau (1893) followed this worldview in his essay "Walden," as did Mahatma Gandhi (1948) and followers of Buddha. Evidence that this worldview is an emerging trend is apparent in surveys such as Ray's (1996) *The Integral Culture Study,* the World Values Survey (1990–91, qtd. in Rifkin 2004a), Gallup's Health of the Planet Survey (1993), and the World Environmental Law Survey (1998).

So how do we live simply? A simple life means sustainable economic development, with shifts in diet, transportation, consumer patterns, and increasing recycling of nonrenewable resources. It furthers economic justice by narrowing the gap between the world's rich and poor. It develops new kinds of community (e.g., eco-villages) with greater participation in politics that value self-reliance and cooperation.

If we live simply, our relationship and identity with the natural world shifts. What humans once considered apart from our realm of activity becomes an interconnected living organism with which we live in harmony. Domination shifts to a relationship of symbiotic stewardship. We become one with nature, and our stewardship extends to the planet as a whole. We cannot protect the environment in the United States but neglect it in developing countries. Political boundaries are arbitrary in the global commons. So how do we achieve global sustainability?

## DECISIONS TO MAKE: THE UN LOOKS AT GLOBAL SUSTAINABILITY

The UNEP acknowledges this interconnectedness. *Global Environmental Outlook 3* (2002), a product of this group of thirty-seven collaborating centers—including universities worldwide, environmental groups, and public-policy research institutes—provides a retrospective analysis of environmental conditions and trends and policy responses. In the outlook section for 2002 to 2032, the group offers four future scenarios to ensure the future of our fragile world.

First, the markets-first approach essentially places trust in the globalization of corporate wealth and market-based approaches to create new enterprises and to ensure against or pay to fix social and environmental problems. The weakness of this approach is that it raises major questions about its sustainability and desirability. Many skeptics are concerned that under such an approach our children will inherit an impoverished and fragile world caused, in part, by the encouragement of lifestyles founded on individualism and greed, which seem to pervade a global consumer culture.

Second, the policy-first approach basically relies on governments, our public governing institutions, to specify environmental goals and plan and regulate them via treaties, tax breaks, and other incentives. The major limitation of this top-down approach is that it is highly technocratic and slow, and it has not "engendered a widespread shift in basic attitudes and behaviors" that may be necessary for sustainability (UNEP, 2002, p. 337).

Third is the security-first focus, which assumes a world in which vast disparities exist and conflict and inequality prevail. As a result, affluent communities and nations enhance their security by vigilant antiterrorism surveillance, military power, and the control of arms and financial flows. This approach does not target social and environmental concerns; therefore, tension increases around these disparities and creates an atmosphere in which more violence ensues. Poor people increasingly migrate to richer countries and "affluent groups respond with growing xenophobia and oppressive policing of borders" (UNEP, 2002, p. 342).

Fourth is the sustainability-first scenario, which evidences a new environmental and development paradigm supported by new, more equitable values and institutions (UNEP, 2002). This scenario is ripe with new-paradigm thinking, as it would involve collaboration across government, industry, and nongovernmental organization sectors, as well as dialogues among small groups of interested citizens across regions. The scenario also recognizes the importance of partnerships, as regional efforts (e.g., the European Union) connect with others (e.g., the Russian Federation) to "form a web of global public networks," such that "values of simplicity, cooperation and community begin to displace those of consumerism, competition and individualism" (UNEP, 2002, pp. 346–47). Traditional indigenous societies are called upon to educate others about the legacies of their own diverse cultures. Moreover, the scenario emphasizes a move away from reliance on exported raw materials toward producing more locally added value as well as actions to preserve biodiversity hotspots together with the involvement of indigenous groups.

Thus, at the global level, scientists in multiple disciplines and policy makers are looking at our environmental problems and proposals in a way that evidences new-paradigm thinking. This should be encouraging to us, especially since we are now barraged on a daily basis with new stories about environmental changes such as global warming or the thinning of glaciers in Greenland, which may have irreversible, long-term effects. In the short term, we can expect greater fluctuations in weather patterns and more frequent natural events such as hurricanes. The question is, how long is the long term when we can't stop the collision course we're on? At the very least we should be encouraged by the growing involvement of our own profession in this dialogue about the environmental world "problematique," or set of crucial problems.

## SOCIAL WORK AND THE ECOLOGICAL IMPERATIVE

The good news is that over the past twenty years, social workers have begun to see the bigger, longer-term picture and to recognize a larger meaning of person-in-environment. Social workers have responded with practice roles and policy proposals that illustrate a new paradigm of thinking about our place in the natural world.

Carel Germain (1979) was an early pioneer in ecological social work who wrote about the importance of space and the physical environment, asserting that healthy environments create growth and adaptation. Berger and Kelly (1993) were among the first to refocus social workers' attention on the environmental imperative with their call to action for social workers to embrace a new global ethic of global stewardship. They also offered social workers an ecological credo to help us expand our practice from an ecological perspective. Mary and Morris (1994) call for a global perspective on the interconnected problems facing our global village. In connecting environmental devastation with poverty and worldwide consumption patterns, they suggest that current environmental trends may present a greater threat to national security than that of warfare (we'll see a little later how warfare and military expenditures are connected to environmental deterioration).

Hoff and McNutt's *The Global Environmental Crisis* (1994), a groundbreaking work that addresses the environment and implications for social work, provides theory and frameworks for integrating the environmental crisis into our social work response and case studies to illustrate its relevance. Hoff contrasts the "industrial scientific paradigm" with the "ecological and feminist paradigm" (p. 21) and its emphasis on wholeness, diversity, sustainability, and balance. She notes that eco-feminist theory adds to the conclusion of social work scholarship that the dualistic worldview has led to environmental destruction. McNutt, in his assessment of social welfare models, suggests a new sustainable model that encourages locally oriented self-help organizations to achieve human-scale economic development, or the idea of small is beautiful. He suggests that social workers modify their roles to act as facilitators and activists in efforts toward sustainability; one model of practice could be a social development approach.

Katherine McMai Park (1996) also offers both macro and micro (i.e., individual or clinical) interventions in "ecological social work." Pointing out that the revised 1994 NASW policy statement on environmental issues commits us to action, she provides the following examples of practice arenas: environmental justice and civil rights arena, such as the Southwest Network for Environmental and Economic Justice; urban housing, such as housing and schools established on toxic sites; youth programs, such as fisheries and community gardens near Salt Lake City; and clinical practice in which wilderness programs and other nature outings help clients in their search for understanding.

Over the past twenty to twenty-five years, community-based initiatives have also provided fertile ground for social workers to help develop environmentally sound economic and social enterprises. For example, the Hawaii Alliance for Community Based Economic Development (2007) has been a driving force since the early 1990s in encouraging community-based economic development. In a

more urban environment, Boston's Dudley Street Neighborhood
Initiative (2007), conceived in 1984, has rebuilt the communities
of Roxbury and North Dorchester through holistic community
change efforts that focus on economic and social development
that are congruent with environmental sustainability.

Perhaps the most encouraging movement in social work and
the environment is the Global Alliance for a Deep Ecological Social Work. Participants at the first annual symposium of this alliance shared four principles that articulate the core, new-paradigm values of the initiative (Besthorn, 2001):

1. Expand our connections with the diversity of life, human and
   all life forms.
2. Reclaim a sacred relationship with the earth.
3. Honor and defend both human and earth communities.
4. Immerse our lives in hope.

These values clearly mirror the thinking of Capra and Steindl-
Rast, Wilber, Berry, and many others (whose work we will explore
in the next two chapters) in the understanding of the web of life
and the need to reconnect the material with the spirit. As these
ideas have been expanded, Coates (2003) articulates essential
characteristics of an emerging paradigm toward sustainability and
social justice, and new roles for social work, in *Ecology and Social
Work*. In Coates's view, we have learned four lessons from our new
knowledge of the universe and our place in it. First, everything is
one; that is, we are interdependent and self-organizing. Second,
each element has a unique place in a larger exocentric (living)
community. Third, the universe is complex and diverse. Last, the
earth's resources are finite.

In summary, the importance of the environment is by no
means a new concern of social work. For most of the past century,
we have used a person-in-environment practice perspective. However, the knowledge of the connection between the health of the
environment and problems such as poverty, employment, and disparate consumption patterns has led us to consider new theories
and new paradigms. Theories such as Gaia, voluntary simplicity,
and deep ecology offer us, in varying degrees, new-paradigm
thinking about our identity with and our responsibility for the natural world. This thinking has begun to translate into strategies in
clinical, community, and policy practice (Coates, 2003; Derezotes,
2005; Hoff & McNutt, 1994).

The primary implication of these theories for us, as social workers, is that the environment is no longer context. This may mean shifting our current emphasis on individual and personal development to one of the individual embedded in relationships with others in community with the natural world. It shifts from treatment to a meaningful relationship with others and with the planet (Coates, 2003). If we become stewards of the planet (Berger & Kelley, 1993), we cannot construct our interventions with families and communities apart from their effects on the natural environment that supports and nurtures them. Only through a support of communal goals will sustainability prevail.

In short, we can spend our time helping individuals move to more stable and comfortable deck chairs on the other side of the *Titanic*, but if this is all we do, we may prolong the inevitable sinking of us all. We must work together to build a stronger ship. A ship with no first-class cabins but livable ones for all passengers. An ark, if you will, that will carry all species while protecting the water, land, and air that sustain us all.

Should social workers not be talking about these things? Social workers can and should initiate dialogue in every arena about the need to live more simply. In today's world, especially in the West, the primary metaphor for human interaction is the marketplace and the primary role for people is as consumers. When we are depressed, feel alienated, or need entertainment, self-esteem, or child care, we do not turn to nature; we visit the mall. These ideas of living simply may be radical to some of us, but step-by-step, through dialogue and action, social workers may be able to play a part in personal and social transformation that helps avert the modernist path from destruction to survival.

## ADDITIONAL THINGS TO THINK ABOUT

1. If we expand our HBSE worldview to consider ourselves as having a sacred relationship with the earth, how does this affect our approach to understanding human behavior?
2. Consider the professional mission of social work. To play a role in environmental sustainability, must we become geologists, biologists, or ecologists? What is our role and responsibility to the environment as a social worker?

3. Consider the following fields of practice. What is the relevance of a sustainable natural environment to the social welfare of these groups?

   - Elderly people with chronic conditions such as arthritis, cancer, or heart disease

   - People diagnosed with conditions of unknown etiology (e.g., spectrum disorders such as autism, attention-deficit hyperactivity disorder)

   - People living in poverty in inner cities

4. You are a medical social worker at an HMO. Your responsibilities involve both direct client contact on various units and collaboration with other community agencies in community education and health promotion. How does the principle of sustainability of the natural environment relate to your job?

5. Social work with client groups who live in self-contained environments (e.g., nursing homes, juvenile detention centers, forensic mental hospitals) are often alienated from the natural environment. Can you see any benefits in trying to reconnect them with the natural environment? If so, how could you do that?

6. The ecological imperative is not new to many indigenous populations, which have been marginalized, are victims of industrial progress, and are now vulnerable to extinction. Can we connect such treatment of indigenous populations with our devaluing of diversity and inattention to environmental sustainability?

7. Imagine that you are a social worker who practices case management with people with developmental disabilities. Your responsibilities are primarily direct client contact, although it is expected that you help scan for needed resources, including support and educational services for clients. You have a caseload of clients who live under the flight path of a major international airport, and you have become aware of research studies that suggest that they are more vulnerable to birth defects, miscarriages, chronic respiratory conditions, and cancer than is the average population. Is there anything you can do to change this vulnerability within the purview of your job? Is there anything you can do outside of your job responsibilities?

8. Duane Elgin suggests that we live in greater voluntary simplicity. Does this reading compel you in any way to reexamine your own relationship to the earth, such as your consumption patterns, transportation, or diet?

## MAIN POINTS

1. Problems such as poverty, environmental degradation, political unrest, social injustice, and warfare are interconnected; solutions must sustain environmental, social, and political systems in the long term.
2. Sustainability involves the principles of valuing all life, fairness and equity, decision making that involves participation and partnership, and respect for the ecological constraints of the environment.
3. Long-term sustainability involves protecting the diversity of all life forms, as they are symbiotic.
4. Voluntary simplicity is an approach that involves living lightly on the plant.
5. The Gaia theory views the earth as a single living organism, with dynamics of self-renewal and self-transcendence.
6. The UNEP's sustainability-first approach to the future involves collaboration, partnerships, valuing the diversity of indigenous cultures, and preservation of local biodiversity.
7. Deep ecology suggests a new relationship between people and their natural environment in which the earth is sacred and entreats humans to live in harmony with it.

### For Further Reading

Coates, J. (2003). *Ecology and social work: Toward a new paradigm.* Halifax: Fernwood Publishing.

Elgin, D. (1993). *Voluntary simplicity: Toward a way of life that is outwardly simple, inwardly rich.* New York: William Morrow.

Schumaker, E. F. (1973). *Small is beautiful: Economics as if people mattered.* Point Roberts, WA: Hartley and Marks Publishers.

Weiner, J. (1990). *The next one hundred years: Shaping the fate of our living earth.* New York: Bantam Books.

Wilson, E. O. (1992). *The diversity of life.* Cambridge, MA: Harvard University Press.

# CHAPTER 3

# New Systems Thinking and a Web of Life

Social work involves making change with individuals and families and with larger systems such as organizations and communities. In studying these systems, we have used behavioral theories of human development and social theories about the structure of society and how social change occurs. Before taking a look at what new systems thinking has to offer, let's examine how we came to understand the systems we work with.

Systems theory originated in the 1940s and 1950s, and social workers embraced it in the 1960s and 1970s in part as a reaction to psychodynamic theory, which, in its narrow focus, failed to consider the social world in dealing with human problems (Payne, 2005). There are two forms of current systems theory: generalist and ecological. In the generalist theory, whether you work with a small family system or a larger neighborhood, you need to place that target system within a larger context to understand how forces in the environment affect human behaviors. The social worker, then, widens the lens to look at the relationships, the process that occurs among people and organizations and forces in their environment, and the patterns of interaction that may enhance or suppress people's growth. This attention to context and interplay among systems does not negate theories of individual development; rather, it broadens our understanding of the forces operating at individual and social levels.

Ecological systems theory, which emerged out of general systems theory in the 1970s (Germain & Gitterman, 1980; Siporin, 1975), focuses our attention on the place at which the person meets the environment. The aim of social work becomes an effort to better the fit between people and their natural and social worlds. The target of change could be some aspect of the self and the context, but emphasis is placed on the interface or place of interaction between the two. The social worker's goal is to help individuals navigate their worlds with attention to that interface (e.g., home, school, work, community).

A major criticism of both these theories is that a system is conceived of as an entity continually striving for stability and homeostasis and that is resistant to change. As theories of equilibrium (Hudson, 2000), the focus of systems theories is not so much on change in the environment as on the ability of the individual or target system to cope with, adapt to, and negotiate the exigencies of the external world. The change that occurs is more in reaction to external forces than it is an action upon them. The elements of the system can be viewed as hierarchical, such as nesting boxes where smaller boxes fit inside larger ones (Germain, 1979) and interface with one another.

Kondrat (2002) suggests that Giddens's structuration theory (1984) may more aptly describe the relationship among systems, as it attempts to bridge the macro-micro understanding of behavior by asserting that the relationship between humans and their social structures is recursive. That is, social structures shape human activity, but participants in any type of social encounter continually create and re-create these structures. Thus, the notion of environment moves from all-powerful determinant to both the medium for and the outcome of activities of individuals and groups over time (Giddens, 1984). This conceptualization is quite relevant to social work, especially for social workers who use a strengths and empowerment perspective with families and communities and view the target system as acting upon the environment rather than as a passive reacting system. For the most part, ecological systems theory is the most common systems theory presented in social work programs today, as it emphasizes homeostasis and the striving of the target system to fit into or create a niche in the environment.

However, a new holistic approach to both the physical and the biological world is evolving—the web of life. We will briefly explore the boundaries in systems, which is important if we view systems as having influence on and acting on one another. We'll also look at chaos theory and its new ideas of how systems change and evolve. Finally, we'll apply some of these ideas to real-world social work problems.

# THE WEB OF LIFE: INTERCONNECTEDNESS OF OUR PHYSICAL AND SOCIAL WORLDS

Over the past two decades, new-paradigm thinking has come to touch on areas from physics to biology and ecology, to psychology, economics, and political science. During the first half of the twentieth century, biologists who study organisms helped develop systems thinking in terms of context, relationships, and connectedness. The result was a revolution in Western scientific thought: it rejected the former Cartesian paradigm, which asserted that the system of the whole could be understood by understanding the properties of its parts, and provided evidence that individual properties were not intrinsic and could be understood only within the context of the larger whole. The solid material objects of classical physics dissolved at the subatomic level into wavelike patterns or probabilities of interconnections, such as the dual nature of light and matter as both particle and wave, that have no meaning as isolated entities.

On the basis of systems thinking, Capra (1996) and others propose that the physical world is not a machine but an interconnected web of living organisms that is in a constant state of renewal and self-organization, with a high degree of flexibility and plasticity (Capra, 1996).

Fritjof Capra (1982, 1996), a theoretical physicist and philosopher, has described this new way of thinking as the web of life and asserts that it applies to natural and social systems. There are five criteria of this model of understanding living systems (Capra & Steindl-Rast, 1991). First is a shift from the part to the whole. That is, the properties of the parts can only be understood from an understanding of the dynamics of the whole. In fact, what we call *part* is not a part at all but a pattern in a web of relationships. Thus, "in quantum theory you never end up with 'things'; you always deal with interconnections" (Capra, 1982, p. 80).

Second is the shift from structure to process, which is not unrelated to the age-old adage that form follows function. In the old paradigm, the focus was on fundamental structures such as the cell. The force and mechanisms through which these structures interact give rise to processes. However, the new paradigm asserts that every structure is a manifestation of underlying processes in a web of relationships that is constantly changing and intrinsically dynamic.

Inherent in this process is the principle of self-organization or self-renewal. Life forms continually adapt, learn, and evolve. Capra and Steindl-Rast (1991) illustrate this shift from structure to process with the example of a tree:

> In the old paradigm I would say the tree consists of certain fundamental structures. . . . In the new paradigm I would say the tree is a phenomenon that connects the sky and the earth . . . with the process of photosynthesis, which takes place in the leaves. For maximum efficiency, the leaves are distributed on the branch in a certain way so they all turn toward the sun. They need to be nourished, and this is why you need a trunk and . . . roots. You have the nourishment from the earth and the . . . the sun, and the two mix in the tree. Lots of processes are involved and those processes create certain structures. (p. 131)

With the third criterion, how we see or study the world shifts from objective science to epistemic science, or from positivism to constructivism. In the old paradigm, scientific descriptions were objective, independent of the observer and of the process of knowing. In the new paradigm, the understanding of the process of knowing is explicitly included in the description of natural phenomena. In other words, you cannot separate the subject of study from the process of studying it. Thus, nonconceptual ways of knowing such as intuition, affection, and mysticism must be included in epistemology.

The fourth is a shift in the metaphor of knowledge from a building to a network. In the former paradigm, basic building blocks of matter are fundamentals upon which further principles are built. In the new paradigm, the network replaces the building blocks of knowledge. The network asserts that there are no absolute hierarchies; nothing is more fundamental than anything else. Instead, reality is a network of relationships, and our descriptions form an interconnected web of observed phenomena.

Finally, scientists do not deal with absolute truth in phenomena. Just as Einstein's theory of relativity has forced us to abandon the notion of an absolute space as a dimension separate from time, if things are constantly self-renewing, all concepts, theories, and findings about phenomena are approximate descriptions of reality. We can approve these approximations, but any one is subject to revision at any time (Capra, 1982; Capra & Steindl-Rast, 1991).

In summary, this new systems paradigm suggests the metaphor of a web of interconnections to understand both natural and social systems. Thus, new systems thought rejects absolute reality to accept different groups' constructions of reality. Systems are ever changing, self-organizing, unpredictable, and may have similar processes emerging at different levels (e.g., violence in the community may mirror violence in the family).

## A NEW UNIVERSE: A CLOSED SYSTEM WITH PERMEABLE BOUNDARIES?

Adding to our knowledge about the ever-changing web of life of physical and social systems is a new understanding of the planet we live on as a whole, closed system. Social work scholar John Coates, author of *Ecology and Social Work* (2003), echoes Capra's views in his own unfolding paradigm, which identifies lessons that we have learned from new knowledge in physics, ecology, and complexity science, such as chaos theory. He adds a new understanding of boundaries to the principles of connectedness, subjectivity, and complexity. Essentially, this means that the earth is a closed system with limited resources and capabilities that require sustainability, and that the universe has evolved with us as a part of it, not in control over it.

This does not mean that boundaries are impermeable. On the contrary, the human body or the planet must have permeable membranes to manage the intake and use of energy from and into its environment and to exclude undesirable influences, poisons, or predators. Nowhere is the notion of a closed system better expressed than in Russell Schweickart's (1983) description of his experience as a lunar module pilot for the *Apollo IX* Earth orbital flight. The following excerpt from his reflection "No Frames, No Boundaries" poetically describes the paradigm shift:

> You look down there and can't imagine how many borders and boundaries you cross, again and again and you don't even see them. There you are—hundreds of people in the Middle East killing each other over some imaginary line that you're not even aware of. From where you see it the thing is a whole, and it is so beautiful. You wish you could take each in one hand . . . and say, "Look. Look at it from this perspective. Look at that. What's important?"

> Later on your friend goes out to the Moon and he looks back at
> . . . the contrast between that little blue and white Christmas tree or-
> nament and the black sky. . . . And you realize that on that small spot,
> that little blue and white thing, is everything that means anything to
> you—all of history and music and poetry and art and death and birth
> and love, tears, joy, games, all of it . . .
>
> And you realize that from that perspective that you've changed.
> . . . You know all those people down there and they are like you, they
> are you—and somehow you represent them. . . . And that becomes a
> rather special responsibility and it tells you something about that re-
> lationship with this thing we call life.
>
> And all through this I've used the word "you" because it's not me
> . . . it's you. It's we. It's life that's had that experience. (16)

This is indeed a radical departure from perceiving our world as a
static structure apart from us, its inhabitants. We are all part of the
fate of the earth.

This new perspective also suggests that there is no linear chain
of events in unraveling the causes of individual or social problems.
Rather, multiple events, including humankind's daily footprints
on the planet, interact and may contribute to the unfolding of
events; the most minute occurrence may tip the scale in some
changing pattern (e.g., failing Communism, glasnost, and the fall
of the Berlin wall in 1989 were only a tipping point in the sociopolitical changes in Eastern Europe). This leads us to the notion of chaos theory.

## COMPLEX SYSTEMS: CHAOS THEORY

In the classical systems view, sometimes referred to as the functional
approach (Parsons, 1951), systems are considered reactive and
mechanistic, and their elements always readjust toward a state of
equilibrium. This view also perceives systems in a linear cause-effect
mode; the larger system places stress on the smaller ones, which
usually forces the smaller ones to adapt in order to survive. Evolving from a wide range of disciplines over the past fifteen to twenty
years, newer systems thinking, sometime referred to as complexity
or complex systems thinking, is about the spontaneous, active, and
self-organizing nature of both social and natural systems (Waldrop,
1992). These ideas challenge linear cause-effect thinking.

Among the complexity theories that some social workers are exploring in an attempt to better understand complex social systems is chaos theory, the study of unstable, complex, dynamic systems. This theory proposes that complex systems are unpredictable and spontaneously move from disequilibrium toward new states (Derezotes, 2005). Examples of such systems are the stock market, the weather, electroencephalogram (more widely known as EEG) patterns, and many social systems (Hudson, 2000). To put it simply, chaos theory challenges simple cause-effect explanations of human behavior.

The public's interest in chaos theory was piqued in the movie *Jurassic Park*. My guess is that most people focused more on the impression the male scientist was trying to make on the female paleobotanist than on any scientific notion. However, the scientist's idea was as follows: even though scientists and technicians involved in the twentieth-century resurrection of dinosaurs thought they had everything under control, there may be other forces that come into play as the inhabitants of this world assert themselves to cocreate themselves and survive. The message sent to the general public by this blockbuster may have been, "Don't mess with Mother Nature." Nevertheless, Michael Crichton, as he often does in his novels, may have done us a service by heightening the general public's awareness of or at least curiosity about chaos theory.

So, how is chaos theory relevant to social work? The social work scholar Christopher Hudson (2000) delineates some concepts of chaos theory and their relevance to social work. First is nonlinearity, which contrasts with the assumption of a direct relationship between cause and effect (i.e., "If you cut twice as much from the welfare budget, twice the number of recipients will be dropped" [Hudson, 2000, p. 5]). Feedback from one or more variables is more likely to create curvilinear relationships in both natural and social systems.

Second is sensitivity to initial conditions. Small, seemingly insignificant behaviors may affect outcomes over time. Lorenz (1972) refers to this as the butterfly effect: a butterfly flapping its wings in Brazil can result in a tornado in Texas, or in the social work context, a small intervention on the part of a social worker can have major effects on client outcome. For example, one mentor may help build resilience in a child that helps him or her take the many subsequent steps to escape a life of abuse. It is implicit in this principle that the specifics of future behavior can never be precisely defined (Hudson, 2000).

Third is that systems' patterns never repeat themselves exactly because of strange "attractors" or other processes that intervene. Prior to chaos theory, it was assumed that change in systems always tended toward a fixed point or stable equilibrium; systems could fluctuate but always returned to steady state. However, it has been discovered that some systems, though they may follow a familiar pattern, will never repeat themselves (Devaney, 1989).

Fourth is the critical threshold, or the straw that broke the camel's back (Hudson, 2000, p. 5). Patterns, if they sufficiently replicate themselves, will spread to other systems. For example, a new approach to intraagency management-staff collaboration may reach a point in its effectiveness when it begins to increase the degree of interagency collaboration among the other organizations that do business with an agency.

Fifth is self-organization, the notion that organisms and systems are in a constant state of self-renewal. In contrast to the idea that systems simply adapt to the external environment (natural or social), this concept posits that systems exist in a constant state of change and continually create new organized states of resolution that result from negative and positive feedback from the environment, as well as from mechanisms from within. So, a family's mode of conflict resolution may evolve to a different pattern instead of returning to the old one.

Last is self-similarity, or parallel processes or patterns that emerge and repeat themselves at different levels. For example, a micro process of poor, ineffective treatment of clients may begin to emerge as an organizational pattern of abusive staff relationships that feeds the process at both levels.

Hudson (2000) points out that chaos theory has been applied to the fields of economics, psychology, and medicine—and examples can also be found in organizational behavior and decision making. But chaos theory has been little noticed by social workers. If we are interested in understanding the patterns in individual and organizational lives, then perhaps we should examine the theory. If we can accept that we may never be able to predict therapeutic outcomes but can gain a better understanding of overall trends and processes, the theory may be quite useful. We may want to become more skilled at research designs such as time series, which looks at phenomena over time, versus the slice-in-time cross-sectional approach. We should also explore nonlinear dynamic phenomena through qualitative research methods, with which we can dig deeper into understanding phenomena that are not directly observable but may affect subsequent patterns (Hudson, 2000).

There are additional reasons why we should look at the concepts in chaos theory. First of all, the theory supports some notions that social workers have had instinctively since the inception of the profession: contrary to evidence-based practice, human beings are complex systems and nothing about assessment and intervention is simple. A second instinct of social workers is that patterns of behavior, such as violence, seem to repeat themselves across systems. Consider a couple that experiences domestic violence that has increased since the father returned from Iraq. They happen to live in a neighborhood where gang violence influences neighborhood norms. Their fourteen-year-old son is getting into more fights at school and has shown a recent interest in ice hockey (a much more aggressive sport) over soccer. The story goes on and on. Can, for example, modeling explain all this violence? Is it not more complex or perhaps interconnected?

The principle of self-emergence is that individuals, families, or groups compose self-renewing systems that are empowering. It suggests that we do not simply react to external forces but can turn to the internal capabilities and motivations of ourselves and our colleagues or friends, our social organizations, to generate new responses to changes in our lives and in our world. If individuals and groups are in a constant state of reorganization, and evolving new and unique responses to natural and social conditions, then we no longer will rely on natural selection and social selection as primary explanations for social change. This has enormous implications for understanding, for example, the life choices of the immigrant, a family of mixed-race children, or even the coming together of religious leaders to address global warming.

Finally, there is the phenomenon of interconnectedness of systems. At the onset of this book, we looked at the interconnectedness of problems that threaten our social welfare on global and local levels. Understanding these connections may be a vital key for how we intervene and solve the problems of the long-term sustainability of our species and our home.

Let's look at how these ideas of new systems thinking are relevant to social work practice with global, community, and organizational systems.

## GLOBAL POVERTY

If we want to examine global poverty, we cannot separate it from global economics, environmental pressures, international and national politics, or culture. In *The End of Poverty*, Jeffrey Sachs (2005), an internationally renowned economic adviser to governments around the world, shares that, though he has worked with governments for the past twenty years, it was only when he began working closely with the villagers and women in local economic development projects that he really understood the interconnectedness of extreme poverty with other pieces of the puzzle. Those other pieces are AIDS; a country's physical geography, agronomic conditions, economics, and trade infrastructure; the fiscal framework of government spending on social welfare; patterns of governance; and cultural norms related to economic development. These pieces represent a shift in thinking from the part to the whole. While Sachs previously focused much more on economic problems, his recent work with the Earth Institute at Columbia University is a cooperative approach that involves many kinds of scientists, including policy experts, environmental scientists, ecologists, and pubic health experts, in a cross-disciplinary approach to the challenges of poverty and sustainable development.

This holistic understanding is reflected in the goals of the UN Millennium Project (2002), which were heavily influenced by Sachs. The plan, a broad and comprehensive approach to reduce world poverty significantly by the year 2015, targets goals in the following areas: hunger reduction, achieving universal primary education, promoting gender equality and empowering women, improving in areas of maternal health and child mortality, combating diseases such as HIV/AIDS and malaria, and achieving enduring environmental sustainability. The final goal is to form a global partnership for development, with strategies that challenge the failing structural adjustment modes of the past. Sachs emphasizes in his book that these goals are reachable, but only if we make a global commitment to all these interconnected needs.

These goals are connected to furthering social justice and human rights, and they are connected to global security. "The war against terror is bound up in the war against poverty" (Bono, quoting Secretary of State Colin Powell, in Sachs, 2005). "Poor countries and hungry societies are much more likely than high income societies to fall into conflict over scarce vital resources. . . . Poor countries are more likely to have weak governments. . . . Resource scarcity can provoke population migrations, displacements . . . and young people without productive alternatives may turn to violence . . . or feel a sense of hopelessness, despair and rage" (UN Millennium Project, 2002, p. 6).

· The process of understanding poverty, then, has broadened from an isolated, discipline-specific, expert-economist worldview. Furthermore, it involves more than just collecting data and reports from various disciplines and having the economists carry out the solutions to world poverty. In another arena, it involves more than having a multidisciplinary team meeting of nurses, physicians, and social workers at the table, with the information filtered, controlled, discounted, and interpreted solely by the dominant professional. New science thinking means a genuine acceptance, validation, dialogue, and processing of each member's offerings, and it means solutions that are more effective because they arise from multiple perspectives.

This interdisciplinary, cross-cultural, cross-interest-group approach to understanding systems means getting the client, patient, or villager to the table, too, with an equal investment in and responsibility for setting the goals and carrying out the plan. This is congruent with social work's value of involving people who are invested and knowledgeable and have experienced the effects of social problems in their definition and solution of those problems. In a nutshell, this approach is an epistemic view rather than an objective view.

If we embrace the notion of approximate realities, then these notions of various professionals and constituents are validated, and the search for solutions and strategies results not in the best answer or the real truth, but in a reconciliation of various perspectives, or views of the elephant. Thus, the goals of combating global poverty involve framing the examination within the interconnectedness of natural and sociopolitical systems. Strategies, then, involve both professionals and laypeople, at the national and local

level; validate their unique disciplinary and experiential worldviews; and are sensitive to an array of cultural values and ideology.
Solutions, then, to problems such as water shortage in a local village in the Philippines are not cookie cutter in their approach.
Rather, they are unique, depending on the mix of conditions and
players involved in the process.

In evaluating the results of strategies to reduce poverty, the expectation shifts from a return to a steady state (by adding a building block to the former structure), to acknowledgment of the ap-
pearance of new organized states or interactive processes of
self-renewal. We are not moving one step further in the building
blocks of world prosperity or that much closer to the apex or ultimate answer. For example, the success of developing countries
does not simply mean a building up of their economies to mirror
that of the United States. Rather, conditions of world poverty and
health are constantly in a state of flux or, in the terminology of
chaos theory, self-organization. The steps to improve other countries' economies or health occur through a constant evolution of
new solutions toward a new organized state of functioning that is
similar but not the same as the former one.

Chaos theory also requires that we pay attention to connections across levels of systems. The element of self-similarity is evident, for example, in the relationship between the subjugation of
and interpersonal violence toward women in household and village life and the state of civil unrest and violence and the threat to
human rights at a national level. Whether our focus is Afghanistan
or Los Angeles, we need to examine and influence the parallel
processes of violence, both in domestic and larger-scale social and
political unrest.

## COMMUNITY DEVELOPMENT

The principles of new systems thinking can also be applied to problem definition and solution at the community level. Following the
fall of the Berlin wall, a movement in this country emerged, over
fifteen years, to turn the country's swords into plowshares. With the
escalated closures of military bases and a real possibility of a peace
economy, communitywide attempts to diversify the former military-
dependent economies of cities and regions cropped up across the

country. From Maine to Minnesota, to San Francisco, communities brought disparate groups to the table to collaborate on planning for military closures. California's Center for Economic Conversion, a nonprofit group headquartered in Mountain View, facilitated this process, which was supported at the national level by the National Commission on Economic Conversion. The commission joined a coalition of more than fifty national peace and justice organizations and sponsored televised town meetings to discuss the adjustment of spending patterns from military to civilian priorities (Mary, 1994).

One of many examples of success includes the conversion of the Brooklyn Naval Yard as part of a job development, clean-up, and beautification program to provide summer employment for youths and to house a post office and forty-five businesses, such as crystal importers, printers, and pipe-fitting manufacturers (Brown, 1990). The strategies of these efforts often involved town meetings and task forces of multiple constituents including large businesses; manufacturing owners and laborers; local military personnel; environmental, housing, and peace activists; and local politicians. Tactics often involved consensual or collaborative modes such as community education, committee work, and political advocacy over more adversary ones such as strikes and boycotts. The focus of this community development was often on understanding the whole.

Working together, key interests came together in communities to examine the bigger picture of the impact of military expenditures on a community and to envision alternative enterprises that address the needs of the environment, the workforce, and the overall health of the community (Mary, 1994). In short, it was a holistic, interconnected, cross-disciplinary, interest-group approach. Challenging the old paradigm of economic development as absolute (e.g., the best strategy being one that raises the tax base), groups dialogued from San Diego to Maine about the multiple uses of former military land and facilities to meet various local needs. These projects were, indeed, tailored to each city's needs, as articulated by the various constituents involved. Thus, what emerged were multifaceted economic conversion strategies that unfolded as approximate descriptions of economic development rather than top-down, singularly focused solutions by economic experts.

## A COMMUNITY DEVELOPMENT CASE

My experience with a local project illustrates a shift from an old paradigm to a new paradigm of community development (Mary, 1996). Facing targeted closures of the naval base, shipyard, naval housing, and naval hospital in the early 1990s, my hometown government's economic development staff began to plan, informally, for possible reuse of the land. The government held preliminary discussions with the local university for a business incubator and with the port for possible expansion. However, a local group of citizens emerged, surveyed various community sectors, and concluded that many city leaders and constituents, including elected officials, were unaware of the upcoming closure. Aware that legislation on base closure mandated the involvement of the community in the planning process, this group decided to engage city and military officials and other constituents and interested parties in a town meeting. The purpose of this venue was to raise the awareness of the community to the issue and to inform them of ways to obtain ongoing and greater community input over the subsequent months. The group thus challenged the narrow business-as-usual mode of economic development by injecting a participatory, multiple-interest-group process of problem definition and solution.

The town meeting featured an update from various speakers on the problem and the possibilities for economic conversion; military and city officials as well as representatives from the Center for Economic Conversion shared facts on the necessary planning process as well as visions for the future. Various constructions or approximate descriptions of the problems and possible solutions resulted from these speakers. Questions and comments were invited. Following this, interest groups broke down into discussion sessions, structured in small circular venues that task-force members facilitated. Groups came up with suggestions for reuse, which were then prioritized and shared when all got back together. The task force formalized the data into a report with recommendations on specific reuses. In addition, the route by which community citizens could remain involved became clear: they would be invited to ongoing public hearings on reuse planning. This participatory process assumed an interdisciplinary, cross-cultural, and cross-interest-group approach. No one expert had the final word; all views were values and all participants equally respected.

The worldviews of local economic development officials and the multi-interest task force were very different. The city's main concern was reuse of the land and increasing the tax base to improve the economy in a trickle-down manner. The city considered needs for local educational facilities or more housing secondary priorities not connected to opportunities for economic development. In contrast, the worldview of task-force members was one of interconnectedness. In a win-win approach, the group proposed a multiple use of the former navy housing land, and it viewed housing, jobs, education, and economic development as interconnected. Therefore, the group proposed four uses: (1) naval housing to house homeless people, (2) a local school, (3) a job development program for youths and young adults, and (4) an industrial job incubator for cutting-edge industries such as recycling and renewable-energy ventures. In addition, the group envisioned connections across the programs (e.g., the homeless could enter the workforce through jobs at the school and industrial park).

The two groups disagreed on how to reuse the land, and in the end Washington officials intervened and mandated that city officials plan to accommodate interests in a mixed use of the land (which was the task force's recommendation from the start). The two sides arrived at an approximate best answer and agreed to develop housing, a job corps program, an industrial park, and possibly a school.

The outcome of this process validated a unique process of community planning that involves diverse interest groups and worldviews and at least compromise, if not total collaboration. In addition, attention shifted from one focus (economic development) to several areas of social welfare: work, education, and business development.

## THE WEB OF LIFE IN ORGANIZATIONS

A major breakthrough in organizational management theory occurred when we began to shift our focus from the maintenance of cogs in a well-organized machine, or scientific management, to a concern for human relationships and people as invested actors in complex work environments (Argyris, 1964). In the 1960s and 1970s, our thinking evolved from workers are lazy and need constant supervision to humans give meaning to their work, to organizations are efficient to the extent that they use the assets of their workers. Over the past few decades, we have made perhaps an even bigger shift from the organization as a static structure to the organization as a living organism.

A central focus of this new thinking is the learning organization, wherein collective learning is the key to change and the concepts of the web of life are apparent. Peter Senge, a leader in this movement, suggests that learning organizations continually renew themselves "where people continually expand their capacity to create the results they truly desire . . . and [learn] to see the whole together" (1990, p. 3). With a focus on learning at the organizational level, a learning organization "facilitates the learning of all its members and continuously transforms itself" (Pedler, Bergoyne, & Boydell, 1991, p. 1), and is characterized by "employee involvement in a process of collaboratively conducted change" (Watkins & Marsick, 1992, p. 118). In the learning organization, individual and organizational goals are connected, tension and change are constants, dialogue is critical, and organizations are continually aware of their interactions with and interdependency on the environment (Kerka, 1995).

Senge and colleagues' (1999) more recent work further supports new systems thinking. The new metaphor for the organization is a garden. Companies are like live organisms that we have tried to fix by forcing change. Instead, we should think about them as embodiments of nature, living things that grow and renew themselves. So, instead of forcing change from on high, we should recognize that change results from dialogue, feedback, and patterns of relationships, and we should create new opportunities for self-regulation and growth. Change in relationships requires openness and reciprocity in place of control and compliance (Senge et al., 1999).

Organizational systems scholar Margaret Wheatley also supports these ideas. She has been writing about the new science and its relevance to organizational behavior for at least ten years. With a background diverse in education and experience, she coauthored with Myron Kellner-Rogers *A Simpler Way* (1996), in which they apply ideas of new science to individuals and organizations.

Organizations are intelligent, creative, meaning-seeking entities. Their structures are not imposed but spring from the process of doing work. Evaluating them must equally involve a look at what they hope to accomplish and the degree to which they nurture human relationships. Leadership does not involve elevating someone to a position of hero; that is, searching for the individual who can outsmart the competition. Rather, leadership is fostering interdependence by supporting and creating new combinations of resources that can contribute to and expand the organization's potential. Therefore, information needs to be shared and free flowing; "when we shrink people's access to information, we shrink their capacity" (p. 82). They assert that "the systems we create are chosen together. They are the result of dances, not wars" (p. 44).

Drawing on the work of Fritjof Capra and chaos theory, in 1999, Wheatley turned her attention to management and change in organizations. Challenging the notion of equilibrium as a desired organizational state, she, too, posits that organizations are not machines but living open systems. Three processes are critical to organizational growth: self-renewal, self-reference, and stability over time. When an organization has an identity and knows what its goal is, it can respond to changes both external and internal in ways that are flexible yet consistent with itself. It stays in business, over time, by staying open to new opportunities, learning new skills, and creating new markets, all while maintaining its overall stability and integrity (Wheatley, 1999).

These principles affect the way that organizations function. For example, most administrators in organizations, especially in large bureaucracies, seek order and believe they have to defend themselves against their employees through strict rules and regulations against every possibility of upset. This explains their rigid chains of command and processes of communication and decision making. If, however, administrators perceived their organizations as more open systems, then they could recognize conflict, disorder, and imbalance as precursors to new, more vital organizational forms and processes that respond to changes in the environment. Change agents would re-create the organization in order to maintain it (Wheatley, 1999).

## LEADERSHIP AND COLLABORATION

How does this type of organizational change occur? Recent literature on leadership and collaboration helps us understand the process of change. Leaders are not superheroes. Leadership is not a position but a process; it happens at all levels. For Senge (1999), first-order leaders are the line-level workers who are committed to talking to constituents and to change. Then, from an original group seed carriers evolve. The internal networkers or community builders who get people talking to one another. Executive leaders, who may act as coaches or mentors, add to the interplay of the three communities.

Key ingredients in helping change take root are the personal stake of the members of the organization and their trust in one another (Webber, 1999). This is congruent with many of the ideas in transformational leadership theory, which, since the 1980s, has received much attention and research (Northouse, 2007). This theory is appealing to the arena of social work because it is value based and involves a participatory, empowerment approach to leadership. Key concepts of transformational leadership that evidence new systems thinking are that it depends not on leader traits or characteristics, but on a process that occurs between leader and follower, and that the success of the organization depends on the connection between personal values and goals and those of the organization.

Literature that has been emerging in interagency, intersector collaboration over the past fifteen to twenty years also evidences some attention to the processes by which organizations tackle metaproblems. Liz Beth Schorr's (1997) review of social programs shares many case studies of how organizations can become unstuck from intransigent responses to social problems by seeing the bigger picture, working together, and refusing to view change as either top down or bottom up but rather as interactive. Some of the ideas from collaboration scholarship reflect web-of-life thinking, such as the importance of bringing entities with divergent views or constructions of the problem to the table (Gray, 1989), the need to make new connections across sectors (Austin & Drucker Foundation, 2000), and the attention to context, consensus decision making, and the development of long-term sustainable, collaborative relationships (Mattessich, Murray-Close, & Monsey 2001; Winer & Ray, 2000).

We have been exploring new systems as living, interconnected entities, both in nature and in the social world, and applying some of these ideas to global and community problems as well as to organizational life. One of today's most profound crises and opportunities is the split between the material and spiritual ways of knowing the world. Let's explore these ideas further before we enter the great divide of science and spiritualism.

## ADDITIONAL THINGS TO THINK ABOUT

1. How do these theories and concepts affect our understanding of the problem and solution of an international policy dilemma? A community or neighborhood problem? An organizational challenge? An individual or family scenario?

2. What are the risks or disadvantages of assessing national problems without a global context?

3. What are your thoughts when someone says, "Of course there is an absolute reality, we just haven't figured out the way to get at it yet?"

4. How does this theme of an interconnected web of life influence research? Does it influence the research question? The design? The methods?

5. How is valuing diversity relevant to new systems thinking?

6. How are the principles in the NASW Code of Ethics consistent with or divergent from this thinking? From the International Federation of Social Workers Ethics?

## MAIN POINTS

1. The web of life, one new systems theory, sees the world as an interconnected web of constantly changing patterns, which rejects the older Cartesian view of the world as a more static structure or machine.

2. The web of life calls for four shifts in thinking about natural and social systems: (1) from part to whole, (2) from structure to process, (3) from building blocks to networks, and (4) from objective science to epistemic science.

3. Chaos theory, another new systems theory, suggests that systems constantly renew themselves; are nonlinear, complex, and unstable; and can never be totally predictable.

4. A new view of our planet suggests that the world is all one closed interacting system with limited resources.

5. This thinking can be applied across all levels of systems.

## For Further Reading

Capra, F. (1983). *The turning point: Science, society and the rising culture.* New York: Bantam Books.

Capra, F. (1996). *The web of life.* New York: Anchor Books, Doubleday.

Korten, D. (2006). *The great turning: From empire to earth community.* San Francisco: Berrett-Koehler Publishers.

Wheatley, M. J. (1999). *Leadership and the new science.* San Francisco: Berrett-Koehler Publishers.

# CHAPTER 4

# Spirituality and Science: Today's Modern Dilemma

If human-made institutions in part cause the problems facing the world today, and if human beings are complex cultural beings who bring their values and belief systems to the problem-solving process, then we cannot ignore the important functions that spirituality and religion can play in moving us toward more sustainable worldviews. This chapter will identify new ideas that connect science and spirit at macro and micro levels.

First, let's define religion and spirituality. The dictionary does not help us much in defining spirituality. David Steindl-Rast, a Benedictine monk and scholar, defines *spirituality* as "an encounter with mystery" and as "religion, translated into everyday living" (Capra & Steindl-Rast, 1991, p. 13). Spirituality can be viewed as "the dynamic way that a person creates purpose and meaning in life" (Hutchison, 1998, p. 57). For purposes of our discussion, I define *religion* as a religion; that is, a "complex of systems, organized or unorganized, by which people relate to deity and to their own existence with spiritual and moral values concerning personal life, work and other people" (Day, 2000, p. 33). In general, religions provide a communal organization or institution offering an organized set of beliefs and values, ritual and worship, a moral code by which to gauge one's behavior, and support and mutual aid to individuals and families and the raising of children.

Social work historically is closely connected to the values of religious traditions. In the Middle Ages, help for the poor and sick depended on the charity of the church. As the U.S. colonies were populated, they turned to the Protestant traditions of England, which were based on early Judaic teachings of social justice, love, and charity. The connection between religion and social work continued with the development of the Charity Organization Society, temperance and social gospel movements of the nineteenth century, and the civil rights movement of the twentieth century (Day, 2000). The connection between the church and nonprofit community-based organizations has become even more critical in the life of U.S. communities over the past two decades, as the direct social welfare role of the government has diminished (Cnaan, Sinha, & McGrew, 2004).

Religions have done and can do much good in the world. They provide ideas and inspiration for peace, charity, social justice, and good stewardship of the earth. Local efforts such as those of interfaith councils have developed resources such as housing, food banks, and programs for the homeless. National organizations such as the Association of Community Organizations for Reform Now (better known as ACORN), with local state chapters, have combined efforts of unions, churches, and other community-based organizations to advocate for myriad social justice issues from voters' rights to farmworkers' conditions and justice for janitors. For many of us, religions have at their core a vital message: all humans are connected to one another and affect one another's fate and the fate of the world, and people must find within themselves a moral compass that will help orient them and their environments (Ornstein & Erlich, 1989).

But there is a darker side of religion. At a religion's worst it can help provide a rationale for destruction, war, and terrorism. John Mack (2003), the recently deceased Pulitzer Prize–winning professor of psychiatry of Harvard University, explores the role of worldviews in terrorism. He discusses immediate causes, such as hatred of people who are willing to sacrifice their own lives to destroy their enemies, and proximate causes, such as the history and economics of the Middle East. He then identifies the more fundamental or deeper causes, which he claims may involve dysfunctional worldviews that are reflected in our thinking and the institutions we create to solve problems.

For example, patriotism or nationalism is also often connected to religion. It can manifest itself in generosity, courage, and loyalty, but it also can give way to extreme chauvinism and hatred of the "other." People in the United States are religious and patriotic (Putnam, 2000; Rifkin, 2004a). Americans' religious beliefs often affect their political views. For example, 48% of Americans believe that the United States has special protection from God (Pew Research Center, 2002). Six of ten Americans believe that "our people are not perfect, but our culture is superior to others" (Pew Research Center, 2002). The 1990 World Values Survey asked respondents in different countries to choose which of two views of morality best reflect their own values: "There are absolutely clear guidelines about what is good and evil. These apply to everyone, whatever the circumstances," or "There can never be absolutely clear guidelines about what is good and evil. What is good and evil depends entirely upon the circumstances of our time." Most Europeans, Canadians, and Japanese chose the second, while Americans were more likely to choose the first. Connected to chauvinism is the reality that religions and religious institutions can polarize and instigate violence or unite others to rise above it. There are, for example, passages in the Bible and the Koran that promote universal love and lasting peace; there are also passages that promote exclusion, division, and holy wars. It is a matter of what you select, how you interpret it, and how you use it in your actions.

Rifkin (2004a), in his comparison of attitudes of Europeans and Americans, remarks that it will be difficult for Americans to adjust to a world with increasingly connected webs, networks of relationships where people and countries are interdependent on one another for their global well-being. "What happens to the American sense of being special, of being a chosen people, in a world where exclusivity is steadily giving way to inclusivity?" (Rifkin, 2004a, p. 23).

But another concept identified by Mack may be the most problematic to long-term survival: dualistic thinking. The "mind divides the world into conflicting polarities—good and evil, God and the Devil, for or against, friend or enemy, deserving or undeserving." Acknowledging that the polar mind may be a necessity in instinctive survival mode, he points out that it is also the mind of revenge and war: "This is a war of good against the evildoers," or "We must destroy America, the Great Satan." This dualism "must be transcended if we are to survive, as a species" (Mack, 2003, pp. 13–14).

Another danger in dualism is its dominance and disconnection. The great chain of being, a classical conception of the order of the universe that sustained into the Renaissance, was based on the premise that every living thing existed in a divinely planned hierarchical order. At the top was God, followed by angels, humans, animals, plants, and finally the inanimate objects of earth, water, fire, and air. Though they are interconnected in the sense that phenomena at one level may mirror those at another, the dominance of each realm over the next maintains order. Furthermore, as modern science developed in the Age of Reason, this hierarchy was maintained, with the debatable spirit world somewhere out there and above the real world, mankind below, and finally the rest of the natural world (Brooklyn College, 2006).

For most of civilization, this dominator model extended down from mankind ruling nature to men ruling women (Eisler, 1995). Scholarship points to a period before the fifth century BCE, when older Neolithic cultures existed with greater egalitarian relationships and a predominance of goddess religions, wherein people and nature lived in harmony and the goddess represented Mother Nature. When invaders from the north began to conquer these societies, a wave of male supremacy began, accompanied by male-dominated religions. It is Eisler's (1995) contention that this dominator model of society is prevalent in the world and supports both the continued oppression of women globally and the degradation of a natural environment that we perceive ourselves as disconnected from, to rule over, and to use or abuse for our benefit alone.

## DOES MODERN SCIENCE FALL SHORT?

Modern science began in the sixteenth and seventeenth centuries when philosophers and scientists began to reject metaphysics, mysticism, revelation, and faith in the understanding of their world. They sought to verify reality through empirical observation and experimental prediction, and they developed a process of hypothesis testing to confirm their observations. These methods led to breakthroughs in physics, astronomy, chemistry, and biology, and eventually in the nineteenth and twentieth centuries, to social and behavioral sciences (Kurtz, 2003). The assumptions of logical empiricism, upon which modern science rest, are three. Objectivism holds that the scientist or observer can hold the objective world at a distance and study it apart and separate from him- or herself. Positivism asserts that everything in the real world must be physically measurable. Reductionism aims to understand the whole world or system by examining the behavior of its elemental parts or fundamental particles (Harman, 1994).

In modern society, there is no single worldview or way of understanding the world that all agree upon. We could say that we have two competing worldviews: one of the humanities and religions that focuses on values, morals, and spirituality, and a scientific one in which these are irrelevant. Thus, if science is the only recognized definer of truth, important realms of human experience are invalidated. But as we enter the twenty-first century, is science enough? Can we adequately assess the pros and cons of communications technology and the way it has altered our human experience of space and time simply through the study of the nanosecond? Today's warnings of global warming come to us primarily from the scientific community. Why, then, are religious leaders claiming this issue as part of their domain on which to speak out? Why is one-third of the American population turning to alternative health care, including methods such as meditation and spiritual healers (Ray, 1996)?

Because the global forces of the 1980s and 1990s have shrunk the world, we find ourselves reexamining the metaphysical nature of our universe. Harman (1994) suggests that our conception of it has changed, and that much evidence from the natural and social sciences leads us toward what he calls a complementary holistic science, in which the physical world and consciousness have a complementary relationship. But can we really hold religion and science in the same hand?

## SCIENCE AND RELIGION: ARE THEY COMPATIBLE?

Science without religion is lame; religion without science is blind.
—Albert Einstein, *"Science, Philosophy and Religion: A Symposium"*

In 1914, the sociologist James H. Leuba surveyed scientists and asked them about their beliefs in God. Of respondents, 42% believed in a personal God, which was less than the general public at that time. In 1996, the same instrument was readministered to a group of scientists. Researchers found no real change in the number of believers, which was greater than 39% (Larson & Witham, 1997). So, why the great divide?

Chet Raymo (2003) helps us to understand the debate. He points out that traditional religious faiths have three components: a shared cosmology (story of the universe), spirituality (personal responses to one's place in the universe), and liturgy (public expressions of gratitude, ritual, rites of passage). The antagonism, of course, is almost entirely in the cosmology, the age-old battle between evolution and creationism or the more current intelligent design. The battle of whose story is the real story. Can we reconcile this?

Many scientists say we can. Eugenie Scott (2003), a physical anthropologist, suggests that there are four ways that religion and science have interacted historically:

1. The warfare model: "Either religion trumps science or science trumps religion"; there is no place for both in the world.

2. The separate realms model: "Science explains the natural world; religion the world of the spirit."

3. The accommodation model: Science and religion are directly engaged. Evolution is accepted and reframed, but it is more of a one-way street on which science is the source for the reinterpretation of religion, rather than the reverse.

4. The engagement model: Science and religion interact with the idea that both epistemologies will contribute to a fuller understanding of both the natural world and the supernatural world.

The first two perspectives support this separation of the two. Scott concludes, however, that most scholars who study science and its place with religion identify with the latter two schools.

Fritjof Capra and David Steindl-Rast have published a remarkable dialogue about the compatibility of science and religion in the spirit of the engagement model. Capra, a physicist, and Steindl-Rast, a monk and scholar of modern religions, have collaborated in the comparison of the application of these principles to science and religion, which results in remarkably compatible scientific and religious worldviews. In *Belonging to the Universe: Explorations on the Frontiers of Science and Spirituality* (1991), in an attempt to formulate a more holistic way of looking at the universe, they provide an example of new-paradigm thinking that seekers of truth regarding the nature of both life and spirit can perhaps embrace. Essentially, they are saying that if we value the religions of the world, the contributions of science, and the debt we owe to both, it would behoove us to recognize and consider possible common ground between the two. In this consideration, Capra and Steindl-Rast apply the five shifts of thinking about systems we explored previously in the web of life to similar shifts in theological thinking.

In the first shift from part to whole, science views the understanding of the whole system, be it a tree or a person, as primary to understanding the relationships among its parts. Similarly, while the old theology focused on the sum total of dogmas that add up to reveal the truth, the new theology shifts its attention and starts with revelation as a whole. Individual dogmas can only be understood by starting with the dynamic interrelatedness of the cosmos, God, and humans.

The second shift in the scientific worldview is from structure as paramount to process. Natural phenomena such as mountains, or social phenomena such as communities, are understood not from what appears to be a static structure, but from examining the underlying constantly changing dynamics of these entities. Similarly, in theology, the shift is from a static and timeless set of supernatural truths to a dynamic and nonlinear process of revelation, revealed historically but intrinsically ever changing over time.

The process of knowing the real world, both physical and spiritual, shifts from a positivist or objective view as the only way of knowing to nonconceptual ways of knowing in science and in theology. Science and faith are social processes, constructed by those who experience them. This allows for the intuitive, the affective, and the mystical in both scientific and theological discoveries.

The fourth shift from knowledge as building blocks to knowledge as networks means that the laws of science and theology are only temporary states. In theology, the old paradigm places God as architect, apart from humans who are discovering the elements of the building blocks. The new paradigm of theology suggests that theology is an interconnectedness of different perspectives on transcendental reality. Thus, through dialogue, theology is constantly being rebuilt not as an edifice, but as a web of networks of constantly changing beliefs, experiences, relationships, and connections among faiths.

Finally, theology, like science, can never provide a complete and definitive understanding of all the mysteries of the universe. Rather, in new-paradigm thinking, both provide approximate descriptions of reality. Theological truth lies not in dogma, but in an ongoing exploration of God, the universe, and humans' relationship to them.

One can see in the above comparison how the principles posited in the web of life of interconnectedness, an intercultural and interdisciplinary approach, and approximate realities are made evident in this science-spirit connection. This connection asserts that the world can be understood from both a material and metaphysical perspective, and that each religious tradition sees the world through a different prism. No one way is the only way. This is evidenced, for example, in how the world's peoples mark time. Most of the alternatives to the Gregorian calendar used in the Western world come from different religions and reflect past traditions. In 2006, Jews started the year on September 26, Hindus on October 21, and Muslims on January 31. People accept with little rancor these differences in how religions mark time. However, we continue our boisterous battles, particularly here in the West, between the evolutionists and the creationists in their attempts to assert the real creation story.

The idea of perennial wisdom could be a uniting force in the traditions and beliefs of religions (Huxley, 1945). Perennial wisdom comprises universal ideas that have existed in every religion, such as that nature is directed from within by a higher intelligence or mind; that mental or physical rituals can sometimes affect what they symbolize or set the certain processes or conditions in motion for the desired events or results to occur; prayers, thoughts, or mental projections might directly aid in the healing of ill people; and all individuals have a strong motivation to discover and identify with a high self, which in turn connects them to some kind of universal force or mind (Harman, 1994).

In the spirit of this tradition of perennial wisdom, Chet Raymo (2003) offers a new story, a story of the world that attempts to unify cosmology. The story begins with seeds and hydrogen and stars and a planet that accommodate species, human consciousness, and invisible spirits who light up the sky. It is a universal story that emphasizes the connectedness of all people and all things, "a cosmic unfolding of space and time" that "teaches our biological affinity to all humanity" (p. 340). We are responsible for our lives and the future, but we may accept the "Unnamable One" (p. 341). In short, it is an evolving story that accepts creativity and observation; it is a story that will never be finished. "When the story fails we change it" (p. 340).

But what is the human mechanism that enables us to connect these two worlds and these two stories? It is what makes us unique, so far as we know, in all species. It is our consciousness. Let us consider for a moment how this can happen.

# CONSCIOUSNESS: BRIDGE BETWEEN THE TWO

For centuries first philosophers and then behavioral scientists have grappled with the notion of the mind. What is it? How do we measure it? Is it just the brain? What about emotions? What follows is not a thorough review of the literature on consciousness, as it is broad and vast. The Institute of Noetic Sciences is a useful resource for a more in-depth view of some of the efforts to understand consciousness and its relationship with the natural world. However, the work of Ken Wilber is worth mentioning, as it has great merit in making sense out of the material-spiritual and mind-body-spirit connections.

Ken Wilber's contribution to a postmodern worldview of consciousness is truly remarkable. It is difficult to summarize succinctly, as his collected works, much of his life's work thus far, comprise eight volumes (Wilber, 2000). In short, Wilber attempts to integrate the physical, mental, and spiritual worlds. To begin with, in a vein familiar to us by now, he makes a case that science needs to include the subjective or interior domains of experience. His main achievement is to have brought together our two great orienting generalizations of evolution and spirit—the former a relatively recent discovery in science, the latter an "ancient, and perennial, discovery of religion and mysticism" (De Quincey 2001, p. 11).

I will attempt to elaborate on a few of Wilber's ideas in the hope that it further stimulates exploration of this fascinating work. Wilber's approach is to reconcile spiritual knowledge in the great chain of being or the great wisdom traditions from Taoism to Vedanta, Zen to Sufism, neo-Platonism to Confucianism (Lovejoy, 1936), with scientific materialism; in other words, to bring together premodern religion and modern science. He does this by broadening our conceptualization of knowledge of the universe into four quadrants: the interior or subjective quadrants are individual consciousness and collective consciousness; the exterior or objective quadrants are the individual world and the collective or social world (Wilber, 2000). Individual consciousness is intermeshed with each other quadrant: the objective organism and brain; nature, social systems, and environment; and cultural settings, communal values, and worldviews. Wilber (2000) also illustrates where scientists and their theories fit into each quadrant.

To understand Wilber's theory from the brief explanation I have offered is not possible. I offer it, however, to give you a hint at some efforts that attempt to connect our subjective inner world of consciousness with our perceptions of the outer world of society and culture. Notwithstanding that Wilber is considered one of the most widely read and influential philosophers of our time, his writings are prolific and extremely dense and complex. But the significance of his work is his attempts to link inner, outer, and spiritual worlds and to bring to the attention of Western minds the ancient psychologies of the East. This has resulted in an important theoretical paradigm that takes consciousness beyond ego and incorporates legitimate spiritual and mystical experiences as attributes of healthy people (Cowley, 1993).

In summary, Wilber's contributions to our understanding of the connections among mind, body, and spirit are his attempts to depict a full spectrum of human consciousness in human behavior. He has revealed that the interior life of individual and collective subjectivity is as complex, differentiated, and interrelated as are the immensely complex physical worlds that physical sciences reveal. His works have engaged multiple disciplines—including philosophy, metaphysics, natural science, and spirituality—toward a greater, more inclusive understanding of the evolution of human consciousness. They have also been translated into therapeutic practice, which we will discuss later in this chapter.

Thus far, scholars in fields other than social work have examined the worlds of science and spirit. Let's take a look at the work of our fellow colleagues in bridging the gap between the material and the spiritual.

## SOCIAL WORK SCHOLARSHIP, POSTMODERNISM, AND THE GREAT DIVIDE

Toward the end of the twentieth century, social work scholars began to take another look at postmodernism and the challenges and opportunities it offers social work. A postmodern view, from a social work perspective, "rejects objectivism and absolutism and stresses pluralism, relativism, and flexibility" (Laird, 1993, p. 2). As early as 1987, Ann Weick espoused the need for a more holistic conception of social work. She traces our thinking from the medieval to the modern mathematical mind, and then looks at quantum principles as a bridge to the postmodern holistic world. She suggests that changes in modern physics have led us to view the world as an interconnected whole rather than a collection of parts. Drawing, in part, from Capra's work, Weick asserts that the metaphor of the universe has moved from "the great clock, whose workings can be tested and toyed with by an army of white-coated mechanics . . . to a universe where all matter is involved in an elaborate, unchoreographed dance . . . with action, uncertainty, color, illusion, humor, passion" (Weick, 1987, p. 43).

In this holistic worldview, the knower is connected to the known in an act of cocreation; thus, a new epistemology is born. The major implications for social work are that (1) an understanding of the world where everything is connected cannot occur without seeing every phenomenon within its larger context, and (2) if knowledge involves participation, then intuition is acknowledged as an element in knowing.

In the 1990s, the postmodern debate continued. Meinert, Pardeck, and Murphy (1998, pp. 17–18) lay out the core ideas of the postmodern perspective, with a focus on acknowledging clients' multiple worldviews:

- "Reality must be treated as socially constructed through language use."
- "The methods used to gather information, the knowledge base for clinical decision making, should be attuned to the different language games that are operative in society."
- "The interventions that are chosen should reflect . . . the 'interpretive community' in question."
- "The ethical principle that should guide intervention is to protect the integrity of the client's worldview."

The debate on how we come to know the world continues from the perspective of postmodern critical theory. We will return to critical theory a little later, but essentially critical theory posits that we can never be free of our own values when we are observing and researching the world around us. Thus, religion and our belief systems come into play in terms of how we experience and explain the world.

One challenge for social work, especially with respect to its code of ethics, is to try to acknowledge relative cultural and religious worldviews with some understanding of universal human

values. Can we explore new paradigms without compromising social work ideals of human rights and social justice? One way to
consider this postmodern challenge is to not succumb, again, to
the false dichotomy of abandoning one worldview to embrace another. The important thing is to focus on the process of thinking
and to "stress the importance of openness and uncertainty, re-
sponsiveness to context, resistance to imposed agendas and values and rejection of arrogant professionalism which privileges expert knowledge over lived experience" (Pease & Fook, 1999, p.
228). This is relevant in any context, working with peers, clients,
students, or other groups.

As students and teachers of social work, then, we should expand our research frames to include paradigms that accommodate and give credence to postmodern holistic and interdisciplinary worldviews. This means a shift from reliance on a more
positivist research approach to the paradigms of critical theory
and constructivism. A critical theory research framework assumes
that there is no such thing as objective reality; instead, the ideolo-
gies of the researcher are made manifest and guide the research
problem and subsequent actions that may result from the research. Constructivism assumes a subjective reality, which is discovered in partnership with research participants; in the process,
joint constructions of reality evolve unique to the time and place
of research (Morris, 2006).

## WHAT PRACTICE THEORIES DO SOCIAL
## WORKERS USE TO RECONCILE THE
## MATERIAL AND SPIRITUAL WORLDS?

In chapter 2, we expanded our notion of person-in-environment
to include the natural environment and the imperative of environmental sustainability. In that discussion, we noted the contribution of deep ecology to the understanding of our connection to
the natural world. Deep ecology is only one of many eco-theories
that not only broadens our view of systems but also bridges the
gaps in our biological, psychological, social, and spiritual well-
being. Multiple ecological disciplines have led us to consider our
relationship with Mother Earth, and social ecology, eco-feminism,
eco-justice, and eco-psychology have linked traditional social work

issues of the oppression of people with the oppression of the environment (Derezotes, 2005).

Social workers also use the postmodern critical theories of feminism and Afrocentrism in their practice to bridge the physical and spiritual gap. Feminist theory and feminist practice models embrace the relationship between the physical and metaphysical worlds. Specifically, Van Den Bergh and Cooper (1986) offer five principles that apply to both research and practice and are congruent with much of our discussion thus far: (1) the elimination of false dichotomies, (2) reconceptualizing power, (3) equal valuation of process and power, (4) the validity of renaming, and (5) the personal as political. We can see how valuing process with product and connecting the personal with the political reflect the interconnectedness we have been exploring. However, the first principle is most relevant to our current discussion on bridging the gap between science and spirituality. Eliminating the false dichotomy between science and spirit allows us to validate the role of spirit and religion in our understanding of individuals, groups, and larger social systems. Thus, we see the whole person or system as encompassing a spiritual aspect, which we cannot separate from the organism in our study and our work.

Afrocentrism makes similar connections between the spiritual and the material worlds. This paradigm asserts three major assumptions about human beings: (1) human identity is collective, (2) the spiritual (or nonmaterial) component of human beings is just as important and valid as is the material world, and (3) the affective (or intuitive) approach to knowledge is valid. Afrocentrism embraces the spiritual nature of human beings; it finds God reflected in all elements of the universe. It sees the soul, mind, and body as interdependent and interrelated, and spiritual alienation as the cause of many of the world's problems (Schiele, 1996). Thus, we must examine the extent to which the individuals and communities of African descent with whom we work see their worlds from an Afrocentric paradigm and approach our work in a holistic manner.

The willingness to consider a postmodern view of the world and a place for spirituality and religion is critical to social work as a profession. Social work is a value-based calling to make change for the better in individuals and society. Social work is work with human systems. If we acknowledge intuition, the client's interpretation of reality, or the various worldviews of the cultural groups that we study and work with, how can we ignore religion and spirituality? The vast majority of social workers in this country do not practice in an international arena. However, whether or not we recognize it, we practice within a globally interconnected context. Every day when we read the news, we learn of a world conflict or dilemma stemming, in part, from the struggle between civil society and religious or cultural norms. Whether it is the coexistence of Palestinians and Jews in the West Bank or the roles of women in the rebuilding of Iraq, we know that the centuries-old discord and destruction is a result, in part, of the widespread belief that there is only one way to reach the one true god. Clearly, there is no place for fundamentalism in religion or in science if we strive to live in greater harmony on a sustainable planet.

Furthermore, the social policy debates in the United States are often tied to this false dichotomy of the spiritual and material world. The purpose of the separation of church and state is, after all, religious tolerance, to ensure that no one religion becomes the state religion. The purpose is not to declare religion or spirituality dead or irrelevant to the lives of people who are struggling in so-called welfare reform programs, people who are aging and in need of social welfare support, or children in need of safe homes and communities. Clearly, Americans are religious and spiritual. But if we cannot find a way to infuse the wisdom of our forebearers, such as the psychologist and metaphysical philosopher William James, or members of the faith community, such as Martin Luther King, into our public life and to acknowledge the role their wisdom played and continues to play in the form of social responses to human problems, we deny our human history.

I would also submit that if we cannot find a way to explore spirituality and religion as part of the human condition in educating our future citizens, we are denying the multicultural reality of our citizenry and are, in fact, making the absence of spirituality and religion the de facto state position. It is now time to challenge our creativity by introducing a new way of thinking about the connections between the material and spiritual worlds. As advocates for children, elderly people, people with chronic disabilities, individuals with chemical dependency, or victims of domestic violence, we cannot ignore the roles that spirituality and religion play in the policy context and in the communities in which these people reside. How does this affect our social work values?

With its strongly value-based code of ethics, the social work profession has perhaps found it easier than other helping professions to acknowledge that our work is both science and art. However, new systems thinking, especially in the connection between the natural and spiritual worlds, allows us to expand and revalue spirituality in human behavior as well as in our symbiotic relationship with the natural environment.

David Derezotes (2005) suggests some areas of application for social work. Americans are moving from a time of individual spiritual growth into a time of collective spiritual activism. In a country of many cultures, social workers are more openly acknowledging spirituality in, for example, rituals, forgiveness, shamanism, sacred sexuality, sacred medicines, psychedelic plants, and therapy. In this process, we may need to take a more systematic look at the revaluing of social work practice as it relates to spirituality. The following are some positions that Derezotes (2005, p. 185) suggests we might take or responses to infuse spirituality in our lives and our practice:

- Revaluing the purpose of life to align ourselves with the meanings we have created
- Taking responsibility for our own consciousness and further developing it throughout our lives
- Taking responsibility for our own sexual health in relationships and in the larger society
- Taking responsibility for the impacts (positive and negative) of religion on others' biological, psychosocial, spiritual, and environmental well-being
- Stopping violence in our personal relationships, institutions, and local and global communities
- Taking responsibility for the biological, psychosocial, spiritual and environmental development and healing of all humanity and the earth

Scholars and theologians have identified both the contributions and the threats that religions can pose to a sustainable world. Interdisciplinary studies have attempted to connect spirituality and religion with both social and physical sciences in an attempt to break the dualism of spirit and flesh, of this world and the other world. Critical theory paradigms such as eco-theory and practice approaches such as feminist practice and Afrocentrism contain elements of this science-spirituality connection.

## IMPLICATIONS FOR SOCIAL WORK PRACTICE: INDIVIDUALS AND FAMILIES

How can we apply our knowledge of bridging the physical and metaphysical worlds to individual, community, and global social welfare issues? First of all, in their work with individuals and families, social workers who are concerned with physical disease and mental illness are slowly being exposed to alternatives to a medical model as they confront conditions closely related to stress, diet, drug abuse, sedentary living, and environmental pollution. The causation of these conditions is more complex than germ theory. Thus, the need arises for a new paradigm of understanding health, disease, and the human body.

One area of application of this paradigm is alternative health care, the use of which is growing in the United States. In 1990, approximately one-third of the population turned to alternative health-care solutions (Ray, 1996). There are two major reasons people are turning to this model of healing: (1) our increasing multicultural society and an understanding that illness and healing are products of the history of groups of human beings and exist within those environmental and cultural contexts, and (2) the belief that health is a state of balance in the interdependence of mind and body and acknowledgement of the influence of the surrounding environment.

Eastern health practices, for example, emphasize the whole and the interconnectedness of phenomena. In Chinese medicine, "the healthy individual and the healthy society are integral parts of a great patterned order, and illness is disharmony at the individual or societal level" (Capra, 1991, p. 313). The importance of cultural diversity in the definition of illness and health illustrates the principle of approximate descriptions of reality in understanding health problems versus an absolute definition of health.

Although alternative health practices are gaining momentum in traditional medical centers throughout the country, social workers are only just beginning to be educated in these practices (Vest & Ronnau, 1997). In the past decade, however, research and overall interest in alternative and holistic approaches to healing have increased, with particular focus on modes most appropriate to diverse cultural groups. Some examples are touch therapy with a group of Mexican Americans with diabetes and their families (Vest & Ronnau, 1997), an approach with indigenous Alaskan women using indigenous values and spirituality, cultural symbols such as the talking stick, cultural teaching traditions such as the talking circle and storytelling (Hurdle, 1998), and the use of shamanic healing techniques such as inducing altered states of consciousness, in addiction counseling "in order to find healing, harmony, wholeness for self and others" (Rioux, 1996, p. 59). See table 1 for other nontraditional approaches.

**Table 1   Alternative Health Care Used by the U.S. Population (1994)**

| Alternative Treatment | U.S. Pop. (%) |
|---|---|
| Chiropractic | 15.73 |
| Exercise/movement | 11.58 |
| Prayer or spiritual practice | 9.85 |
| Diet programs | 8.30 |
| Relaxation | 6.95 |
| Massage | 5.69 |
| Herbal therapies | 4.25 |
| Folk remedies | 2.12 |
| Spiritual healing | 2.03 |

Note: Partial listing. Source: Ray, P. (1996).

Narratives have been collected acknowledging the emergence of spirituality in social work over the past fifteen years and reflecting social workers' experiences and approaches to spirituality in their work with various populations (Abels, 2000). Some of the stories reflect, for example, group work with people who are incarcerated (Sheridan, 2000), the use of Christian faith in a hospital setting (Kreutziger, 2000), Native American storytelling in the Sanish and Hidatsa nations (Lowery, 2000), and the role of faith in the construction of Kwanzaa (Karenga, 2000).

In a review of anthropological research on traditional healing in Abels's (2000) work, Alean Al-Krenawi (2000) notes that a significant number of studies point to psychotherapeutic elements in traditional healing, and that more traditional healers are becoming interested in learning about modern health care. The author notes that Western-trained mental health practitioners tend not to be as interested in traditional healing, but the main point is that there are many and deep connections between modern and traditional approaches, and that we should investigate them within the contexts of our diverse clientele. Al-Krenawi believes that we

can bridge the gap. His concluding remarks support the importance of the mind-body-spirit connection in working with individuals, their families, and their communities: "Because social work
intervention is often based on intuitive as well as empirical knowledge, traditional healing can readily be integrated into practice
with people of various cultures" (Al-Krenawi, 2000, p. 26).

Finally, transpersonal psychology, another practice approach,
has been referred to as the fourth force of psychology because it
moves beyond the influences of the first three movements of
Freudianism, behaviorism, and humanistic psychology (Robbins,
Chatterjee, & Canda, 1998). Heavily influenced by Ken Wilber, the
transpersonal psychology movement emerged in the 1960s and
1970s and began to take hold in the social work arena in the 1990s
(see Canda & Smith, 2001; Cowley, 1996).

Clearly, we can see in clinical work how to bridge the gap between the material and the spiritual. However, given the problems
that this gap has caused us, globally and over time, what can we do
to help societies and countries find common ground?

## LARGE SYSTEMS: NEED FOR A
## GLOBAL DIALOGUE

As mentioned previously, the study of the connection between the
mind and body, and the physical and spiritual worlds has been the
focus of the Institute of Noetic Sciences, in Sausalito, California,
since 1971. Efforts to apply this connection in larger societal and
global realms are not new. Many movements illustrate this trend,
including the recognition that intuitive powers, sometimes thought
of as psychic abilities, are not necessarily pathological but can be
used for understanding and transformation; individuals' increasing commitment to individual and group experiential modes of
spiritual practice; the increasing recognition of the power of extraordinary experiences such as near-death experience to expand
our identity and open us to empathy and relationship; and the
emergence of new sociopolitical forms such as nongovernmental
organizations at the UN, which enable a wider range of citizens to
take part in international relationships in spiritual exploration
(Mack, 2003).

A major global attempt was made, in 1991, to create a bridge
between scientists and religious leaders concerning the crises

threatening the earth. As reported in *Nature* on February 1, 1990, under the heading "Global Change":

> Astronomer Carl Sagan and 22 other well-known researchers chose Moscow as the unlikely venue for an appeal to world religious leaders to join scientists in protecting the environment. The appeal came at a recent conference on the environment and economic development which attracted over a thousand religious, political and scientific leaders from 83 nations. . . . The conference was sponsored by both the USSR Academy of Sciences and the Russian Orthodox Church.
>
> The appeal states that "efforts to safeguard and cherish the environment need to be infused with a vision of the sacred. Among those who have given their backing are physicist Hans Berthe, biologist Stephen Jay Gould and former MIT President Jerome Weisner. . . .
>
> The appeal reached a global audience. Parts of the conference were televised and reached an estimated audience of 2,000 million in 129 countries. Later, at the conference, more than one hundred religious leaders joined to hail the scientists' appeal as a "unique moment and opportunity in the relationship of science and religion." (Shulman, 1990, p. 398)

In 1997, ten Nobel laureates, five heads of state, and "a galaxy of moral authorities" (Marquand, 1997), including the Dalai Lama and Václav Havel, met in Prague for four days to discuss the health of civilization and crises of values, and to try to agree upon common moral imperatives. In that same year, the American Association for the Advancement of Science hosted a conference in Chicago, titled "The Epic of Evolution," to promote a dialogue between science and religion. At the conference, physical, biological, and social scientists teamed with theologians to discuss the implications for evolution (Scott, 2003). These gatherings are not new, but they have been more frequent since the end of the cold war. In November 2005, the Dalai Lama was invited to inaugurate the Society for Neuroscience meeting in Washington; he gave a lecture on the neuroscience of meditation. Causing quite a stir in the context of today's intelligent design controversy, the Nobel laureate is attempting to join science and spirituality for the "betterment of humanity" (Schmidt, 2005, p. B11).

In February 2006, another interesting meeting of science and religion occurred. Eighty-five evangelical Christian leaders proclaimed their support for legislation to combat global warming that the White House had opposed. In response to renewed consideration of the Climate Stewardship Act, first introduced in 2003 by Senators John McCain and Joseph Lieberman, pastors, religious broadcasters, and presidents of Christian colleges sponsored a full-page advertisement in the *New York Times*. The campaign included national television spots as well, with the message "With God's help we can stop global warming for our kids, our world and our Lord" (Eisner, 2006, p. 1).

## WHAT IS OUR ROLE IN THIS DIALOGUE?

As one of the only professions charged with environmental as well as individual change, social work should take a lead in these kinds of dialogues at the community, national, and global levels. We have expertise, in both micro and macro systems, in bringing various interest groups to the table to confront problems and, through dialogues and consensus, to design a strategy to address them. There are a number of arenas in which we could catalyze dialogue, including interfaith alliances, church social-action committees, peace groups, nonprofit groups, city governments, environmental action groups, neighborhood associations, and other groups that witness such problems in their neighborhoods as discrimination, economic and spiritual alienation, and gang warfare.

The result of such organizing could be a conference, a dialogue, or a community symposium on the role of the church and religion in addressing these problems. Where there are no interfaith alliances, we could help build them. Where there are no courses in the intersection of religion and science, we could advocate and develop them. Many communities have no human relations commissions or advisory groups to deal with intercultural clashes. We could help initiate them. If we assume that all organizations can be learning organizations, we can create forums for cross-cultural, cross-religion, or science-religion dialogues in hospitals, community centers, schools of social work, universities, state capitols, or any number of international venues.

Education, of course, is the best long-term strategy for consciousness raising, cross-cultural exploration, and tolerance. Michael Lerner, whose work we will visit in a later chapter, is a rabbi and a scholar who has suggested activities in educational settings to achieve these ends that social workers involved in education at any level should consider. Asserting that high school sophomores are capable of hearing alternative views and making their own judgments, Lerner (1997) offers some suggestions in an approach to teaching about religion in high school.

First, he suggests that U.S. high schools should teach all religious traditions, except for any that specifically acknowledge a belief that certain groups are fundamentally inferior to others (groups that explicitly teach racist or sexists ideas). In this process, he asserts that schools should give major religious communities the opportunity to present their material on videotape in the spirit of education and not proselytization. Others should also be able to present their approaches to spirituality, including advocates for philosophical and spiritual ideas not represented in major religious traditions. Finally, Lerner suggests that local school districts be free from using the religious advocacy series but prohibited from teaching religion in a one-sided manner that offends members of minority religions (Lerner, 1997).

Imagine the possible long-term effects of educating high school students about the vast richness of perennial wisdom. The prohibition of religious ideas that discriminate is not an easy task to consider. But would we not benefit from having our high school students explore various world religions, in an attempt to understand the worldviews of our global neighbors? In fact, should we not begin this development of knowledge and understanding about diversity in primary school?

To summarize, our examination of spirit and science has revealed some shortcomings of attempts to make one or the other the sole container of truth. There are dangers of dualism and fundamentalism in religion; there are also dangers in putting science on the pedestal, particularly logical positivism, as the sole source of truth in a world where human beings hunger for meaning and purpose in life.

In our exploration of this web-of-life worldview, religion, spirit, and the environment are closely connected. We have discussed some of the threats to a sustainable future if we continue to devalue Mother Earth. We have also discussed how some degree of reconciliation of the material and spiritual worlds may be necessary if we are to continue to evolve as human beings, in harmony with our planet. Let us now turn to our human-made institutions of economy, systems of governance, and technology. For if systems are interconnected, to what extent do our current institutions reflect a sustainable world?

## ADDITIONAL THINGS TO THINK ABOUT

For the following questions, consider how you have learned some new ways of looking at spirituality and religion and their relationships to science that challenge the separation of the physical and metaphysical worlds within both small and larger systems.

1. What are your thoughts about the nature of the relationship between science and spirituality? Between science and religion?

2. Social work has been called a science and an art. What makes it an art? How does this relate to the dualism of science and spirituality?

3. Where do you get the knowledge you rely on to understand the world? Are intuition and metaphysical or spiritual experiences valid ways of understanding individual human behaviors and problems? Larger social systems and the problems therein?

4. Many people believe that their god is the true god, and all religions have false gods. Some people view this as the root of violence and conflict. Can this belief be reconciled with living peacefully in a multicultural, multifaith world?

5. Most people do not think of *spiritual* as a word to describe politics. Do you believe that there can or should be more of a connection among spirituality, morality, and politics? If not, why not? If so, how can that come about?

6. Consider Derezotes's suggestions. Do you think that these are relevant to social work intervention? Do they help bridge the divide between the spiritual and the material worlds of our clients?

7. What has been your exposure to eco-theories, feminist practice theories, or Afrocentrism?

8. Refer back to table 1. Have you used any of these methods of alternative care? Have your clients reported using any of these? What has been your experience?

## MAIN POINTS

1. Religion can be a polarizing force in our society if it fosters dualistic thinking such as patriotism or nationalism and conflictual, violent solutions to problems.

2. New connections are being made between science and religion that suggest that neither science nor theology are absolute but processes of knowing, with different perspectives on reality.

3. Objectivism, positivism, and reductionism of modern science may not adequately reflect reality, given our new understanding of interconnectedness of self and our physical world.

4. Postmodern thinking can help social workers bridge science and spirituality by acknowledging multiple worldviews.

5. Science and spirituality are bridged via the construct of consciousness.

6. The bridging of science and religion or spirituality has implications for social work research approaches, values, and practice at micro and macro levels.

7. Eco-theories, feminist practice, and Afrocentrism offer approaches to social work that can bridge the gaps among the environment, spirit, and science.

## For Further Reading

Capra, F., & Steindl-Rast, D. (1991). *Belonging to the universe: Explorations on the frontiers of science and spirituality.* San Francisco: Harper Collins.

Cowley, A. S. (1996). Transpersonal social work. In F. J. Turner (Ed.), *Social work treatment* (pp. 663–698). New York: Free Press.

De Quincey, C. (2001, March/May). A theory of everything: A critical appreciation of Ken Wilber's collected works. *Noetic Sciences Review.*

Derezotes, D. (2005). *Revaluing social work: Implications of emerging science and technology.* Denver, CO: Love Publishing.

Payne, M. (2005). *Modern social work theory.* Chicago: Lyceum Books (see chapter 11, "Feminist perspectives").

Schiele, J. (2000). *Human services and the Afrocentric paradigm.* New York: Haworth Press.

# CHAPTER 5

# Redefining Economy

But while they prate of economic laws, men and women are starving. We must lay hold of the fact that economic laws are not made by nature. They are made by human beings.

—Franklin D. Roosevelt,
*speech to 1932 Democratic National Convention*

It could be empowering, particularly for those of us who tend to shy away from economics, to remind ourselves that economics is a social science. Human activities and belief systems fashion the institutions and rules of economics; they do not exist on stone tablets or as immutable laws of nature. According to *Merriam-Webster Collegiate Dictionary*, 10th edition, the study of economics is the "description and analysis of production, distribution and consumption of goods and services." Modern economics is "the scientific study of the choices made by individuals and societies in regard to the alternative uses of scarce resources which are employed to satisfy wants" (Dodda, 2004). Hmm—choices, wants. It's good to remind ourselves that these are human constructs not scientific laws. This means we can change them.

It is also important to set some parameters for our discussion of the function of economics. Politics influences the decisions regarding who produces, distributes, and consumes; thus, the policies of economic institutions such as banks, corporations, and businesses that determine how jobs, money, and resources are made available to people are political ones. It is hard to separate the two. But we will try, in the ensuing discussion, to focus the exploration of economics on production, distribution, and consumption of goods and services and the occurrence of these events in a global context. I'll reserve discussion of how the populace, government, and corporate world get involved in making decisions for chapter 6, when we discuss principles of sustainable politics.

Let's begin with a little theory for context, and a little history of the U.S. economy. Then we'll look at some limitations of the current definition of success in a sustainable world, using the principles of sustainable thinking as guidelines. We will then turn to some new ways of conceptualizing economics that reflect these principles as well as holistic systems thinking. We'll focus on areas of rapidly changing technology that are affecting nature and the world of work and that pose challenges as well as opportunities to a sustainable world. Finally, we'll identify what social workers are doing and what they could do more of by articulating a more holistic approach to development and by connecting groups together in sustainable community projects.

## A LITTLE BIT OF THEORY

Over the past two centuries, the major debate in economic theory has been around two kinds of economic systems: capitalism and socialism. The main features of capitalism are that productive wealth is held in private hands, economic life is ordered around market principles (e.g., supply and demand), commodities have a monetary market value of exchange, and self-interest and profit drive enterprise and work. In contrast, socialist economies are based on common ownership of productive wealth, with varying degrees of state ownership; economic organization is based on planning, which is often centralized; a system of production is based on use, geared, in theory, to meet human needs; and work is a cooperative effort from a desire for the general well-being (Heywood, 2002). There are pluses and minuses to both systems. Market capitalism is said to be efficient, to promote innovation of new products, and to allow for freedom of choice. Its downsides are said to be the generation of material inequality and poverty, the elevation of personal greed and inattention to broader societal needs, and instability and insecurity in the populace as a result of fluctuating market trends.

Some of the advantages of socialism are its focus on the material needs of society (rather than profit), that planning is based on human decisions rather than market whims, and that society is less vulnerable to rapid instability and crises. Disadvantages of socialism are that it does not promote innovation or efficiency, central planning by the elite may not serve the populace, and a focus on stability and central bureaucracies may encourage mediocrity in products and services (Heywood, 2002).

By the mid-twentieth century, a third ideology was evolving, but this one was environmental. Sometimes referred to as eco-socialists, these thinkers were precursors to the current ecological environmental school within the discipline of economics. This postmodern view, embraced by many of the new systems or trans-formational thinkers, is that capitalism and socialism are different manifestations of a larger view, industrialism. That is, both ideolo-gies serve industrialization, which exploits both labor and the nat-ural environment. The primary concern of eco-socialists is not who owns the means of production but the destructive relation-ship between humankind and the natural world (Schumacher, 1973). We will return to some of this thinking when we explore al-ternative definitions of the economy later in this chapter.

## THE RICHEST COUNTRY IN THE WORLD

The economic progress of the United States has occurred within a system of capitalism, driven by rapid economic growth since the 1800s. Before that time, population and economic growth pro-ceeded at a gradual rate. The past two centuries of modern eco-nomic growth have evolved out of the industrial revolution, be-ginning in the United Kingdom and spreading rapidly throughout the West and more slowly in developing countries. This growth has changed the way people live in every way (Sachs, 2005).

Urbanization shifted work from the farm to factories. The production of new goods and services, and the development of new means of transporting them, opened up new jobs, creating so-cial mobility and population migration within and immigration into the country. Technological breakthroughs fueled these new opportunities, from the steam engine to the railroad, electrifica-tion, and multiple uses of fossil fuels. All these transitions changed the family structure and gender roles, as women worked outside the home, families moved away from grandparents, and a devel-oping education system moved children from home to school.

The most dramatic economic changes occurred in the last quarter of the twentieth century, when globalization started to take hold. The capitalism and privatization that occurred in the

Unites States began to occur internationally. Trade and banking became international. Private capital began to flow to developing countries, encouraging the extraction of natural resources (e.g., timber, minerals, oil) as well as manufacturing, services, and other commodities. Our current economy is global in every way, in labor, trade, banking, communications, and the use and abuse of the natural resources in its support.

Are we better off with this global economy? Indicators of progress include increased affluence in major cities in the developing world. Relatively speaking, we have moved from almost universal global poverty to a place where more than half the world is experiencing economic progress (Sachs, 2005). However, one-sixth of the world lives in extreme poverty, which is often connected to unstable governments, failures of foreign assistance, environmental destruction, and the low status of women (Sachs, 2005). The modern premise upon which economic success is gauged is, "Growth is better." The greater the output in goods and services, the greater is the volume of trade, the higher is the standard of living, and the better is the economy. More often than not, the United States is seen as having the optimum standard of living to which developing countries should strive.

The question is this: is the current economic system sustainable? The aforementioned principles of sustainability will be used to address this question: Does the economy respect environmental constraints? Does it value the quality of all life on the earth? Does it result in social justice, fairness, and equity? Does it promote participation and partnership in its citizenry?

## RESPECT FOR THE ENVIRONMENT: THE LIMITS TO GROWTH

In the late 1960s, a multidisciplinary group of futurists began to develop an empirical comprehensive methodology for projecting the future of the current industrial order. Known as the Club of Rome, this group issued a report called *The Limits to Growth* (Meadows, 1972), wherein it concluded that five trends, if left unchanged, would endanger our life on the planet: accelerated industrialization, widespread malnutrition, depletion of nonrenewable resources, rapid population growth, and a deteriorating environment (Garbarino, 1992). In the early 1990s, researchers at the University of British Columbia began to calculate the amount of land needed to supply national populations with resources and to absorb the populations' wastes. They coined this calculation the ecological footprint of a population. The researchers concluded that sustaining the whole world would require a land area the size of three Earths (Gardner & Sampat, 1998). Similarly, the 2005 special issue of *Scientific American* concluded that trends in population, water, energy, biodiversity, and poverty are endangering our ability to sustain life on the planet.

With this growing recognition of the limits to growth and our planet's finite resources, a new branch of economics, ecological economics, has emerged (Boulding, 1992; Daly & Cobb, 1989; Schumacher, 1973). Ecological economists challenge the mainstream classical economic thinking that continued economic growth can prevail, and that negative effects on the environment and quality of life for any species can be adequately mitigated. Traditional economists see these negative effects as minor externalities or social costs that strategies such as recycling, cleanup, or levying taxes on the polluters can address.

However, many ecological economists have come to the conclusion that we can no longer pretend that the global economy operates within a limitless ecosystem: we live in a finite biosphere (Daly, 2005). These economists believe that we are minimizing the negative effects of growth, such as pollution and species endangerment. Natural capital of our freshwater and ocean fisheries, the forest and the wetlands, and the atmosphere support life on the planet. Therefore, we must preserve these in a manner that can sustain future generations of species.

## DOES THE CURRENT SYSTEM OF ECONOMICS VALUE QUALITY OF LIFE?

Do current economics value quality of life? "Well, it depends on how you define *quality*, and whose life we are talking about!" OK. But sometimes the simplest ideas are the most profound and take us the longest to get our heads around. Our definition of economics describes the functions of economic activities. But what is our end goal? What is the purpose of an economy? Given a finite system of resources, is it enough to adhere to classical economic thought and its goal of simply producing the most goods and services at the greatest efficiency (or the lowest monetary cost)? Should an economy contribute to the overall enhancement of the quality of life of humans, their communities, the species with whom they share life, and their home, Mother Earth? If this is a rational function of an economy, is ours meeting that goal?

In the media and in the formal speeches of our national leaders, we are told that America is progressing. The indicators are the stable, though meager, increase in the gross domestic product (GDP), the stock market, the index of leading economic indicators (ILEI), the balance of trade, the rate of inflation, consumer confidence, housing starts, and other similar measures. The GDP tells us, in monetary terms, the growth of goods and services. The ILEI can help businesses forecast whether to expand, invest further capital, or downsize operations. The consumer confidence index tells us what consumers are saying about what they are willing to invest in or purchase. If exports are strong, inflation is stable, consumers are spending, interest rates are low, and the GDP is rising, we have come to believe that we are doing well.

But what does all of this really signify in terms of the overall quality of life in our communities? Does the GDP tell us whether people are working in jobs where they earn a livable wage? Do the leading indicators tell us how healthy our citizens are? The quality of our air and water? How children are faring in school, and whether they are learning the skills to become economic actors in the workplaces of the future? The usual indicators of economic success cannot answer these and other questions about the health, productivity, and happiness of the populace; health and happiness are not the primary focus of our economy. Perhaps we need to change our thinking.

## DOES THE GLOBAL ECONOMY SUPPORT SOCIAL JUSTICE, FAIRNESS, AND EQUALITY?

Social workers should know a thing or two about inequality. The gap between the rich and poor has continued to widen. More than 80% of the world's income is concentrated in 20% of the world's countries Among all advanced industrial countries, the United States leads in this idea: the wealthiest one-fifth of the population receives almost half of all U.S. income (Sivard, 1996) The consumption patterns of industrial countries are in sharp contrast to living conditions in much of Asia, Latin America, and Africa: the leading importer nation, the Unites States contains 10% of the world's population.

Neither development nor trade benefits all nations in any semblance of equality. Foreign aid to developing countries is totally inadequate; as of 2002, the world's rich countries gave $53 billion to the developing world, or 1.2% of the rich world's gross national product (Sachs, 2005). Foreign aid has decreased. Structural adjustment policies accompanying foreign aid over the past two decades have forced countries to focus on paying down their debt to institutions such as the World Bank. Market strategies of privatization, belt tightening, and good governance have become the order of the day (Sachs, 2005). The result has been distorted development (Midgley, 1995), with negative consequences on the environment and the neglect of local input into economic development strategies.

We know that combating inequality is a human rights issue and the right and moral thing to do. But we need to move beyond naive altruism. We are all interconnected. To create a sustainable world we must move toward greater peace and harmony within and among species. Jared Diamond, in his recent book *Collapse* (2005), shares lessons about the factors that interplay with environmental stress to force civilizations over the brink. He asserts that it is clear that inequalities, over time, create conflict, civil wars, weak governments, land grabs, terrorism, and desperate behavior in every living system, from the individual to the country.

History has shown us that countries that are environmentally stressed are prone to government collapse. And when people in those countries are desperate, undernourished, or without hope, they will blame their governments—or any invading ones. They will try to emigrate at any cost. They will fight one another over land. They will kill one another. They will start civil wars. They figure that they have nothing to lose, so they become terrorists, or they support or tolerate terrorism (Diamond, 2005). The effects of this violence and chaos are not contained within the boundaries of any one country in today's global world.

The global economy, controlled largely by Western industrial corporations and countries, has provided some relief to the developing countries of Asia, Latin America, and Africa. But global economics has fallen short in the race to a sustainable global commons. This is a race we must win. Scholars in many disciplines, including ecological economists, suggest that more of the same will not keep us from an eventual collapse. Our common sense tells us that we cannot measure economic success solely on the basis of monetary or technological growth indicators, real or electronic. You cannot eat, drink, or breathe money. We are in need of a new approach to economics that conforms to the needs of the planet and its inhabitants. If everything is interconnected, then our global welfare depends upon "how well underlying economic, political, and intellectual models correspond with the realities of the environment" (Garbarino, 1992, p. 21).

## WHAT IS A HEALTHY ECONOMY?

Economies are constructed to serve people and should preserve the earth; the earth does not exist to serve and preserve us. We must live in harmony with the earth. If this is true, then human institutions such as industry and business, education, and social welfare are all connected to the economy. A holistic way to conceptualize a healthy economy is to ask ourselves, what makes a healthy society? One could argue, for example, that a healthy society relies on four things: (1) a clean, sustainable natural environment, (2) a physically well populace (3) educated citizens, and (4) meaningful activity (e.g., work, recreation; Closson, 1992). In this definition, *economy* has to be congruent with the resources and institutions that support a healthy society.

This is a much broader concept of the economy than most people hold. The more common view of the economy, as Hazel Henderson (1991) points out, is the market economy that we have talked about; that is, those products and services that can be assigned a cash value and the labor associated with them. But if economy has to do with the use of natural and human-made resources and their consumption, then don't family and the environment have to be considered part of the equation? Henderson posits that we are living in an age of interdependence, wherein the threats of persistent poverty, environmental devastation, and nuclear catastrophe are interconnected (Henderson, 1988). She offers an expanded view of our economy as a layer cake, which is shown in figure 1.

**Figure 1   Paradigms in Progress: Life Beyond Economics by Hazel Henderson (1991)**

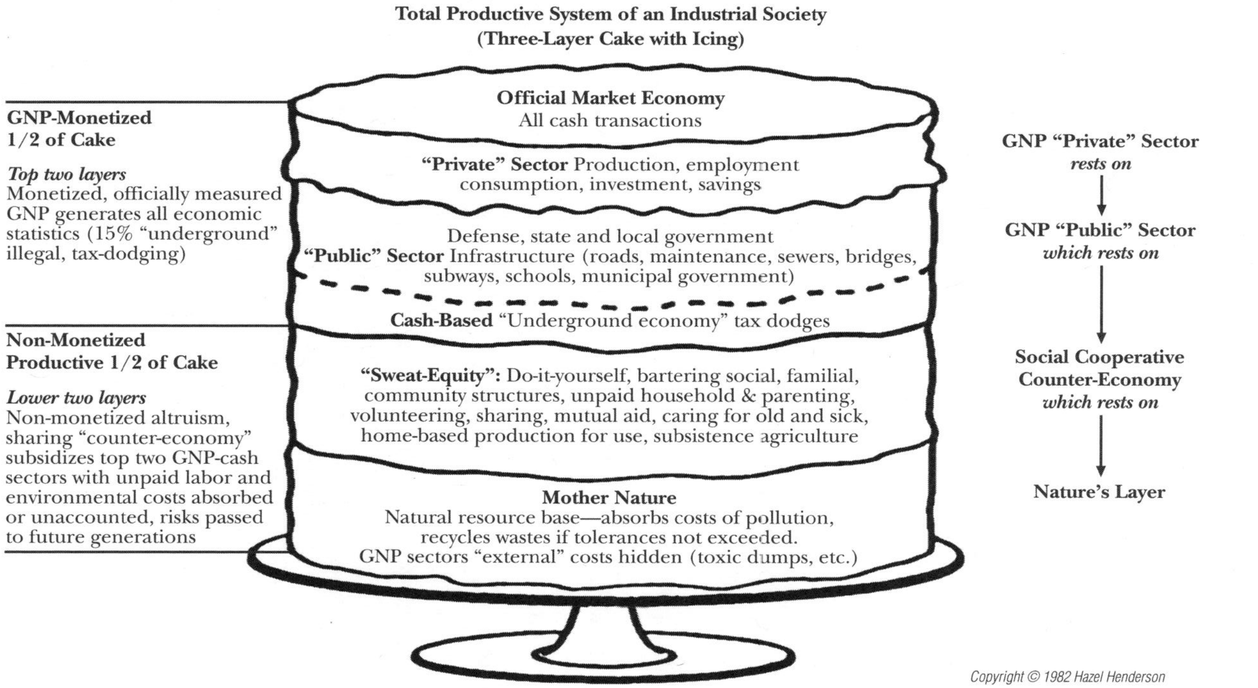

**Total Productive System of an Industrial Society**
(Three-Layer Cake with Icing)

**Official Market Economy**
All cash transactions

**"Private" Sector** Production, employment
consumption, investment, savings

**"Public" Sector** Infrastructure (roads, maintenance, sewers, bridges,
subways, schools, municipal government)
Defense, state and local government

**Cash-Based** "Underground economy" tax dodges

**"Sweat-Equity":** Do-it-yourself, bartering social, familial,
community structures, unpaid household & parenting,
volunteering, sharing, mutual aid, caring for old and sick,
home-based production for use, subsistence agriculture

**Mother Nature**
Natural resource base—absorbs costs of pollution,
recycles wastes if tolerances not exceeded.
GNP sectors "external" costs hidden (toxic dumps, etc.)

**GNP-Monetized
1/2 of Cake**

*Top two layers*
Monetized, officially measured
GNP generates all economic
statistics (15% "underground"
illegal, tax-dodging)

**Non-Monetized
Productive 1/2 of Cake**

*Lower two layers*
Non-monetized altruism,
sharing "counter-economy"
subsidizes top two GNP-cash
sectors with unpaid labor and
environmental costs absorbed
or unaccounted, risks passed
to future generations

GNP "Private" Sector
*rests on* →

GNP "Public" Sector
*which rests on* →

Social Cooperative
Counter-Economy
*which rests on* →

Nature's Layer →

We have noted that one principle of sustainability is respect for environmental constraints. In this model of the economy, the bottom layer is Mother Nature. This natural resource base is the foundation layer that we must preserve, as it supports all the others. Resting on it is sweat equity or social cooperative economy, where volunteer work, caring for family, maintaining community and mutual aid, and child rearing takes place. As social workers, we know a lot about this nonmonetized yet essential realm of activity. Without this family-based home economy that raises future citizens, the productive activity of our public and private sectors are compromised. The sweat equity sector of the economy is sometimes referred to as producing social capital; that is, the social networks developed among individuals and groups that help support families and neighborhoods (Putnam, 2000). Social capital is the glue that holds families and communities together.

The next layer, the public sector, rests upon the home and neighborhood economy. It is the public economy that supports the infrastructure, via government at the municipal, state, and national levels. These are the necessary political institutions and public works that contribute to cash flow, maintain social stability, and provide infrastructure such as highways and parks. The top two layers of the cake are the ones that generate most of the attention of current economic definitions and statistics. These are the private (for-profit and nonprofit) sectors and official market transactions. As the figure shows, each layer depends upon the stability of the layer below for long-term sustainability. This is a much more comprehensive, holistic view of an economy. This model helps us begin to connect the home economy of healthy households and families, the social capital of institutions of care in communities, public goods and services, and private capital with the importance of preserving the resources of the natural environment upon which they all rest.

It should not be difficult for social workers to accept this expansion of economic parameters to include social care and the work of the home. Mutual aid, social networks, and social goods, and the role they all play in healthy communities, are right up our alley. However, social workers know the importance of these aspects but do not usually think of them as indicators of a healthy economy. This conceptualization is a rethinking of the paradigm of economy and success because it expands the idea of the economy to include elements of a healthy society. In this model, there is much more to success than money, as it acknowledges the interconnectedness of functioning families, social networks, and public and private institutions. Thus, indicators of economic success need some expanding as well.

## NEW INDICATORS OF ECONOMIC SUCCESS: THE QUALITY OF LIFE

If we think more broadly about the purpose of an economy, our measures of economic success broaden. In the 1990s, new indicators redefining wealth and progress opened our eyes to worldwide problems and changed the direction of human societies toward sustainability (Henderson, 1996). An early example is the index of social progress developed by the social work professor Richard Estes. Begun in 1974 and summarized in his *Trends in World Social Development: The Social Progress of Nations, 1970–1987* (1984), this measure consists of ten indicators of the health of a country: education, health status, status of women, defense effort, economy, demography, geography, social chaos, cultural diversity, and welfare effort.

Other indices include the physical quality of life index, devised in the mid-1960s by Morris David Morris and colleagues at the Overseas Development Council; the high-profile 1990 UN human development index; and the core indicators for measuring development progress, which include poverty, education, gender equality, reducing mortality, promoting reproductive health, and protecting the environment. The gender empowerment measure introduced by the UNDP tracks worldwide gender inequalities in human progress (Estes, 2005).

Although the United States collects large quantities of socially relevant data, we have yet to embrace a national scorecard on the quality of life or social health. In response to this, over the past fifteen years, some cities (e.g., Jacksonville, Florida; Racine, Wisconsin; and Seattle, Washington) have developed their own social reports. These efforts have often involved much community participation and have formed the basis for needs assessment, goal creation, and the monitoring of the city's progress toward certain economic, social, and health standards (Estes, 2005).

What you choose as your goals or indicators of quality of life will also reflect the degree of fairness and equality in your local or global community. For instance, Jacksonville's quality indicators for progress track such indicators as the number of students attending desegregated schools, the gap between African American and total unemployment, and the percentage of the community that reports racism as a problem (Jacksonville Community Council, 1994). Using this broadened model of the economy, we will now turn to economic strategies that are sustainable.

## SUSTAINABLE DEVELOPMENT

A shift in thinking toward sustainable development is emerging internationally, at both national and local levels. As social workers have been involved in community problem solving since its inception, this is a natural area for their greater involvement. Social development is a "process of planned change designed to promote the well-being of the population as a whole in conjunction with a dynamic process of economic development" (Midgley, 1995, p. 25). Sustainable development has emerged from the eco-development approach (Farvar & Glaeser, 1979; Glaeser, 1984). As defined by the Brundtland report (World Commission on Environment and Development, 1987), sustainable development is an approach to the development of economic enterprises that ensures that "natural resources are replenished, and that future generations continue to have the resources they need to meet their own needs" (Midgley, 1995, p. 137).

If we think globally, sustainable development should occur at all levels of systems, from global to local, and should move us toward ecologically sustainable and equitable human development (Henderson, 1999). Two proposals at the global level are especially relevant to social work values and practice. First is the promotion of the protection of the global commons, the notion that the planet's resources belong to all of us and that we must assume a caretaker role. The commons are those natural resources that we all share and, therefore, have some responsibility for nurturing. This includes the oceans, atmosphere, space, Antarctica, the planet's biodiversity, and airways that carry electronic communication such as the Internet. Social workers should indeed become more aware of treaties, such as the Kyoto Protocol and the UN Agenda 21 developed at the Rio de Janeiro Earth Summit, as they can advocate for their adoption.

The second is peacekeeping and the adoption of alternative methods of greater citizen involvement to maintain peace. If we are to pursue a sustainable economic future that enhances all life, we cannot afford to continue international problem solving through warfare, which ensures death and destruction. Pursuing disarmament and demilitarization needs to occur at every level of economic activity, including new roles that the UN could play, such as strengthening the International Court of Justice as an alternative to warfare (Henderson, 1999; Morrison, 1995). The Ottawa Process, begun by Nobel Peace Prize recipient Jody Williams, a concerned citizen, produced the Treaty to Ban Landmines, which more than 160 governments signed (Henderson, 1999). This organizing of nongovernmental organizations provides a model of citizen engagement, illustrating how ordinary people, such as ourselves, can make extraordinary changes.

The connection between the world's military expenditures and environmental degradation is a direct one. Mention should also be made here of the enormous opportunity cost of military expenditures. *Opportunity cost* is an economic term that simply means that when you spend money on one thing, you do not have money for something else. The Pentagon's fiscal-year 2004 weapons procurement stood at $73 billion; slightly less than half the money goes to fund the twenty top weapons systems (Worldwatch Institute, 2003). The production of jet fighters, combat helicopters, destroyers, attack submarines, high-tech missiles, and munitions may raise the country's GDP. But the use of such technology does not promote human welfare; it kills people, destroys their infrastructure, and devastates the natural environment to a state of toxic waste.

The renewed growth in world military expenditures redirects money and attention from many of the world's unmet needs in the areas of general human well-being, education, health, and environmental protection. "Estimates suggest, for instance, that the prevention of soil erosion worldwide would require something on the order of $24 billion annually; the elimination of starvation and malnutrition, $19 billion; reproductive health for all women, $12 billion; safe, clean drinking water, $10 billion; prevention of acid rain, $8 billion; and elimination of illiteracy, $5 billion. Although these are substantial sums, they pale in comparison with the funds made available for military purposes" (Worldwatch Institute, 2003, p. 119).

The effects of squandering an immense portion of our social surplus on military weapons and the costs of war are felt at the local level. Though currently our military budget has been increased, and our commitment to Iraq appears to be never ending, this country continues to downsize its military bases. Local conversion projects, though they wax and wane in the political winds, provide opportunities for social workers and other community interests to become involved in the community planning and conversion of former government-use lands. Projects that provide useful civilian assets, such as parks, housing, and employee-owned industrial and health-care companies, may result in such planning (Mary, 1994, 1996).

Now let's look at strategies of sustainable development at the local level. Democratizing finance involves giving local communities greater interest in and control over their own economic ventures. These projects can take the form of cooperative commercial banking, community development corporations, credit unions, and cooperative savings banks. Chicago's South Shore Bank is a good example of this type of venture in the realm of housing. The bank works with business, nonprofits, and faith-based communities to help low-income people access housing. Community economies are mixed economies that may include co-ops, individual businesses, partnerships, public or government organizations, and corporations. Corporate forms and wage labor are not prohibited; rather, their nature and size are transformed into viable community-based firms instead of transnational corporations with little commitment to or control by the local community. Examples of players in these efforts are the Industrial Cooperative Association of Boston and national and local Jobs with Peace campaigns. For community economics, the ideal of a socially viable or competitive firm must include issues such as fair competition, a livable wage, working conditions, worker ownership, environmental protection, and human rights (Morrison, 1995).

Current global and local economic development approaches have involved top-down strategies with corporate and finance leaders at the helm. Meanwhile, most of the world's populace are the passive passengers being taken down the river. The exception to the traditional approach is projects such as the Seikatsu Club in Japan and the Mondragón Cooperative Corporation in Spain. These enterprises include elements such as a social wages, organic food co-ops, and alternative-energy resources development in attempts to promote economic democracy and a more healthy and sustainable planet. A more recent example is Vauban, a development of more than 2,000 homes on a former military base outside of Freiburg, Germany. A successful experiment in green urban living, Vauban's small homeowners cooperatively designed and built their homes from scratch, using a master plan that enables the 4,700 residents to travel via bicycles and live virtually car free. Economic enterprises supporting the local economy, such as solar panel installation and wastewater purification account for 3% of jobs in the region (Forum Vauban, 2002).

These projects are built on the notion of partnership, in which the goals of development must be choices made that creatively and constructively involve members of the community. The model challenges the old industrial paradigm of unlimited progress and instead promotes initiatives based on new-paradigm principles such as the evolution of cooperative systems and projects that involve relationships and networks rather than hierarchical structures, all through a process of revitalized democracy.

This thrust can be accomplished through micro- or individual-focused economic enterprises. Ramanathan and Link (1999) identify roles for social workers in these kinds of efforts. For example, the recipient of the 2006 Nobel Peace Prize, Muhammed Yunus, was rewarded for his creation of the Grameen Bank, created in Bangladesh in the 1970s. The Grameen Bank extends loans mostly to groups of women to set up their own businesses. Now, individual development accounts modeled after this approach are operating all over the United States. The accounts offer opportunities for social workers to help local residents learn clinical skills, group process, organizing, and social development strategies. Communities in developing and advanced industrial nations suffer from the effects of globalization, such as low-wage job markets, toxic environments, poor physical infrastructure, and the lack of housing. Social workers can help develop community groups, partnerships, and collaborative efforts to begin the dialogue about what is needed and then to assist in the formation of a response.

Strategies of sustainable development are operating at both local and international levels to build more democratically and ecologically balanced community ventures. But all this is happening in a world in which rapid technology changes not only affect the economy but also change the way we think about time, space, and even relationships. What are some of the implications of technological change for social welfare and a sustainable future?

## WHAT IS TECHNOLOGY?

In the end, the fate of children depends on our ability to use technology constructively and carefully. The connection of the children and technology is not simply a matter of seat belts, safe toys, safe air, water and food, additive-free baby foods, or improved television programming. These are all important issues, but to stop here is to forget that today's children will soon be adults. Technological decisions made today will determine, perhaps irrevocably, the kind of physical and social world we bequeath them and the kind of people they become.
—Kenneth Kenniston, *All Our Children*

Many people born after 1980, when asked, "What is technology?" probably think, "Technology. Oh yeah. Computers. Cell phones. E-mail. The Internet. My iPod." Yes, it is all these and more. Technology is, simply put, the practical application of science, as it translates discovery into every arena of our economy. For example, science is working to develop a blood coagulant from snake venom. Technology takes that element and puts it into a pill that helps people with heart disease manage their heart condition. Science is discovering the atom. Technology develops nuclear power plants to produce energy or creates the atom bomb. Science is the discovery that, over a large number of studies, behavioral intervention combined with cognitive therapy helps people with alcohol dependency stay sober. Technology is the development of self-help or clinical counseling groups that use these techniques in mental health clinics.

The postindustrial, old way of thinking maintains a positivist approach to science that separates the observer from the observed. Thus, science is value free, and the technology developed from scientific discoveries is separate from science. In other words, a scientist would say, "We have no responsibility for the use of this destructive biological organism; we just discovered it; you technicians decided to use it." In this old paradigm, humankind is separate from nature and dominates it. Technology, then, reflects this relationship. Nature's resources are ours to use in the march toward progress—progress for the human race, that is. Progress, or the lack thereof, for other species is not central to decision making regarding technological innovations. Is this sustainable thinking?

Derezotes (2005) believes that we have conceptualized technology as a religious movement that has influenced civilization for more than a thousand years. However, new trends are making us rethink this paradigm. The globalization of information, work, resource extraction (e.g., oil, human and plant DNA), the pollution of the natural world, and the extinction of species are all moving us to reconsider technology within a framework of sustainability. That is, we must pull back one photo frame to include a new composite and reflective view. This frame forces us to consider the effects of what we observe and create on the larger web of life, on our ability to live in harmony with nature, to preserve the diversity of species and future generations (Henderson, 1996).

Technology is posing new advances and concerns for our economy and social well-being. I have chosen to talk about four areas: energy, biological diversity, jobs, and the age of access (Rifkin, 2000).

## WE'RE RUNNING OUT OF FOSSIL FUEL

We are beginning to transition from an economy based on petroleum to one based on other energy alternatives, including hydrogen. Recent estimates suggest that the global production of cheap crude oil could peak before the year 2010, but no later than 2020 (Campbell, 1997; Hatfield, 2001). That means that half the estimated ultimately recoverable reserves of oil in the world have been produced (Rifkin, 2002). Energy is a geopolitical problem. "While globalization can be understood from many perspectives, none is more important than the energy equation. . . . Geopolitics has been, to a great extent, synonymous with politics of oil for five generations" (Rifkin, 2002, p. 7).

The need to diversify our energy is not a controversy; it is a daily reality. We have now invaded a country, Iraq, in the next major move in a protracted war on terror. This move was the next step in a continuum of warfare following September 11, 2001, which began in the first Gulf War. The roots of this conflict can be traced to colonial years when Western governments and oil companies, in concert with Arab strongmen, established their presence in the Middle East for the purpose of securing cheap crude oil for the United States and other consuming nations.

We are also receiving reports of a slower yet equally devastating kind of death. In recent decades, the Arctic has warmed, which will affect the entire world. The Arctic Council, which comprises government representatives, scientists, and indigenous groups, reports that the warming is among evidence that more clearly shows the effects of global warming and the greenhouse effect (Pew Center for Global Climate Change, 2007). Some of the local effects are declining reindeer herds, crumbling infrastructure (e.g., pipes, buildings, roads), relocation of coastal villages inland, insect infestation in forests, and projected decline of seal and polar bear populations. The military and environmental costs of our global dependency on oil substance are enormous. They cannot be sustained. How can we, as individuals and citizens, move the public will to bring these threats closer to us all?

Social work's professional policy statement on the environment embraces energy alternatives. "We advocate for fossil fuel elimination or reduction to be replaced, where feasible, with clean energy such as solar, wind and water" (NASW, 2000). Rifkin (2002, pp. 227–40) offers three strategies to move us from a global economy reliant on oil to one based on alternative energy sources:

- The democratization of energy via distributed generation associations. In the United States, Touchstone Energy, an alliance of 550 consumer-owned electric cooperatives, provides electricity to 16 million customers in thirty-nine states. Other models for development, in the United States and other countries, are credit unions, community development corporations, and public utilities.

- Political advocacy with world lending institutions and national governments to help provide fiscal and logistical support for the creation of a hydrogen-energy infrastructure.

- The provision of stationary fuel cells for every neighborhood and village in the developing world; developing countries would no longer depend on the flow of crude oil.

In stark contrast to these suggestions, there is a recent surge of interest in building nuclear power plants. This is understandable, in the short run, given the estimates in additional energy capacity needed over the next twenty years. One option being proposed is fourth-generation, high-temperature, gas-cooled nuclear reactors that expel their heat into the earth or the air, thus lessening the chance of another Chernobyl (Grant, Starr, & Overbye, 2006). However, even putting the dangers of accidents or targets of terrorism aside, it is questionable whether the long-term buildup and storage dilemma of nuclear waste has a sustainable solution.

In addition to hydrogen as an energy source, some people today are proposing that we move toward greater reliance on a solar economy as part of our necessary shift to renewable energy resources. The scale of these projects, however, is important to consider, as renewable power can come from destructive, massive hydroelectric dams and other large projects (Morrison, 1995). A primary reason, then, to support solar energy as a soft energy path is its potential to transform the social relationships that support the industrial system. Some people assert that the exploration of solar energy may help create a movement toward decentralized, democratically controlled, and environmentally sensitive innovations (Lovins, 1977).

These are some of the challenges of our future energy needs. But what about another facet of technology from the perspective of sustainable life on earth: messing with Mother Nature?

## THE CHALLENGES OF BIOTECHNOLOGY

We are rapidly entering an era wherein we have the ability to alter our own bodies as well as the bodies of other living things. Rifkin, in his book *The Biotech Century* (1998), examines both the potential and the challenges of the biotechnology era. The combining of genetics and computer technology is enabling us to recombine genes, to artificially produce plant and animal organs, and to produce life patents in a global life science industry. Here are just a few examples of how we are remaking our natural world.

In bioengineering, energy companies are starting to experiment with renewable resources as a substitute for coal, oil, and natural gas. Ethanol, from sugar and grain crops, may provide up to one-quarter of U.S. motor fuel by the middle of the twenty-first century. Animal husbandry scientists are experimenting with "super animals." In Australia, scientists have transplanted the genes of genetically engineered sheep into normal sheep to make their wool grow faster (Ford, 1988). Mosquitoes are being engineered genetically to make them unable to spread illnesses such as malaria. Researchers have deleted the muscle-regulating gene that produces a protein that regulates muscle growth in mouse embryo cells, in the hope that this will lead to new treatments for human diseases such as muscular dystrophy. A current, fairly controversial issue is the expansion of human stem cell research, whereby stem cells from frozen embryos that would have been destroyed may be used to explore the potential for treating human neural disease and dysfunction. Two scientists are working on growing women's breasts in the laboratory. Researchers around the country are also experimenting with the development of fabricated lungs, hearts, livers, and pancreases made of human cells (Rifkin, 1998).

Rifkin provides a cautionary note in his discussion of the potential of biotechnology. He observes that many ecological scientists are taking a more integrative approach in agriculture and medicine to better understand the relationship between environmental influences and genetic mutations. In agriculture, this means reliance on crop rotation, organic fertilization, integrated pest management, and other sustainable methods to make agricultural production compatible with ecosystems in the regions where crops are grown. Similarly, in medicine, rather than focus on altering genes to correct disorders, the approach would be a more scientifically based understanding of preventive health. A holistic approach to human medicine, in line with new-systems thinking, would involve the study of genetic predispositions and how they interact with toxins in the environment, metabolism of different foods, and lifestyle changes.

At the global level, as the interdependence of the environment and development become more clear, the UN General Assembly adopted the World Charter for Nature to try to protect the value of species and ecosystems. The four general principles of this charter are as follows:

- The genetic viability on the earth shall not be compromised; the population levels of all life forms, wild and domesticated, must be at least sufficient for their survival, and to this end necessary habitat shall be safeguarded.

- All areas of the earth, both land and sea, shall be subject to these principles of conservation; special protection shall be given to unique areas, to representative samples of all the different types of ecosystems and to the habitat of rare or endangered species.

- Ecosystems and organisms, as well as the land, marine and atmospheric resources that are utilized, shall be managed to achieve and maintain optimum sustainable productivity, but not in such a way as to endanger the integrity of those other ecosystems or species with which they co-exist.
- Nature shall be secured against degradation caused by warfare or other hostile activities. (UNEP, 2002, p. 10)

So, what values do we, as social workers, apply to messing around with Mother Nature? Biotechnology may affect every aspect of life, from whom we marry, to how we conceive and raise our children and where we work, our politics, our faith, and how we see our place in the world (Rifkin, 1998). Therefore, might we consider the application of the principle of "Do no harm," which has long been revered in medicine? The more powerful a technology is at changing the natural world, the more likely it is to disrupt long-standing networks and to create unanticipated imbalances somewhere else in the surrounding environment. Which of two visions of biotechnology—genetic engineering or ecological practices and preventive health—is more radical and most likely to cause disequilibrium, and which is the more conservative approach and least likely to cause unanticipated harm down the line? (Rifkin, 1998). In the social work response to the potentials of biotechnology, we should consider the principles of sustainability and then dialogue, in many arenas, about the impact of these developments on the well-being of humanity, the earth as a whole, individual and community involvement in decision making, and distributive justice (e.g., equal rights, access to biotechnology; Derezotes, 2005).

Much of the discussion has focused on the impact of technology on our environment, the base layer of the cake of our new model of economics. Let us move to the level of sweat equity. Is it possible that this nonmonetized but vitally important sector of work that develops social capital through activities such as caregiving, parenting, and community volunteerism can be validated in its role in a healthy economy?

## WHAT IS WORK?

In the past, when new technologies replaced workers, new sectors have always emerged. Today, all three of the traditional sectors of the economy—manufacturing, agriculture, and service—are experiencing technological displacement resulting in millions becoming unemployed. The wholesale trade industry, hard hit due to information technologies, lost 60,000 jobs in 1992. Since 1989, the wholesale sector has lost more than a quarter million jobs (*Monthly Labor Review*, 1993). General Electric, a world leader in the manufacturing of electronics has reduced worldwide employment from 400,000 in 1981 to fewer than 230,000 in 1993. Its sales have tripled in that time (U.S. Department of Labor, 1990). There are similar staggering figures in the appliance, housewares, and laundry equipment manufacturers. It is important to note that none of these losses have occurred because of growing imports or falling demand (*BusinessWeek*, 1993).

The only real new sector is the knowledge sector, a small, elite group including scientists, entrepreneurs, professionals, educators, computer technicians, and consultants. This sector is expected to make up a small fraction of the millions who will be unemployed in the next several decades (Rifkin, 1995). A major question, then, is, what is the future of work in our global economy? What will be the productive jobs that are so important in shoring up a healthy economy?

Global markets are expanding. So is the gap between the haves and the have-nots. As machines replace humans in both manufacturing and service industries, where are the jobs for our children? The small number of jobs created in the information industry may not be adequate to redirect employment opportunities to millions of people.

Some are suggesting that globalization of the social economy or development social capital may be an answer. Nongovernmental organizations are forming networks north and south to redevelop local communities through cooperatives, intervillage trade networks, and microenterprises. Although many of these are rural, they could be expanded to the suburbs, as Morrison (1995) suggests. This rise of worker-owned, self-managed enterprises and of bartering, sharing, self-help, and mutual aid is documented by the Institute for Local Self Reliance, the Cooperative League of the U.S.A., and in publications such as *Mother Earth News* and *Yes! The Journal of Positive Alternative Futures* (Henderson, 1988). In an address to social work educators at the 2004 Annual Program Meeting of the Council on Social Work Education, Rifkin offered several recommendations for the development of a social economy.

He asserted that we should empower communities and help them become more politicized in efforts to accomplish the revaluing of social care, the transformation of education to involve greater civic participation, sales of businesses on the notion of partnerships that revalue social care, and advocacy for government reinvestment in social capital (to save money on, e.g., health care, mental health, welfare). At that conference, he placed these activities at our doorstep when he stated, "We are the only profession that bridges social capital with the world of work and commerce—the person and the environment."

So, what is a social wage? The major principle of a social wage is the creation of a mechanism to provide some income to all; it is the second tier of Henderson's layer cake. A spectrum of economists have embraced this idea, in various forms, from Milton Friedman's guaranteed annual incomes to Bill Clinton's earned-income tax credit and Lyndon Johnson's pilot work projects. Given the range of useful work that needs to be done at the home/caring community infrastructure levels of the economy, a social wage could be opened up to include socially useful work that is now typically unpaid or underpaid, such as hospice work, child care, and education.

The community can determine what is useful labor in the context of a broad mandate of responsibilities and rights for all community members. These responsibilities are based on what Mahatma Gandhi called the "need for all to perform bread work" (Morrison, 1995, p. 210). The mechanization of jobs, the high-tech revolution, and the rise of the service industries that have created a gap among rich and poor workers are all evidence that suggests a larger role for the caring sector in sustainable community economies.

How does a social wage work? Social wage ideas are reflected, in part, by proposals for reduced work hours; many European countries, such as Germany, have reduced weekly work hours. However, a social wage aims to provide all people with decent clothing, shelter, medical care, education, and recreation in a bundle of social benefits and entitlements, not all in cash, in exchange for so many hours of work per year, or over a lifetime. Although a social wage is an attempt to move away from the world of industrial production and consumption as an all-absorbing focus of life, people could choose to work more or less and to receive a smaller share of the social wage, depending on their need and interest. A social wage aims to optimize the individual's realms of personal freedom, family, and community (Morrison, 1995).

For example, in Minneapolis, a group of unemployed single parents on welfare who call themselves the Mothers' Union have joined together to offer one another mutual support—from housing and child care to crisis intervention and tutoring for their children. In New York City, the Youth Action Program, with a board made up of 75% young people, has relied on the energies and initiatives of teenagers to rehabilitate houses for the homeless and a senior citizens' activity center where young people serve as escorts and companions. Also in New York City, Cooperative Home Care, consisting of more than one hundred African American and Hispanic women, many formerly on welfare, now run their *own* home-care business and earn incomes above the industry average (Forest, 1991).

Efforts that bring community members together involve participation in face-to-face exchanges and the building of intimate and collegial support networks. Yet every day we are bombarded by a virtual reality. What does this virtual reality have to do with quality relationships? Let's take a look.

## THE AGE OF ACCESS TO GOODS AND SERVICES

A rapid global trend is a new commercial worldview; that is, the movement from the production and consumption of goods to the evolution of access to services (Rifkin, 2000). Due to the power of the Internet and e-commerce, access is replacing property as the valued global asset. Simply put, we no longer value owning something, such as a compact disc; we value access to it, so we can download it on our computer, cell phone, or iPod, and even remix it on our computer music-making software. We no longer deal in hard cash or even plastic; we transfer our assets electronically. In other words, the production of factory-produced goods is being replaced in the information era by access to experiences.

Though the potential to connect the world's people in a global village has long been asserted, the reality is that 65% of the world's population has never made a phone call and 40% have no electricity. Highly industrialized countries accounted for more than 88% of Internet users in 1998, though they account for less than 15% of the population (Rifkin, 2000). However, things are rapidly changing. Not so long ago, middle-class parents of school-age children would purchase fifteen volumes of the encyclopedia in a onetime transaction from the door-to-door salesman. We now no longer have ownership to this information; rather, we have access, via a long-term relationship with upgraded features. Another example is time-shares, which provide us with a time-limited vacation experience. We can own a home or we can purchase a way of life through common interest developments, gated communities of like-minded folks with all the necessary resources contained therein. We can purchase our movies or have them delivered to us by Netflix. The dematerializing of goods and services could result in monetary and natural resource savings. For example, if all American commuters leased cars that were maintained over fifteen years, and transportation access companies were rewarded by both the longevity of the product and the length of the relationship, rather than the fast turnover of new vehicles, the resulting drop in production costs of labor and material would be enormous. Can we give up the desire to own our own vehicle?

A major concern and topic of much international debate in the age of access is fairness and unequal distribution of the costs and benefits of technological development. Concerns include technology transfer, intellectual property rights, appropriate technologies, trade-offs between security and privacy, and the potential for information-poor countries to find themselves on the wrong side of the digital divide (UNEP, 2002, p. 325). Once again, if the goal, in the economic use of technology, is primarily profit, then there will be some major winners and many more who will have no access to the information highway. If more and more communication is reliant on the information highway and some people don't have the means to get on, how do we make the right to access a universal one?

There is another issue that is posing a real danger in continued reliance on this technology for our work, play, and socialization: the potential of information to commoditize and change the way we experience human relationships, not necessarily for the better. Traditional communities involve face-to-face relationships, with long-term commitments and social contracts. Commercial or market contracts are of shorter duration and serve the individual interests of the customer and supplier. Why are these differences important in assessing the nature and quality of human relationships?

As social workers, we value empathy, diversity, and cultural understanding. Understanding people and other cultures involves immersing oneself in the rich details of their lives and, where possible, in their worlds. Accessing facts about various cultures via the Web plays an instrumental role in learning. But how important are empathy and engagement in the development of social trust in learning about diversity and cultures, and how does cyberspace compromise these (Rifkin, 2000)? True, the Internet lets us connect with people all over the world, but what do we gain? What do we give up? These questions are just a few of the many we are already wrestling with as we enter the age of distance learning, online courses, online therapy and support groups, and indeed, online communities.

## WHAT CAN SOCIAL WORKERS DO?

There are many roles that social workers can take in the shift to a more sustainable economy. The previous case study of social workers and a more holistic approach to economic conversion is an example of the role of social workers as a catalyst to bring people to the table around a community issue that pertains to economic and social development. The Rivers Communities Project (Baum and Twiss, 1996), involving the University of Pittsburgh School of Social Work, is another example of social workers assisting communities in economic and environmental struggles resulting from military downsizing. From the mid-1980s to 1993, social work students, professors, and administrators played the roles of action researchers, facilitators, and policy advocates toward the betterment of ailing communities in western Pennsylvania.

Social workers can be researchers of more comprehensive social indicators of the health of a community or a country. They can help poor women develop their own home-based business or cooperative. They can be catalysts for community participation in local planning and development projects, such as community development corporations, local credit unions, or a sweat-equity child-care and house-cleaning cooperative.

They can be advocates for treaties that protect the global commons, limit land mines, or decrease the production and sale of arms. They can help establish an interdisciplinary center at their university that unites social work, economics, political science, geography, and other departments to identify community needs and develop service-learning partnerships in response to them. Social workers need not be experts in economics, housing, real estate, or banking. They need only be themselves, experts in engaging people in dialogue, getting them to the table around common interests and concerns, helping identify what is needed, and then mobilizing them to partnership and action.

Social workers should be actively involved in individual and community dialogues about the role of technology in the lives of the citizens with whom they work. This means that they are advocates for jobs with livable wages and for revaluing volunteer and family work as work, in practice and policy. We live in a time when, unfortunately, the role for which we are valued most by society is not citizen, parent, worker, or student, but consumer. Given the problems of consumption, social workers should take a hard look at this role. We should question and advocate the questioning of the adage, "More technology is better," in family, community, or global economic and social life.

## ADDITIONAL THINGS TO THINK ABOUT

1. How has the infusion of technology changed your life or your family's life in relation to the kind of work you do and how you do it? Are there negatives and positives? For the clients you work with?

2. If as a country we were to invest a lot of money in the development of alternative energy resources, what kinds of additional jobs might we create related to this development?

3. Some might argue that the virtual reality or online networks we create have potential as communities. From your understanding of what communities are and what they do for people, to what extent do you agree with this point of view?

4. For some time now we have been messing with Mother Nature in the transplant of organs and limbs as well as the creation of artificial ones. Now we have real possibilities to clone and plan the makeup of human beings. What ethical ramifications are there in these activities?

5. If we developed the ability to cure deafness in 99% of the population via prenatal in vitro intervention we could, theoretically, cause communities like Martha's Vineyard, Massachusetts—

which in the nineteenth century became home to a community of deaf people and influenced the development of American Sign Language—to become extinct. Is this a good thing or a bad thing?

6. Interview an older person and have him or her share with you how he or she now uses technology and what life was like before this technology. Talk about the costs and benefits. What did they gain from new technology? What were its negative effects?

7. Consider the community you live in or one with which you work. If you were to develop two indicators of progress most relevant to this community's success, what would they be? What are some strategies that might affect these indicators?

8. Habitat for Humanity is a sweat-equity, community-development strategy that renovates and builds homes for first-time homeowners. Can you think of an area of need other than housing where a sweat-equity or cooperative approach might work?

9. Does the community you live in or the larger county in which you reside have a community development corporation? What is its focus? Its degree of citizen involvement?

10. Find a community that has an established farmers' market where people buy produce from vendors as an alternative to buying from a large grocery chain. Find out how the market got started. Who was involved? Is there a role for social work here?

## EXERCISE: A ROYAL MEETING

Once upon a time, in a Queendom far, far away, there were two young children of the royal family. They were both boys and their names were Economicos and Technologicos. They were not the only children, but their three sisters, Ecologia, Psyche and Philosophia, were much older and had grown up and ventured beyond the boundaries of the Queendom.

Certain conditions made early life for the two younger children very different from what it had been for the older sisters. Not long after the births of Economicos and Technologicos, their mother, the Queen of the land, disappeared mysteriously while out on one of her solitary walks into the forest. Her husband became the new ruler, and being grief-stricken at the loss of his companion, did not take another bride. Further, the new ruler, being a superstitious type, thought the misfortune of losing the Queen was a result of the way they had brought up the first children. Ecologia, Psyche and Philosophia had been given many freedoms and had been allowed a youth full of wonder and imagination.

To rectify his mistakes, the ruler raised the two youngest children in a much more strict and logical way. There was not much time for play or experimentation for Economicos and Technologicos. The Arts and Humanities, and even much of the Social Sciences, played little part in their education.

When Economicos and Technologicos were young adults, their father died, still saddened by the loss of his wife, but confident that he had helped to make amends by reforming the Queendom. He even gave the country a new name, Capitalis. The two brothers then ruled together. Their goals were simple: through innovation, specialization and material productivity, they would increase the material standard of living throughout the land. Those who had the largest schemes and the most resources at their disposal were given the money and freedom necessary for their projects. Others would benefit from the various jobs necessary to keep the wheels of progress moving.

Roads were built, forests were cleared, every kind of machine was invented. New weapons were made and sold to other countries who feared for their security in the fast changing world. Many diseases were eliminated and much toil was reduced. But there were other effects of the rapid advancement as well. The water, soil and air became poisoned. Rivers actually became so full of synthetic chemicals that they caught on fire. For some reason, the rich kept getting richer while the poor got poorer. The weapons of destruction became more and more life-threatening. And people lost their ability to relate cooperatively and without inhibition with each other and the rest of nature. New diseases, related to stress and hazardous substances, took the place of the old ones. And many wars were fought over control of the markets and resources necessary to keep the machine of progress running.

This went on for generations as the male descendants of Economicos and Technologicos inherited the rulership. Meanwhile, the descendants of Ecologia, Psyche and Philosophia developed another society, called Humanitas, in a remote region relatively unaffected by the changes sweeping over a great part of the world.

But finally the changes reached their doorstep too. Having been raised to value the Arts, Humanities and the Social Sciences, the offspring of Ecologia, Psyche and Philosophia did not welcome the intensity of the new thrust toward rationalism, materialism and militarization. Feeling a familial connection with Economicos and Technologicos, their government sent three female ambassadors—named, appropriately, Ecologia, Psyche and Philosophia—to discuss the matter.

The three were received well, though they were generally viewed as being soft and impractical in comparison to those of the society of Capitalis. Two government leaders, also named for their forebears, were selected to discuss the matter with the ambassadors from afar. And so the five gathered together at a retreat center in the hills of the government compound.

Philosophia began the discussion by expressing her people's concern over the spread of the culture of Capitalis. She said that the ambition and materialism of their ways was wiping out the pursuit of higher knowledge of human possibility and deadening the life of imagination and intuition. She said that it was unethical that some should have so much while others do not have even enough to meet their basic needs. She said this was bound to cause resentment and violence. She reminded her hosts that the wisdom of the ancients counsels us to simplify and uplift our desires rather than simply seeking to fulfill them without question.

Economicos and Technologicos responded that life had improved immensely under the influence of Capitalis. They pointed out that freedom and wealth had been extended to many who never dreamed of either before. They reminded their guests that differences in wealth have always existed, and that absolute equality could only come at the cost of giving up our freedom. They said that members of their society were free to choose their material destiny, whether they would be rich or poor.

The three listened with patience. Then, after a pause, Ecologia said that these were noble accomplishments. But, she continued, one of the great learnings of Nature is that life depends on balance. Too much of even a good thing becomes a poison. There is proof of this in the fact that your industry has altered and poisoned the air and water and soil upon which we all depend. We are not outside, but within the fabric of life. The soil and air and water and other creatures are the threads of that fabric no less than we. What is done to one is done to all.

Economicos and Technologicos both felt strange sensations inside. But they did not want to appear weak, so they responded quickly. They assured the three that they were capable of solving the problems of the environment through scientific innovations. They also said that every benefit has its costs and that the benefits of their society outweigh the costs.

Again there was a pause. Psyche broke the silence by saying that sometimes costs are hidden. Sometimes it is hard to place a value on things. What is the value of peace of mind? What is the value of being a whole person, balanced in the skills of thought, feeling, intuition and sensation? What is the value of knowing a wide range of things, rather than being trained in only one area of knowledge? What is the value of uninhibited friendship? What is the value of knowing you are passing on an unpolluted and peaceful Earth to future generations?

Economicos and Technologicos felt strange and disoriented. The arguments that immediately sprang to mind seemed out of place. They knew that the ambassadors were not being hostile and so they resolved to consider their comments. The outcome of their reflections was that they decided to . . .

## A Royal Meeting

### Study Questions

1. What are the goals of economics when it "grows up" disconnected from an awareness which includes ecology, psychology and philosophy?

2. How does this compare with our present understanding and practice of economics?

3. Why do you think the author links economics and technology in the story?

4. Why do you think the author used gender the way she/he did?

5. In your own words, what are the messages that come from Philosophia, Ecologia and Psyche?

- Philosophia—

- Ecologia—

- Psyche—

Are these messages accurate? Are they relevant? Explain.

6. On a separate piece of paper write your own ending to the story.

7. What kinds of changes would economics and technology make if they listened to the insights of philosophy, ecology and psychology? What would the goals of the economy be?

Sustainable Economics: A supplementary curriculum for High School Economics Courses
The Center for Economic Conversion, Mountain View, CA.

## MAIN POINTS

1. Our industrial economy has brought much progress and higher standards of living across the globe. It has also done much damage to the earth, which, if it continues, may not be sustainable.

2. A broader definition of economy includes the environment, social equity, and public and private economic activities which can broaden our goals for a healthy economy, with new indicators of social and environmental welfare.

3. New advancements in energy, biotechnology, and information technology bring advantages and possible dangers to our quality of life. We should consider them mindfully in terms of their contribution to sustainability of physical and social systems.

4. There are many roles for social workers in helping create sustainable systems at the family, community, and global levels.

## For Further Reading

Derezotes, D. (2005). *Revaluing social work.* Denver, CO: Love Publishing.

Henderson, H. (1991). *Paradigms in progress: Life beyond economics.* Indianapolis: Knowledge Systems.

Henderson, H. (1996). *Building a win-win world: Life beyond global economic warfare.* San Francisco: Berrett-Koehler.

Morrison, R. (1991). *We build the road as we travel: Mondragón, a cooperative social system.* Gabriola Island, British Columbia: New Society Publishers.

Morrison, R. (1995). *Ecological democracy.* Boston: South End Press.

Rifkin, J. (1995). *The end of work.* New York: G. P. Putnam's Sons.

Rifkin, J. (1998). *The biotech century.* New York: Jeremy P. Tarcher/Putnam.

Rifkin, J. (2000). *The age of access.* New York: Jeremy P. Tarcher/Putnam.

# CHAPTER 6

# Sustainable Politics

The response of the government to September 11, 2001, was to re-sort, once more, to the old realpolitik of an earlier era, which has only made clear the presenting problems of the terrorist attack and driven the United States' to claim its right to protect its boundaries. *Families in Society: The Journal of Contemporary Human Service* published a series of responses from social work professionals in the aftermath of September 11. These thoughtful reactions provide different perspectives but all point to the need for an alternative to the old thinking. Some suggestions include the need for a foreign policy that reduces the real and perceived barriers to international cooperation (Fischer, 2002), the need to look below the surface to the real causes of global social problems (Newcomb, 2002), and the need to recognize that "meaningful participation in the broader privileges and benefits of productive society is the best defense, in the long run, to the development of terrorists" (McDevitt, 2002, p. 120).

Cheung and Tsui's (2000) comments remind us of our need to refocus on our interconnectedness:

> Worldwide inequalities in resources and power have resulted in extreme disparities and violent responses. Social workers can no longer ignore such strong global economic and political forces and hope to resolve social problems by focusing only on individual or the local systems. . . . We need to think and act both locally as well as globally. . . . Let us turn this nightmare into a dream. Let us renew our profession's mission to include the enhancement of humanity through the inspiration of love, peace and justice. Because we now know that in this global village, everyone's behavior, attitude or belief can and will invariable affect the rest of us. (p. 124)

Perhaps it is time to reexamine the viability of this institution of politics in a sustainable global village. For many, including social workers, the word *politics* conjures up a negative image: dirty business, corruption. Politics is the exercising of power to influence decision making at the individual, community, national, or global level. But it is the power "thing" that social workers have always had a love-hate relationship with. Though we have seen a slow growth in the number of social workers in political office over the past fifteen years, social workers do not report goodness-of-fit between their work and their politics. Comments by social workers' field instructors suggest that the value base and scruples of our profession make it difficult to accept the self-absorption, interest in fame, and power of money in current political arenas (Mary, 2001). Perhaps there is another way of thinking about politics and power that is more congruent with our value base.

## WHAT IS POLITICS?

The term *politics* comes from ancient Greece; the term *polis* means "city-state." So, politics is a system of organization involving the machinery of government, practiced in the halls of legislatures by representatives, lobbyists, and civil servants. This traditional definition, however, excludes most social activities and institutions that people are involved in as outside politics (Heywood, 2002). Simply put, politics is the work of government.

In a broader sense, however, politics is the activity by which people make, protect, and change the general rules by which they live. These decisions may affect their rights, the roles they play, and the resources to which they have access. This broader definition moves politics into the public arena and into a host of organizations, such as associations, clubs, corporations, nonprofit groups, churches, and policy arenas at work, in the boardroom, or even in the family. Although most of these are open to the public and may even have public goals, they are traditionally referred to as civil society or the as the private interest sector, in contrast with the government's focus on the larger public good.

Historically, social workers have experienced these boundaries as blurred. In fact, in the early days of the profession, it was the religious sects, friendly visitors, and community-based settlements that tried to meet the needs of the public when there were few government programs to address them. Government involvement grew as a result of urbanization, population growth, and industrialization, with major increases in the 1930s and again in the 1960s. But governments at both state and national levels have pulled out of many human service programs over the past twenty-five years. One could argue that the public good that the state does is, at best, meeting physical infrastructure and police and fire protection needs of communities, with minimal coverage of education, recreation, and social needs. This government retrenchment in human services coupled with increased media attention to scandals and corruption on the part of some civil servants have perhaps helped fuel our perception as social workers and citizens that politicians are in business for themselves. This may explain the hesitation of social workers to enter the frays of partisan politics. Rather, they support political work indirectly through NASW or through their own field of practice-related interest groups (Mary, 2001). I believe that this may explain the difficulty I have had in trying to convince social work students that they are power players in every arena of practice. They prefer not to think of their work with families as involving the use of power. But influence is power. Let's look at some models of power.

## MODELS OF POWER

In a broader definition, politics is the way individuals and groups influence decision making and agenda setting in organizations and in government. The following models of power have largely been applied to government at community, state, or national levels. But let's consider the previous broader definition of politics and keep in mind our many agencies, work groups, voluntary associations, and clubs, as well as city hall, as we look at these models and think about how influence is exerted and decisions are made.

The first of five models of power is the elite model. Coined by C. W. Mills (1957), in the elite model, power resides with members of the top social strata of the community. This model suggests that, regardless of the issue—be it growth, education, recreation and leisure, or the environment—the same players with money, occupational status, connections, government position, or other powerful assets have the most influence. Second, the pluralist model, while still a hierarchy, places the elite at the top of the triangle but puts emphasis on the myriad interest groups that exert power on the elite, such as business, the arts, labor, environmentalists, and senior citizens. These groups compete for resources and lobby the elite on behalf of their own interest (Dye, 1998). The third public choice model combines the first two, with an emphasis on the free market. Essentially, this model asserts that those interests with the most resources and willingness to invest them have the most influence on decision making.

Fourth, the neo-elitist model acknowledges the elite as well as interest-group access to influence, but it also recognizes the unequal access of those groups to the elite as a result of structural barriers (e.g., money, education). This model asserts, however, that there are those among the elite who are more progressive and in tune with the needs of the broader population, and that they may align themselves with those groups toward social change (Hardina, 2002). Finally, there is the corporatist model, wherein the organized interests of business and industry are granted privileges and strengthened as a result of their close relationship with government (Heywood, 2002). Though there are differences among these models in terms of the potential power of interest groups, they all are based on a hierarchy of power, with elite decision makers at the top.

How are the elite chosen? The basis in Western democracies is by popular elections, in contrast to totalitarian governments, such as North Korea, that allow citizens to vote between the government's chosen candidates, or in monarchies, such as Jordan, where power is passed on through the family. In the United States, political platforms are developed and voters can choose between candidates or parties. These are converted into representation via majoritarian or proportional systems. The first is, in general, a winner-take-all mechanism whereby the most powerful body with the largest influence becomes the majority (e.g., the United Kingdom, the United States). Proportional systems make single-party rule less likely, as the parties are allocated seats in the legislature in direct proportion to the votes gained, as in Germany, Ireland, or the European Parliament. In general, the major weakness of majoritarian systems, and common criticism of the U.S. system, is the lack of access of minority parties, which represent a broad spectrum of opinion. This is in contrast with proportional systems that allow for a broader spectrum of opinion. The major weaknesses of such coalition governments are that they may be unstable over time or unwieldy and inefficient in decision making (Heywood, 2002).

Our government is a representative democracy based on the pluralist model. Strictly speaking, this means that the power is distributed among various interest groups who have access to influence elected representatives. One could well argue, however, that over the past quarter century, the United States, along with many other Western democracies, has become much more of a corporatist model of democratic power. There are several forces that have greatly contributed to tipping the scale of power on the side of business: the waning power of labor, the lack of representation of other political parties in a majoritarian structure, minimal regulation of money flowing to political candidates, and the globalization of capital in an unregulated market.

The price we have paid in the United States for this marriage of democracy and the market agenda has been high, with negative effects on the environment, civil rights, labor, overall social welfare, and the national debt. Since 1980, we have seen the gap widen in income between the rich and the poor. We have seen the government retrench in the interests of human welfare, which culminated in the 1990s in the abandonment of a federal commitment of aid to families with dependent children. Environmental protection, civil rights, wages, and human welfare have all taken a backseat to business; in the same breath, we have had increased funding for military intervention. This decreased social protection and quality of life is occurring in other Western countries as they too adopt market-based policy priorities (Mishra, 1999).

Though the failures at the hand of government over the past couple of decades to maintain a quality of life for people and the environment have been daunting, people have not bailed out of the ship of public life completely. Robert Putnam (2000), in *Bowling Alone*, has traced the decline of Americans' involvement in civil society over the past twenty-five years. There has been a decrease both in traditional political activities, such as voting and active, participatory membership, and downturns in participation in civic life of associations, clubs, and other players that enhance the social capital of communities. A more recent study, however, sheds some light on why the trend of inactivity in traditional political arenas in particular is occurring.

In 1990 and 1991, the Harwood Group, a small public-issues research firm, held ten focus groups across the country and asked people what they thought about politics (Atkisson, 1991). One of the study's most encouraging findings was that people are not apathetic; they are "simply disgusted" (Moyers, 1991, p. 9). People reported that they did care about issues and the accountability of their representatives, but they have shifted their activities to neighborhood associations, schools, and local government issues. They "refuse to associate this activity—or themselves—with politics, which they view as corrupt" (Moyers, 1991, p. 10). Some of this disgust may translate into the perception that the work of government lacks morality or meaning, according to Rabbi Michael Lerner. He contends that many citizens are not involved in politics because they see it as selfish, corrupt, and representing all the excesses of materialism. Lerner (1997) and other transformational thinkers assert that the citizenry is searching for a more meaning-oriented vision for politics and public life. We will explore the need for meaning in politics a little later.

So, we have some problems in terms of truly realizing democracy. Let's now turn to the world stage and the decision makers in the global village.

## GLOBAL POLITICS

*Globalization,* a term that has emerged since the 1980s, refers to the interconnectedness of countries, and it has influenced local, regional, and national events in all countries. Certainly, economic globalization has occurred with the free movement of investment capital and the help of telecommunications. Along with that, a kind of cultural globalization is occurring as global goods and the media flatten out cultural differences across nations (Heywood, 2002). Political globalization began increasing post–World War II, with the development of the United Nations and the North American Treaty Organization, and later with the European Union, the World Bank, the International Monetary Fund (IMF), and the World Trade Organization. But most people hold the prospect of a global state or world governmental structure as very distant.

The power base with the most influence in global decision making is that of multinational corporations. Their ability to relocate capital and production all over the world gives them power to escape much of the democratic control of national governments. The policies of three key players support this power: the World Trade Organization's thrust is to liberalize world trade, the World Bank lends money driven by market strategies to foreign investors, and the IMF controls the flow of international money through the establishment of exchange rates and other mechanisms. All three support a neoliberal political philosophy that embraces market mechanisms such as privatization and deregulation, and that places much constraint on what national governments can do in areas of trade, development, and other policy areas such as labor and the environment (Heywood, 2002). In fact, some have made a strong case that governments no longer have much power over domestic or international issues and that corporations rule the world (Korten, 2006).

The UN is the most advanced experiment in world government to date. Established in postwar 1945, its charter lays out standards for international conduct in peacekeeping and renounces the use of force in international disputes and human rights. Unlike the League of Nations, the UN has remained a steady force. But it, too, is set up as a hierarchy. The most significant body is the fifteen-member Security Council, responsible for the UN's role as negotiator and peacekeeper. The big five of this body are the United States, France, Germany, Japan, and Britain. These members have individual veto power, which means that any one can cancel decisions made by other members of the 192-member General Assembly. All decisions are recommendations, not enforceable international law. Although the UN has considerable moral authority worldwide, its judicial arm, the International Court of Justice, is also limited in its power. Only about one-third of UN members acknowledge its jurisdiction (Heywood, 2002).

Despite these limitations, the legacy of the UN should be acknowledged. Since 1948, the UN has accomplished disarmament, decolonization, protection of human rights, respect for international law, and the promotion of social progress standards for many of the world's citizens. It has assisted some forty-five countries, including El Salvador, Namibia, and South Africa, in holding free and fair elections; in effect, it has helped countries promote democratic foundations—a major force in global stability.

In 1952, the General Assembly overrode South African objections and considered the question of apartheid. In April 1994, the UN observer mission in South Africa oversaw the first nonracial elections in South Africa, which led to the end of the racist system of apartheid. In 1945, some 750 million people lived in dependent territories (nearly one-third of the world's population). Decolonization efforts since then have promoted independence for former colonies and dependent territories, now members of the UN. The International Court of Justice over the years has considered

95 cases and issued 60 judgments and 284 orders, including international tribunals on genocide in Rwanda and the former Yugoslavia. More than 300 international treaties have been developed through the UN's efforts over the past half century.

The UN Population Fund's family-planning programs have enabled people, especially women, to have greater control over their lives. As a result, women in developing countries are having fewer children. In 1960, only 10% of the world's families were using effective methods of family planning. The number now stands at 55% (UN Chronicle, 1995).

In conclusion, the U.S. government has brought us great prosperity over the past half century. It has, in partnership with other institutions, made possible countless inventions and discoveries in medicine, technology, and communications. But it has not lived up to its potential. We have come to a point in human history where we think in new ways about growth, democracy, and power. We have a global body, the UN, that has played an admirable role in galvanizing nations toward peaceful resolutions of disputes among countries. But it is limited in what it can do. We must begin to think differently about world order and sustainability.

## AN ALTERNATIVE TO THE OLD WORLD ORDER

Albert Einstein, after the development of the atomic bomb, stated, "The unleashed power of the atom has changed everything save our mode of thinking and we thus drift toward unparalleled catastrophe" (qtd. in Nathan & Nordan, 1981, p. 376). But horrors of the nuclear deaths and destruction had many thinking that the Big War would be the last one. We had learned our lessons.

But today warfare is pervasive. At any point in recent history, more than fifty large-scale wars are being waged around the globe (Gurr, 1993). In 1945, only eight hours lapsed between the decision to drop the bomb on Hiroshima and the time the bomb fell. By the mid-1980s, that time has been reduced to ten minutes (Beyond War, 1985). The real threat may be the inevitability of a terrorist attack or the accidental use of such weapons.

Nuclear weapons are part of the old way of thinking about how nations can solve local and international conflict. This old world order, which arose in the decades following World War II, is based on a model of sovereign nation-states that have political authority over a given territory with clear boundaries and political, economic, and cultural institutions independent of other nation-states. However, this model is an illusion. Populations have loyalties to multiply religious, political, economic, kinship, and other groupings that cut across national boundaries and are subject to transnational forces. Stronger countries pressure weaker ones; the unintended effects of global processes and events, from global warming to nuclear accidents, affect all. It was only after the wind shifted, literally, that we, in the United States, breathed a little more easily after Chernobyl.

In the old world order, the United State dominated every other industrial country in economic and military power, everywhere but in the so-called second world. As the cold war ended, we entered, in the 1970s and 1980s, an era of a global economy of transnational corporations and world markets, or President George Bush's new world order. New coalitions of the haves began to form, such as the World Bank, the IMF, the General Agreement on Tariffs and Trade, and Bush's favorite, the Gulf War coalition. The aim was to create a coalition of powerful political regimes, corporations, and the military to preserve access to resources. But this is not a new order. The old hierarchical model of power and economic competition is still upheld, wherein the ultimate and often-common mode of problem solving is the law and order mentality of starving and/or bombing into submission those who are targeted as enemies of the aims of the more powerful countries.

The reality of this new world order, or as Richard Falk calls it, "globalization from above" (Falk, 1995), is continued concentration of power, and increased repression and impoverishment of Third World countries, income and resource disparities between the North and South, and numbers of refugees due to warfare, flawed development strategies, and environmental degradation.

## BROADENING THE DEFINITION OF NATIONAL SECURITY

In the old world order, we have defined security as securing our national borders. The often-unstated goal, however, is to secure our interests abroad. A multitude of pressures and instabilities that threaten the very fabric of civilized societies drive today's conflicts. "A toxic brew of growing disparities in wealth, increasing unemployment and job insecurity, population growth, and environmental degradation is provoking more social discontent and polarization, leading to political strife in many countries and to devastating violence in some" (Renner, 1999, p. 34). Because these economic, military, and environmental trends are global in nature, national policies alone cannot contain or remedy these threats. So, what international strategies can reduce threats to global security?

Already mentioned is the role of nongovernmental organizations in citizen involvement in, for example, securing a ban on land mines. However, the UN is an international body that, if supported and bolstered with funds, could play a major role in international peacekeeping. But has the UN lived up to its peacemaking potential? Preventive diplomacy, which involves political, economic, and military strategies at an early stage to discourage or minimize hostilities, has had some success (Hokenstad & Midgley, 1997). However, additional strategies could include more assertive and effective new roles and authority for the UN.

For example, the UN could set up a security insurance agency that could provide member states more security for less money. It could negotiate agreements guaranteeing UN peacekeeping support to countries paying an annual premium for this protection. This could be negotiated among the country, the UN, and the new agency. The agency might require that the country reduce its aggressiveness to curtail its military expenditures before it could be insurable. It could monitor compliance, contract with civil society groups for their professional conflict-resolution services, and make recommendations for contract renewal (Henderson, 1996). Other strategies might include early conflict warning and early deployment networks, with a core of experienced individuals to serve as roving mediators on behalf of the international community.

Ultimately, however, national security is global. This shift toward a global view of security will involve nonviolence, fair distribution of wealth, balancing of the interests of various population groups, adequate job creation, the elimination of poverty, and the preservation of ecosystems (Renner, 1999). There is no single road to ending conflict. Just as Jeffrey Sachs (2005) came to realize in his commitment to end poverty, there is no one road or one discipline that can end conflict. We are a web of relationships, strengths, and problems. We need to pursue the interconnected paths to human security and quality of life for all. We also need to examine and eliminate obsolete strategies at every level.

## VIOLENCE: THE MICRO AND MACRO CONNECTIONS

Violence is not a viable means to security, quality of life, or social justice at any level. Understanding the connection between international and personal violence is the subject of Turpin and Kurtz's 1997 compilation of articles entitled, *The Web of Violence: From Interpersonal to Global.* Political scientist Robert Elias (1997), in "A Culture of Violent Solutions," points out several failures of the use of violence to solve social problems. First, violence intensifies the problems, is counterproductive, promotes resentment and hatred, stimulates new problems, and invites retaliation (Elias, 1993). This is evidenced by the violence of imprisonment (Zoroya, 1993), the war on drugs (Elias, 1993), and violence abroad in such places as the Middle East and Central America. As most violence is used to keep power, not to solve problems, it does not eliminate our enemies; it simply creates them.

Although Elias notes that it is difficult to determine cause and effect, linkages exist between domestic violence and violence in the broader society. Eisler (2005) points out that it is not coincidence that the most warlike societies have been those in which the threat of violence is used to maintain domination—of parent over child, of man over woman. There are differences between Hitler's Germany, Stalin's Soviet Union, fundamentalist Iran, and Idi Amin's Uganda, but all were violent and repressive. And all were characterized by top-down rankings in the family and the state, wherein physical and economic control were maintained by domination of the male half of humanity over the female half, with a high degree of acceptance of violence, from child and wife beating to chronic warfare (Eisler, 2005). We have evidence from the United States as well. Family violence is in part responsible for subsequent violence committed by children who were previously abused (Straus, 1994). The battering of women escalates simultaneously with the structural violence of increasing unemployment (Boulding, 1978), and there are links between the violence of poverty and teenage violence.

The kinds of violence that may be easier for all of us to identify are acts or events such as warfare or personal assaults. There are perpetrators and there are victims. We can label this violence as a violation of human rights. We can intervene, whether with a batterer or with guards in a prison or with peacekeeping troops. We can also identify the victim and sometimes blame him or her, whether the victim be the child who turns to the gang in a poor neighborhood with few alternatives or a country that resorts to civil war over the scarcity of water or land. But the problems of world hunger, AIDS, and poverty are related to the violence of chronic inequality in the systems of government, trade, and market economies that are not equal-opportunity systems. We must acknowledge that the world is not working well for most of its peoples, in large part because of structural violence. Undoubtedly, human beings have the ability to produce enough food for the world, but no fewer than 800 million people are malnourished. We have the know-how to protect children through nutrition, vaccinations, and public health strategies. But every year, more than 10 million children die before their fifth birthday (Kent, 2003). It is not because they are born into a poor world. It is because international political and economic institutions have not found the will to apply the means to more equally meet human needs.

These are our institutions, formed by human ingenuity. Let's say you are a social worker making a home visit on behalf of a disabled child. You find an upper-middle-class, two-parent family who own their own home, with swimming pool and sauna in the backyard. Two of their children are having some friends over, and they are all swimming in the pool. Upon further observation, you conclude that the children have plenty of food and clothing, their own bedrooms, and appear to be well adjusted. You then find that their other child, the disabled three-year-old, is living in the basement with poor ventilation, is malnourished, has lice in his hair, is in rags, appears wary of strangers, and communicates at a developmental level half his age. You would have no problem declaring the situation one of child neglect. You would not blame the child. You would intervene in whatever ways possible to make a difference in the life of that child. But as a country we are in a state of denial regarding these same inequalities on the global stage. What will it take for us to come together as a species for the good of the whole?

If a secure society and sustainable future cannot be built on political and economic systems that support violence and social injustice, then what are our alternatives? Perhaps some new thinking about politics can help us address this question. First let's look at another definition of politics. Then, as we did with our economic systems, let's look at some alternative visions for politics that promote our survival and that of all creatures sharing the planet, and the participation of citizens in developing a sustainable local and global vision based on valuing life and social justice for all people. We will then turn to an alternative model of power, in contrast to the hierarchical model. Finally, we will examine what role we want to play. Do we simply want a piece of the traditional pie? A way in to the inner circle of decision making? Or do we want something more?

## NEW THINKING: POLITICS AS GOVERNANCE

The traditional view of politics is the narrow arena of the state. Government bodies make decisions that affect the larger public good. In contrast, civil society comprises all those other private institutions, such as clubs, associations, family, and businesses, all of which are seen as in business for themselves. Liberal economic theory heavily influences these views and holds that private groups are only concerned with their own self-interest. The power to serve the public good is with elected officials, and the way to influence this power is by somehow getting your agenda to the table of the decisions makers, in competition, of course, with other private interest groups. The reality is that many private organizations serve the public good, both locally and internationally, through their own service delivery, advocacy, and government influence.

Consider the private effort of Jody Williams, founding coordinator of the International Campaign to Ban Landmines. Williams oversaw the growth of the ICBL to more than 1,300 nongovernmental organizations in more than eighty-five countries, and in 1997 received the Nobel Peace Prize for an international treaty banning antipersonnel landmines. As a private citizen, Williams played a major role in catalyzing civil society to bring about international social change. Subsequent to this achievement, she was a distinguished professor of social work and global justice in the Graduate School of Social Work at the University of Houston. What a great role model for social workers in the power of the private citizen and the civil sector!

Perhaps the term *governance* is a useful alternative to the traditional narrow view of politics. Although dictionaries may not distinguish government from governance, the latter is a broader term that has been used to refer to the various ways that social life is coordinated. The modes of governance have been identified as markets, hierarchies, and networks (Heywood, 2002). However, we must be careful to avoid a simple shift in this definition from less government to more free market. Rather, the rationale for a different definition is to broaden our thinking and to acknowledge the decision making and influence that goes on in all of the players in the civil sector as part of politics. The vision of a web may also open up other possibilities of decision making in politics, such as public-private partnerships. A web shifts the construct from a hierarchy of the elite to a more circular web of interaction.

There are many examples of increased citizen involvement in community decision making in public life. One is the Neighborhood Action Initiative in Washington, D.C. (Potapchuk, 2002). Shortly after he took office in 1999, Mayor Anthony Williams engaged citizens in a collaborative city-planning effort with city officials. This effort innovatively opened up the web of governance with citizen summits held with small-group work and laptop computers to facilitate input and setting priorities among citizen suggestions; telephone lines available to citizens watching live summits on cable television; a Neighborhood Action web page; discussion guides published in daily newspapers with feedback forms; and a 2001 Youth Summit, planned because few youths were initially involved in the planning. These kinds of efforts can help build structures and networks with potential for permanent partnerships between government officials and the citizens they represent. But consider, now, a broader vision of governance in terms of where we want to be in a sustainable world.

## A NEW PARADIGM: TRANSFORMATIONAL POLITICS

When I was in the middle of the research for this book, exploring paradigms of politics, I was struck by how futuristic the more popular literature seemed to be. It was rich with new ideas. But I was fearful that academia, once again, had failed to catch up to the outside world and new-paradigm thinking. Then, much to my delight, I came upon *Transformational Politics* (Woolpert, Slaton, & Schwerin, 1998), a product of the Ecological and Transformational Section of the American Political Science Association, which took shape in 1987. The following is a discussion about a new paradigm of politics that reflects the thinking of these political academicians who call themselves transformational political scientists. The principles of these scholars eloquently mirror the thinking of others we have highlighted—those deep ecologists, social scientists, economists, physicists, and scholars such as Jeremy Rifkin. These thinkers cannot be placed neatly within one discipline but they have articulated a new postindustrial way of thinking that, in terms of politics, expands far beyond the new world order.

In 1987, a group of scholars became dissatisfied with mainstream social science research in political science and began to be engaged in scholarship in paradigm shifts. Thus, a new paradigm began to take shape that places change at its core and seeks to transform us and our political institutions in positive, peaceful ways. Their thinking is meant to challenge traditional paradigms and to "offer a theory that is value-based and relatively comprehensive by integrating democratic, ecological, feminist, post-modern and non-Western thought" (Woolpert, Slaton, & Schwerin, 1998, p. xxiv).

The themes that depict this scholarship echo those we have talked about, but they are framed and applied to issues in political science, such as citizen participation, democracy, public policy, and conflict resolution. The following is a brief description of each major theme.

## The Obsolescence of the Prevailing Paradigm and the Emergence of a New Paradigm

The impetus for a new way of thinking about politics was, in part, the sense of a discontinuity between the past and the future in political affairs. Symptoms of this were trends such as accelerating environmental degradation; the end of the cold war; the challenges to the sovereignty of nation-states; and the growing impact of multiculturalism, feminism and ethnic assertiveness, and breakthroughs in technology (Woolpert, Slaton, & Schwerin, 1998). A recognition of the limitations of positivism and the global nature of interconnected changes in technology, economic, and political institutions requires a new look at our political condition.

## An Ecological Focus and Systems Thinking

The five principles related to an ecological focus and systems thinking are reminiscent of our earlier discussion of the new science or web of life:

1. *Interdependence*: The shift to patterns of political interaction rather than a focus on discrete political actors.

2. *Partnership*: The pervasiveness of partnership, symbiosis, and permeable boundaries; these are often downplayed in the current prevailing paradigm, which results in greater attention to conflict and destruction.

3. *Flexibility*: Attention to continual feedback loops and the natural and social environment emphasizes adaptability of structure and processes versus reliance on obsolete doctrine.

4. *Diversity*: Attempts to force homogeneity or replace cultural diversity with a global monoculture lead to massive instability. Diversity enriches and endures the viability of complex communities.

5. *Sustainability*: For a sustainable society, systems thinking must not be allowed to reduce the operation of complex wholes to one-way cause-effect explanations and linear relationships. Concern for the future requires cross-disciplinary study and the awareness of the global reach of politics is essential (Woolpert, Slaton, & Schwerin, 1998).

## Linkage of Personal and Political

A central theme of feminist thought, the linkage of the personal and political reminds us that politics is not just about running for political office, but about how we live our lives. It emphasizes a power with versus a power over paradigm. It also disputes the detached observer and the detachment of political science research and activism. With an emphasis on praxis, or placing theory into action, the political scientist is both scholar and activist, involved in self-critical reflection. Research and action agendas are not value free but value based.

## Inclusion of the Spiritual and Sacred

The inclusion of the spiritual and sacred has to do with a postmaterialist perspective that places great value on self-actualization and the search for purpose and meaning in our roles as political beings, such as citizenship, electoral politics, informed consumers, and policy making in private and public arenas. The goal is "to move beyond the self-interest and self-centeredness of the politics as usual world" (Woolpert, Slaton, & Schwerin, 1998, p. xxiii). This theme is echoed in Lerner's (1997) *Politics of Meaning*, which we will examine a little later.

## WHAT DOES TRANSFORMATIONAL POLITICS LOOK LIKE?

Some of the best transformational leaders who have demonstrated transformational values are people such as Mahatma Gandhi, Martin Luther King, Nelson Mandela, and Václav Havel (Gilbert, 1998). Havel led the Czech Republic's velvet revolution from Soviet rule. Gilbert, from research of Havel's writings, delineates elements that evidence these themes. Essentially, they are behaviors such as seeing the interconnectedness of political realities, viewing events with a holistic understanding of context and meaning, maintaining truth and integrity through self-reflection, and remaining aware of one's spirituality while confronting daily struggles (Gilbert, 1998).

In politics, the Green Party has embraced these values. Many transformational scholars have been active in green politics (Affigne, 1995; Rensenbrink, 1988; Rohter, 1992; Slaton & Becker, 1990). The Green Party's value base includes ecological wisdom, social justice, grassroots democracy, personal and global responsibility, nonviolence, decentralization, community-based economics and economic justice, gender equality and cooperation, respect for diversity, and future focus and sustainability (Coleman, 1994; Rensenbrink, 1988). These values provide key research questions for many transformational scholars.

These ideas illustrate the transformational or new systems thinking we have been exploring in this book. For example, the principle of ecological wisdom integrates the new systems thinking of Capra (1982), chaos theory, and feminist theory (Knight, 1998). It is also echoed in authors we have discussed such as Schumacher (1973), Morrison, (1995), Henderson (1991), and many others. Linking the personal to the political is, of course, a major principle of feminist practice theory, along with redefining power; valuing process equally with product; and challenging the false dichotomies between research and practice, between the observed and the observer (Van Den Bergh & Cooper, 1986). Community-based economics, gender equality and cooperation, and respect for diversity are values of Morrison's (1995) ecological democracy. In the redefinition of power, nonviolence becomes the viable option for sustaining families and countries. The inclusion of the spiritual is part of both feminist practice and the Afrocentric paradigm of social work practice.

## THE POLITICS OF MEANING

The spiritual element is the focus of another notion that Rabbi Michael Lerner calls politics of meaning. This is the articulation of that need so many citizens are expressing to escape the politics of cynicism and embrace one of values, spirituality, and meaning. This notion challenges the popular image that politics is all self-interest and pragmatism, and by nature, lacking in moral integrity. This may provide inspiration for social workers. Lerner, editor of *Tikkun Magazine* and author of *The Politics of Meaning* (1997), is critical of the political right wing's claim of sole ownership of ethics, spirituality, and family values. He is also critical of the political left's failure of empathy, which, he says, acknowledges the economic and political oppression of poor people but ignores the spiritual alienation of all, including the upper class. Lerner asserts that Americans are in a state of spiritual and political crisis because they see no link between the two. They want to experience politics and morality in the same breath. Social problems that are studied and reported on from a unidimensional and/or superficial perspective that does not consider the deeper moral and spiritual aspects of an issue are not illuminating for academics or citizens alike. This kind of research is shortsighted in Lerner's view. He, too, is challenging the great divide between science and spirit:

> Our society insists that the problems be analyzed and dealt with in isolation from one another. We therefore will pour millions of dollars into research to see what genetic factors might predispose someone to crime or to drug or alcohol abuse. But we will not ask, "What are people trying to escape when they deaden their consciousness through drugs or alcohol?" . . . We pour billions into building more jails, but we are afraid to face honestly the breakdown of human

connections, the dissolution of moral and spiritual bonds. . . . [We need] a more systematic critique of society than the proponents of this research care to take on. (Lerner, 1997, p. 40)

Arguing that we cannot separate our institutions of economics and politics from the sense of solidarity and the framework of meaning, or lack thereof, Lerner states that individuals desire to be part of larger "communities of caring" (1997, p. 14). This desire may involve consciousness raising and the evolution of a renewed social contract among people to create more spiritually and ethically sensitive political and economic institutions.

To create communities of caring, the author offers a host of national and community-level initiatives to support families, ranging from family leaves to full employment, housing, and health-care policies. We should teach about religions and spiritual awareness. Tolerance and understanding of various kinds of religions and definitions of spirituality, then, are essential in the education of future citizens and the building of a social contract among people toward developing communities of caring. This social contract may have the potential to transform politics from a self-serving enterprise to more value-based processes and structures of governance, wherein citizens take responsibility for the creation of communities of caring. The following story, by Garbarino (1992), captures this sense of responsibility:

[April 1987] The shoreline of Lake Michigan at Chicago is the scene of a philosophical and ecological struggle. . . . This year the specific agenda for environmentalists is to resist efforts to build a new football stadium . . . [and] to urge the closing of the lakeside airport (Meigs Field) and convert it into park land. The battle pits the "do-gooders" against the "slobs" to put it gently. . . . As I walk along the shore it looks to me like the slobs are winning. Two mallard ducks are paddling close to shore. Three teenage boys approach, rocks in hand. One lets loose and misses the ducks, but not by much. I can't stand it and make bold to intervene: "Hey, guys, don't throw rocks at the ducks. Don't hurt them. Isn't there enough pain in the world?" They hesitate; then one responds, "Do they belong to you?" What a fantastic question. How profoundly discouraging that someone should ask it. Of course, these kids are merely expressing precisely the same attitude as their elders in high places and low. They would exploit and degrade the whole planet with the same cavalier selfishness these boys show in stoning the ducks.

Yes they belong to me, and I to them. (pp. 239–240)

The values of tolerance, caring communities, and nonviolence are alternatives to the violence inherent in the old world order. Our country's involvement in the movements of nonviolence and restorative justice should be acknowledged in our discussion of transformation and a new model of power.

## RESTORATIVE JUSTICE AND NONVIOLENT RESISTANCE: ALTERNATIVE MEANS TO PROBLEM SOLVING

Although a case could be made for the inception of restorative justice in ancient times, the modern movement began in Ontario, Canada, in the mid-1970s. A Mennonite probation officer and a community volunteer decided to fashion a discussion group to come up with a different way of dealing with criminal behavior. Efforts have continued since then in many different countries throughout the world (Wilkinson, 1997). Restorative justice is a philosophical framework for responding to crime and the actions needed to mend the harm done. It is accomplished through a cooperative process involving all relevant stakeholders. Offenders take responsibility to help make things whole. Victims are involved, as well, in coming up with acceptable responses. The community is charged with holding offenders accountable and creating opportunities for them to reintegrate into society (Wilkinson, 1997). Mechanisms such as family conferencing, sentencing circles, victim-offender meetings, and community restorative boards all play a part in restorative justice (Prison Fellowship International, 2007).

A relatively new concept in the Unites States, restorative justice owes a great deal to the experiences of indigenous people in both North America and New Zealand (Neighborhood Reconciliation Services, 2007). Restorative justice occurs in a wide variety of contexts. It may involve the management of high-risk sexual offenders and other prisoners transitioning to the community (Strahl, 2006; Wilson et al., 2007). It may target juveniles with minor criminal histories (Rodriguez, 2007), or involve peacemaking circles to deal with student conflicts across a school district in Minnesota (Umbreit, Vos, & Coates, 2005), or conference with families to deal with intrafamily conflicts in a public housing community in Hawaii (Walker, 2000).

There are many questions and issues regarding the future of restorative justice, such as how to deal with domestic violence or the extent to which it can offer a viable alternative to the current criminal justice system. Nevertheless, it is a growing and relevant alternative movement (consider the South African Truth and Reconciliation Commission) that is having an impact in many communities throughout the world (Umbreit, Vos, & Coates, 2005).

Nonviolent resistance has ancient roots in Christianity, Buddhism, and Hinduism. The discussion of the modern nonviolent movement usually begins with Mahatma Gandhi. At the essence of his philosophy is satyagraha, positive resistance, not to be confused with passive acquiescence or the avoidance of conflict at all costs. The most modern follower and practitioner of this movement in the United States, was the Reverend Martin Luther King, who adopted Gandhi's principles for use in the civil rights movement of the 1960s.

Social workers are familiar with King and his accomplishments, such as the development of the Southern Christian Leadership Conference and his historical Poor People's Campaign, which led more than 500,000 people to Washington in 1963. Lesser known, however, is the long-standing leadership group in fostering nonviolence in America as well as other parts of the world, the Fellowship of Reconciliation. Founded in 1915, the fellowship is the largest interfaith peace organization in this country. It helped create a host of other organizations such as the Congress of Racial Equality, the American Civil Liberties Union, and the National Congress of Christians and Jews. Their many efforts include their assertion of the futility of World War I, the campaign for the cancellation of war debts, lobbying for conscientious objectors, opposition to military conscription, and pressuring the United States to join the League of Nations. The list goes on and on (Wink, 2000). Their members and scholars continue to provide us with alternative avenues to violence in community and global problem solving.

Nonviolent movements in the United States have come a long way, from the opposition to slavery to the civil rights movement, to the creation of peace and conflict studies on many college campuses. In the past two decades, we have seen nonviolence used in a number of international arenas. In 1989 and 1990 alone, thirteen countries underwent nonviolent revolutions. These struggles affected 1.7 billion people—one-third of the population of the world (Wink, 2000). We have a long way to go. But look how far we have come.

In short, we have attempted to redefine and broaden the notion of politics as governance to include decision making in the many domains of public life. Transformational politics embraces the new-paradigm thinking of interconnectedness, linking the material and spiritual worlds and principles of sustainability, such as the value of quality of life, nonviolence, fairness and equity, participation and partnership, and a respect for environmental constraints. Movements of reconciliation and nonviolence remind us of their place in our own country's battle for social justice. But we are still operating with a model of power that is hierarchical, one of power over versus power sharing. Is this a problem? Cultural transformational theory suggests this dominator model is pervasive and unsustainable. In order to realize the goal of sustainable public institutions and greater citizen participation in decision making, a fundamental shift is needed in the model of power, from one of dominance to one of shared power.

## CULTURAL TRANSFORMATION THEORY AND A NEW MODEL OF POWER

Societies have been conceptualized, for the most part, as superior versus inferior models, patriarchies or matriarchies, with one sex dominating the other. Recent feminist scholarship in archaeology, chaos theory, and history proposes a different paradigm of society: cultural transformation theory. Eisler (1995), in *The Chalice and the Blade*, posits that underlying the great diversity of human culture are two basic models of society: the dominator model, which involves the ranking of one gender of humankind over the other, and the partnership model, which involves the linking of social relationships. In her look at prehistorical data, Eisler concludes that the original direction of our society's evolution was toward partnership, but that following a period of chaos and almost total cultural disruption, there occurred a fundamental social shift. Thus, we may be at an evolutionary crossroads that may necessitate a transcendence of conventional polarities of left and right, capitalism and communism, and masculine and feminine (Eisler, 1995).

What is striking about these postmodern ideas is that the main determinant of the future is not technology or economics. Rather, human values and social arrangements will ultimately shape the future, as will the way we conceive of the future's possibilities, potentials, and implications (Harman, 1977; McHale, 1969; Mesarovic & Pestel, 1974). What is most relevant to social workers as future change agents is the suggestion that there were sophisticated civilizations that flourished for generations, such as Minoan Crete, which operated with social stratification systems that did not involve slavery or the domination of one gender over another, and in which warfare was absent. These new data challenge strongly held beliefs that there will always be war, there will always be poverty, or it is human nature to conquer. They give us hope to envision alternatives toward global human rights and social justice (Mary & Morris, 1994).

A summary of the key concepts of cultural transformational theory appears in table 2. The table is based on an alternative model of power but goes beyond this power shift to embrace other concepts of sustainable thinking. Key ideas in this theory mirror those found in new-systems thinking: the bridging of the gap between science and spirituality and the sustainability of major institutions such as economy, technology, and family. To a great degree, this model of power encompasses the four themes of a sustainable future.

**Table 2    Summary of Key Elements of Cultural Transformation Theory**

|  | **Dominator (Blade) Model** | **Partnership (Chalice) Model** |
|---|---|---|
| **Power Relationships/ Polity** | Domination over nature and humans; power based on ranking/shared power | Linking in equal power; win-win model of conflict |
| **Economics** | Limitless growth as measure of success; narrow view of productivity (e.g., GDP) | Sustainable growth; congruent with ecology; expanding definition to include social goods (e.g., nurturing) |
| **Science/Religion** | Western positivist paradigm; separation of object and subject; science is values free; compartmentalized knowledge | Approaches that acknowledge intuition and spirituality; science of empathy; connections among phenomena |
| **Technology** | Destructive technology of defense; subjugation of nature | Life-enhancing technology; living in harmony with the environment |
| **Family** | Hierarchy, male-dominant relationships | Equality of gender relationships |

Table 3 provides a comparison of the dominator and partnership concepts (Eisler & Loye, 1990).

**Table 3    Key Comparisons in Dominator and Partnership Concepts**

| Dominator Model | Partnership Model |
| --- | --- |
| Fear | Trust |
| Win-lose orientation | Win-win orientation |
| Power over | Power with |
| Control | Nurture |
| Manipulation | Open communication |
| Hoarding | Sharing |
| Left-brain thinking | Whole-brain thinking |
| Taking orders | Working in teams |
| Secrecy | Openness/accountability |
| Violence against others | Empathy with others |
| Conquest of nature | Respect for nature |

The dominator-partnership model has been applied to work with children and adults. Eisler and Loye's (1990) *The Partnership Way* offers experiential exercises for group facilitators or educators. Eisler (2002) also applies the approach to the development of relationships in *The Power of Partnership*. *Tomorrow's Children* (Eisler, 2000) offers a framework for transforming education by infusing new data on the history of civilizations into the curriculum. In addition, it offers ways of incorporating partnership concepts into math and science, social studies, literature and humanities, history and current events, love and relationships, and our living planet. Eisler's work clearly has significant implications for the practice of the profession of social work.

## CULTURAL TRANSFORMATION THEORY AND SOCIAL WORK

There is much congruence between cultural transformation theory and other social work theories and approaches; some of these were noted in our discussion of transformational politics. Paulo Freire's (2000) concept of praxis and the empowerment perspective are relevant in their validation of the experiences that shape the lives and values of the individual client or constituent group. Clients are empowered to take their own action (praxis) for political and personal change; professionals have equal exchange and dialogue in this process rather than power over their clientele. The major principles of feminist practice resonate with the concepts of the partnership model, such as the elimination of false dichotomies (e.g., science and religion), the reconceptualization of power, and the connection between the personal and the political (Van Den Bergh & Cooper, 1986).

The interconnectedness of science and spirituality, and working in partnership rather than competition are principles of Afrocentrism (Schiele, 1996). Social constructionism, with its overall assumption that there is no overall truth and that different cultural groups construct reality differently is consistent with Eisler's rejection of the narrow Western positivist approach to science as the only way of understanding the world. The importance of the role of culture in social work practice in multicultural practice (Lum 1996) is also congruent with social constructionism and Eisler's concept of science.

How does this theory apply to how we approach work with social systems? The partnership (chalice) versus dominator (blade) model of society can be applied across various systems as an approach to assessment and intervention (table 4).

There is documented application of Eisler's work to social work. In *Incorporating Peace and Social Justice into the Social Work Curriculum* (1990), Van Soest applied the dominator and partnership models to compare aggressive and nonviolent approaches in human relationships across systems.

Table 4　Application of Partnership and Dominator Models Across Systems

| System | Chalice | Blade |
|---|---|---|
| Individual | Seeing points of agreement; differences are sources of new ideas | Evaluating differences as negative; antagonism, anger, and fear |
| Family | Accommodating differences | Punishing for differences |
| Group | Collaboration; shifting roles according to skill or need | Hierarchies of decision making |
| Community | Including all groups in developing resources | Fighting for scarce resources |
| Nation | Human welfare programs | Defense; market power |
| World | International collaboration | War |

Cultural transformational theory has also provided a framework for an advanced master of social work seminar. Eisler's *The Chalice and the Blade* was the text, and the theory was used to explore interconnections among global threats such as violence and warfare, environmental degradation, and poverty, and the current endeavors of the social work profession (Mary, 1997). Common themes in student papers were linking politics with personal values and product with process, connecting personal identity with the fate of humankind, and the importance of the environment in social policy. The student products were remarkable in their probing of theory and its application to social work.

One student's paper, "Ethnic Cleansing, Diversity and Education," explored the economic and sociopolitical causes of ethnic cleansing. His proposal embraced multiple levels of social work intervention. At the international level, he recommended the involvement of nongovernmental organizations and the UN in sponsoring international dialogues among indigenous leaders. At the state level, he proposed a multicultural educational curriculum with a global focus. At the personal level, he suggested that increasing awareness of one's own ethnic, religious, and national identity was key to the long-term prevention of global ethnic conflict (Steinberg, 1995).

Another paper, "Political Reform for a Transformational Society," challenged the policy-personal dichotomy, making the case that the survival of democracy necessitates a set of reforms in the political and personal arenas. The student's recommendations included ideas such as town councils directly linked to congressional representatives, citizen ombudsman programs independent of congressional influence, daily public education from kindergarten to high school in hands-on democracy, and Ned Cooney's Volunteer for Democracy program to sponsor candidate forums and political discussion groups that would educate and politicize the citizenry (Mary, 1997).

## SO, WHAT IS SUSTAINABLE POLITICS?

Sustainable politics involves several shifts from the current conceptualization of politics. First, it involves broadening the narrow definition of political activity within the mechanism of government to governance; that is, the involvement of citizens in making decisions in government as well as the host of other organizations in civil society. This definition of political activity may allow us to more easily dream of venues and structures, such as those of the students in the aforementioned class, for greater involvement of and accountability for citizens in the decisions of their communities. Second, as transformational politics articulates, sustainable politics involves a value base of principles that support sustainability, such as the interconnectedness of systems, the link between science and spirit and between politics and morality, a respect for ecology, valuing of diversity, and social justice. Third, sustainable politics offers a model of partnership power across all levels of institutions rather than a dominator model. This model has much potential for the revitalization of democracy at all levels of participation. How can social workers experiment with these ideas of sustainable politics?

## SOCIAL WORK'S ROLE

There are many people from all walks of life—feminists, environmentalists, psychotherapists, social workers, teachers, and cultural creatives—who are already engaged in activities in their daily lives based on a progressive politics of meaning. The beginning stages, of course, involve dialogue about new conceptions of politics, power, and politics of meaning. Possible venues for this dialogue include national, regional, or local summits on ethics and meaning, similar to the economic summits held regularly by local and national governments. We could develop networks of meaning-oriented professional dialogues to rethink the role of one's profession in creating caring communities. We could advocate for a rebirth of the public intellectual; that is, professors who see themselves as responsible to the larger community beyond academia and the academic press. In fact, the current trend of community-university partnerships in service learning and civic participation evidence this trend in thinking. Another strategy might be to contribute to journalism that shifts the media's interest from materialism and cynicism to idealism and spirituality (Lerner, 1997).

Dialogue about a partnership model of power can occur within any system. Eisler's *The Power of Partnership* (2002) and *The Partnership Way* (Eisler & Loye, 1990), companion works to *The Chalice and the Blade* (1995), can provide practical guidelines in the form of discussion and exercises for the application of a partnership model of decision making. These could be used in classes, organizations, and therapeutic or self-help venues.

The transition to transformational thinking about the global interconnections among peace, empowerment, and social justice is, of course, the work of social movements. But that is not a new arena for social workers. Beginning at the beginning, with Jane Addams, social work has been the helping profession to connect peace with social justice. This commitment is reflected in our code of ethics, our policy statements (see "Peace and Social Justice," in NASW, 2000), and educational initiatives such as that of Van Soest (1992).

Over the past ten years, we have more clearly connected peace, social justice, and sustainable development. For example, Crosby and Van Soest's *Challenges of Violence Worldwide* (1997) and Hokenstad and Midgley's *Issues in International Development: Global Challenges for a New Century* (1997) both recognize the connections among warfare, environmental devastation, and ethnic tensions. Both advocate sustainable human development as an antidote. We now see that the use of force to solve international and local problems is obsolete. We also see that democratic forms of government that nurture decentralized authority and development need to be pursued to establish peace, social justice, and stability.

Thus, the task for social workers, as peace and social justice workers, is to broaden this mission and the definition of global security beyond disarmament, to advocate a more holistic approach. Security includes the educational system, the economy, health care, and the environment; freedom from economic want; good housing; good schools; and the rejection of militarism (Novotny, 1999). Yes, we must limit violent conflict, which is a major force of destabilization, human suffering, environmental degradation, refugees, and a colossal waste of human resources. But beyond the need to thwart global warfare is the need for a new way of thinking about power as shared power, within a partnership model of decision making at the individual, family, community, national, and global levels.

How do we get to more caring communities? One step at a time, at every level, all the time. The emphasis in these new schools of thought is on ecological wisdom, social justice, grassroots democracy, personal and social responsibility, nonviolence, decentralization, gender equity and cooperation, and respect for diversity. These are congruent with our values, our national and international codes of ethics, and our practice approaches that embrace feminism, empowerment, strengths, and multiculturalism. We might do well to recommit to caring communities and institutions, then, from this broader framework to ensure a sustainable future.

Now, within this sustainable framework of thinking, what are social welfare and social work?

## ADDITIONAL THINGS TO THINK ABOUT

1. Where do you draw the lines when you think of politics?

2. What are your reactions to transformational politics?

3. In studying human behavior and the social environment, we oftentimes see politics as context, acting on, limiting, or at best disconnected from the opportunities of poor and vulnerable people. Does this reading change this view of politics? If so, how so?

4. Can this new thinking help resolve social work's disdain for politicians and the political process?

5. Public policy in the United States is often made without a commitment to the long-term view, due to, in part, the constant turnover of leaders and their goals. If the values of sustainability make sense, do they help us gain a long-term view? What changes would be necessary to commit to that long-term view?

6. Money is the bane of democratic politics. What can we do to make it possible for ordinary people to run for office and for everyone's interests and needs to be more justly represented?

7. Can you think of other ways to move us toward communities of caring and politics of meaning?

8. What are your thoughts on restorative justice as an alternative to the existing justice system?

9. What would it take to move nonviolence as a mode of problem solving into more mainstream thinking?

10. Can you think of other ways to move us from a hierarchy model of power to a model of shared power in government? In other arenas?

11. What do you think of the partnership model of society? Is this realistic? How do we get there?

# MAIN POINTS

1. Old-world-order thinking upholds the competition of individual nation-states, the military domination of Western industrial states, and the hegemony of global economic institutions, which results in continuing warfare and gaps between the haves and have-nots.

2. Reliance on military aggression for global security is an obsolete concept; a new definition of global security includes, for example, fairer distribution of resources, balancing the interests of local and global citizens, the elimination of poverty, and preserving the ecosystem.

3. Violence as a global phenomenon, community violence, and domestic violence may be connected and may be obsolete means of preserving security.

4. Transformational politics is a paradigm of thinking with a focus on ecology and systems thinking, a linking of the personal and political, and inclusion of the spiritual and the sacred in public life, all as alternatives to the old world order.

5. Lerner's politics of meaning is congruent with transformational politics and focuses on the civic responsibility of all citizens to find common values among religious traditions and to create caring communities.

6. The nonviolent (active resistance) movement and the more recent restorative justice movement are alternative models to problem solving in response to transgressions.

7. Eisler's cultural transformation theory is based on a partnership model of society that also embraces ideas of interconnectedness of the spiritual and the material, nonviolence, and a respect for the environment.

## For Further Reading

Lerner, M. (1997). *The politics of meaning: Restoring hope and possibility in an age of cynicism.* Reading, MA: Addison-Wesley Books.

Schell, J. (1982). *The fate of the earth.* New York: Avon Books.

Turpin, J., & Kurtz, L. (Eds.). (1997). *The web of violence from interpersonal to global.* Chicago: University of Illinois Press.

Woolpert, S., Slaton, C. D., & Schwerin, E. W. (Eds.). (1998). *Transformational politics: Theory, study and practice.* Albany: State University of New York Press.

# CHAPTER 7

# A Model of Social Work for a Sustainable World

The premise of this book is, simply, that if social work is to continue to be a viable, meaningful profession that addresses the problems of our age, it must consider a paradigm that will help secure a sustainable future for us all. In our exploration of literature on the interconnectedness of systems, we have seen that sustainability is not just a concept that applies to the natural environment. Our environment is the base upon which all other institutions are built; thus, our polity, our economy, and our social systems must reflect the principles of sustainability. They must value human life and the lives of all species; they must promote fairness and equality, as well as economic and social justice; they must support decision making that involves participation and partnership rather than domination; and they must protect our Mother Earth.

In chapter 1, I attempted to help us shift our thinking about how social workers view the world, from a narrow lens, and focus on the individual and his or her immediate context to a broader lens that allows us to connect individual failings with institutional shortcomings. This is certainly not a new connection. Recent efforts to expand and connect the macro and micro worlds in the study of human behavior and the social environment evidence the growth in our understanding of the interconnectedness of systems.

Other new knowledge suggests that our long-term viability on this planet may also depend on our understanding of two additional critical connections. If we are to create caring communities, locally and globally, we must do so knowing that we are one world, in science and in spirit. This does not mean one world government or one world religion. Rather, it means that from a multiplicity of cultures, belief systems, values, and traditions we can fashion communities and institutions that will both nurture diversity and meet common human needs. We can do this only through a disconnect from the old world order, wherein final arbitrations are made via violence, militarism, and warfare. This old mode of problem solving is ultimately obsolete and will not sustain us or the planet. We must transform our problem-solving strategies to a partnership approach and model of society focused on preserving and nurturing the planet and all its inhabitants.

Our model of practice, then, should inculcate this view of the world, these values, and a mission, policies, and practice approaches that reflect sustainability.

## THE MODEL

How social workers see the world and its problems leads them to a professional mission and strategies of intervention. The model shown in figure 2 is one way of conceiving of a model of social work practice intended to lead us to a more sustainable future.

**Figure 2    Conceptual Model of Social Work**

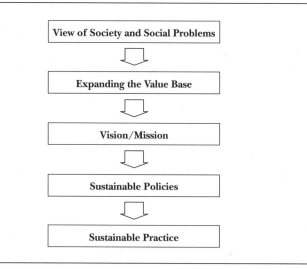

## OUR VIEW OF THE WORLD

Our new understanding of the world comes from viewing the behavior of individual and larger systems through a wide lens. This is how we can see the interplay within and between natural and social systems. Reality is interconnected, holistic, and epistemic, as it is defined by all the groups and interests that make up the social context of any human enterprise, large or small.

Furthermore, the behavior of any system is not totally rational. It acts upon and is influenced by natural forces, politics, economics, cultural values, and individual dreams. It is in a constant state of flux and is not linear in nature. New systems thinking suggests that systems never return to the exact same state as before change or intervention took place. Life on the river is socially constructed. How each person perceives the danger of falling over the waterfall depends on his or her place on the river, in a small vulnerable raft or in a large steamship, or on the safety of the land. Different people experience the journey, the current, differently. Thus arises the relevance of critical theory to this worldview.

## THE VIEW OF SOCIETY AND SOCIAL PROBLEMS

In a new model of sustainable social work, society and social problems are seen from a postmodern perspective. The current view of social welfare and social work holds two perspectives on the nature of society and social institutions, which encompass most if not all of the social theories: order and conflict. The order perspective, sometimes referred to as the functional or systems perspective, views society as orderly and stable, with all institutions working together to maintain order and a consensus on the functions of those institutions. There is agreement on the rules, and all members of society contribute to the support of the institutions (Durkheim, 1972; Parsons, 1951; Weber, 1946). Neoconservative and liberal political perspectives are based on this view. Inequalities and problems necessitate incremental change in otherwise healthy institutions. The order perspective dominates social welfare in the United States (Mullaly, 1997).

In contrast, the conflict perspective views institutions and groups as in constant struggle with opposing interests and views about society and its functions. The power of dominant groups, not consensus, holds together the parts of the system. Inequalities are inherent in the power structure of the capitalist system, and radical change is needed. Competition is natural in such a system. Social democracy and Marxism both hold this perspective of society. These two political ideologies advocate wide participation by workers and citizens, which tends to flatten, if not eliminate the hierarchy, and emphasize shared power.

Social problems from an order perspective are seen as problems of individuals who are unable or unwilling to follow the rules. Through some individual deficit, trait, or inadequacy, those people do not conform to the expectations of society. A more liberal explanation of these deficits asserts that individuals sometimes have difficulty navigating complex modern societies and may need assistance. Changes in their immediate environment or advocacy for greater access to services can help alleviate the casualties of capitalism. Much of social work's early casework was based on an individual explanation of social problems. At present, most social workers trained in the systems perspective do not subscribe wholly to this view and acknowledge a liberal perspective of social disorganization (Mullaly, 1997). Thus, we may need to improve the institutions to deal with problems that individuals in a capitalist economy and dominator society face.

Social problems from the conflict perspective are structural in nature. They do not stem from a personal deficit but are inherent in a system of oppression, where those who have the capital, wealth, and power dominate those who do not. Therefore, basic institutions must change to protect and enhance human welfare.

A third perspective is the postmodern structural social work. At first glance, structural social work appears to be part of the conflict perspective of society and social problems (Mullaly, 1997). This approach, critical of the social structures of the society, has as its major thrust tackling the social injustice and marginalization of many groups in our society, through change from within and without institutions. Its ideology and values are socialist, embracing a radical social work heritage. What distinguishes it as a new paradigm is its postmodern view of society, which is congruent with the thinking we have been exploring.

Structural social work's approach stems from critical theory and challenges false dichotomies, asserting that there is more than one way to conceptualize society and social problems. For example, it suggests that oppression is multifaceted; that is, not just racism or classism. Though the women's movement, the gay rights movement, and indigenous movements may have some commonalities, the groups that constitute these movements feel and experience oppression differently by different groups at different points in time (Mullaly, 1997). Thus dialogue about each group's construction of oppression, a process highly valued by feminist, multicultural, and other critical theory approaches, is an important part of structural social work practice that allows for various worldviews of the social world. Structural social work is congruent with sustainable thinking in its transformative goal and its location of social problems as structural. But some expansion is needed.

The lens on society and social problems again must be widened to see the interconnectedness of all the elements of the social web of life in all the institutions of society, for they all contribute to both the health and the dysfunction of the systems. The thrust of structural social work to change the capitalist economy with the goal of greater social justice will not, alone, ensure a sustainable future. The shortcomings of capitalism must be understood and approached in connection with failings of other institutions such as the excesses of industrialization and consumerism, the lack of involvement of citizens in dialogue and decision making around needed changes, the need for environmental imperatives of resource conservation in global development, the need to achieve human rights, and population stabilization. Social problems are interconnected global problems of survival and must be conceptualized within this broad context.

A sustainable view of society challenges the dichotomy that society is either order based or conflict based. New systems thinking purports that institutions at all levels are in a constant state of flux, not order, and renew themselves through interactions that are consensual and conflictual. Lasting change will not be imposed from the outside or top down but will occur as a process of interaction of the elements at every level. Major movements such as the U.S. civil rights movement, the antiapartheid movement in South Africa, the revolution in Poland, and the demise of communism in Eastern Europe illustrate this social change that involves efforts at multiple levels. Many of these movements used local and global action, nonviolent strategies, dialogue and collaboration, and conflict tactics.

Because the new paradigm of systems thinking is holistic, social problems are the consequence of unsustainable elements in all institutions: the economy of unlimited growth and a global market system of profit over people, political systems that are closed to the direct involvement of citizens, and a societal view of family as consumers and receivers of service rather than active participants in the creation of and solution to social problems. This means that individuals and institutions contribute to social problems and are involved, interactively, in developing the solutions.

Finally, a sustainable view of society and social problems also requires taking a look at the interconnectedness of the material and spiritual aspects of social life and social institutions. In each of the previously mentioned social movements, the contributions of religious figures and moral leaders in opening up dialogue about the meaning of the human struggles was and is as important as any decision by a formal political leader. Consider the words of Václav Havel, a truly inspiring spiritual political leader, who believed in the power of the populace and led the Czech Republic's velvet revolution:

> The only real hope of people today is probably a renewal of our certainty that we are rooted in the Earth and at the same time, the cosmos. This awareness endows us with the capacity for self-transcendence. Politicians at international forums may reiterate a thousand times that the basis of the new world order must be universal respect for human rights, but it will mean nothing as long as this imperative does not derive from the respect of the miracle of Being, the miracle of the universe, the miracle of nature, the miracle of our own existence. . . . The truly reliable path to coexistence must be rooted in self-transcendence. (1994, p. 613)

In summary, society and its problems are conceptualized holistically in a sustainable paradigm of social welfare and social work. Society is the result of interacting and self-renewing systems. The cause of and solutions for social problems are not found in individuals alone, nor in the structure of society alone; they involve both. We must assess what needs to be changed by examining the interconnected unsustainable, degrading, and dehumanizing processes as well as the devastating results on the environment and its species. In short, how we deal with problems cannot be separated from the results we attain.

But how do we know where we want to go? What values ground us as we think about what needs to be done?

## EXPANDING THE VALUE BASE

The history and culture of the United States have shaped the values of the profession of social work, as practiced in the United States. Most of us would argue that, despite the recognition of multicultural worldviews of a vast heterogeneous population of immigrants, the American ethos has embraced, over centuries, core values of the Protestant work ethic, egalitarianism, individualism, patriarchy, Judeo-Christian values, democracy, and capitalism. These have influenced our beliefs that if people work hard in the application of their individual talents, opportunities are endless. They have also influenced our darker side. For when people differ from the American ideal of the Caucasian male, they receive differential treatment in the form of individual and institutional discrimination and oppression (Day, 2000). Thus, Native Americans, women, ethnic minorities, people with disabilities, and other deviantly perceived groups have suffered social injustice in this country.

In the history of social welfare in the United States, social workers have played important roles in fighting this oppression, sometimes aligning themselves with the oppressed. For example, some were members of labor's rank-and-file movement in the 1930s and later advocated and organized for civil rights in the 1960s. However, the current thrust of social work is not on the structural problems of social injustice but on a narrow focus of work with individuals and families and their treatment. We mediate by helping them navigate the interface between themselves and social institutions (e.g., the workplace, the welfare office their child's school). Our current code of ethics supports this focus.

Although the 1999 version of the code expands our responsibilities to include the broader society, only four of the fifty-one standards pertain to social change at a broader level. The core values are service, social justice, dignity and worth of the person, importance of human relationships, integrity, and competence. It is in the translation of these values to the standards where the focus becomes narrowed to clients, colleagues, practice settings, and the profession (Congress, 1999; NASW, 1999). My experience with students over the past twenty years has been that, when asked how what they do relates to social justice, students have had a hard time conceptualizing this value, given the narrow focus of their work. Thus, the response is usually something like, "By offering them assistance and service it contributes to social justice." This may be because one of the aims of the code of ethics is to serve as a guideline for adjudicating those who demonstrate unethical conduct in the workplace and in private practice. But it appears that this purpose has become a driving force behind the narrow focus of the code on the relationship between client as individual and worker.

It is interesting to contrast the NASW's code of ethics with the statement of ethics and principles of the International Federation of Social Workers (2005). The range of models of social work is much greater in the member countries that belong to this federation. The mission and the standards embrace a much broader view of social work in the three categories of human rights and human dignity, social justice, and professional conduct. One could argue that the greater emphasis on human rights is due to the human rights violations in countries where torture or ill treatment of women is more prevalent than in the United States. However, all the statements on human rights and social justice certainly apply to this country. This country affords its citizens many individual rights and freedoms that other countries do not. However, the degree of inequality in income and wealth and social indicators demonstrating differential treatment of minorities and women in areas such as poverty, employment, education, and rate of incarceration do not indicate a country that is living up to its potential for social justice and human rights, given our status as the wealthiest country on earth.

Thus, though the stated values of social work in the United States may be humanitarianism, equality, social justice, the facilitation of self-determination through participation in government, and more equitable distribution of resources, the focus of social work has been to minimize oppressive elements of the system in which it finds itself rather than to change the system (Mullaly, 1997). The values are progressive, but the difficulty comes in trying to realize these ends within the existing institutional order of society.

The existing values articulated in the code of ethics are not bad ones, but they do not reach beyond to a vision of change that is needed to sustain the welfare of species around the globe. Table 5

**Table 5    Expansion of Social Work Values**

| Theme | Values |
|-------|--------|
| **New systems thinking** | View of world and new knowledge as *epistemic;* diversity of "constructions" no "one" reality. *Interdisciplinary* (cross-interest-group) and *interconnected* (nonlinear) assessment of problems and solutions. Maximum *participation* of citizens in the web of decision making. Belief in systems' penchant and abilities to *self-renew* vs. imposing solution from position of power. *Process* and *product* are equally valued. There is no way to peace; peace *is* the way. |
| **Spirituality and science** | Interconnectedness (same as above). *Science* is always *value* based. *Problem identification, solutions* made from spiritual/religious perspectives alongside other disciplines or worldviews. |
| **Sustainability of environment** | New sense of *identity* with the earth. Cohabitants with other species. Responsible as *steward* or caretaker of the earth. Institutions (e.g., economy, polity, family) must develop in harmony with the earth, respecting its limits. |
| **Sustainability of economy** | Shift from capitalist economy to more *sustainable collective model* with planetary and human welfare as goal (vs. profit). *Social justice:* greater equality in meeting human needs. Social capital valued. *Sustainable development* principles (respect for environment, participation, quality of life, social justice). *Technology* driven by *sustainable values and principles* . |
| **Sustainable politics** | *Nonviolence* toward people and environment, including structural violence of poverty and oppression (see social justice above). Development of citizen role of *governance.* *Value-*based politics of meaning. Principles of *transformational politics* (e.g., partnership, diversity). |
| **Partnership vs. dominator model** | Trust, sharing, open communication, win-win model of power, respect for nature, science of empathy. |

delineates values for us to consider for our code of ethics that are connected to each theme of sustainable thinking (value and quality of all life, fairness and equality, participation and partnership, respect for the ecological constraints of the environment, the interconnections among nature and social systems, the need for a holistic approach to connecting spirituality or religion and the material world, and a partnership model of society).

The values of this new paradigm do not counter existing social work values of equality, humanitarianism, and social justice. They are congruent with them. However, these values expand our value base in recognition of the limits to growth and move us beyond the unsustainable costs of a market-driven economy and technology, beyond a model of interest-group politics that stifles public participation, and beyond a dominator model of society that, through its separation of spirituality and science, relies on the power of dominance and violence as ultimate problem solvers. In short, these values provide us with an expanded view of our professional relationship with society. Now, with an expanded value base, how do our institutions need to change? And what is our expanded vision for global social welfare?

## DOES OUR CURRENT WELFARE SYSTEM REFLECT OUR VISION OF SOCIAL WELFARE?

Currently, many people view the United States as a welfare state, albeit it a reluctant one, in contrast to many European countries. We have no universal health care, increasing privatization of retirement and other social service programs, and decreasing commitment of the federal government to social welfare, as evidenced by the 1996 welfare reform legislation, the telltale Personal Responsibility Act. The good news is that we have managed to salvage Social Security. The bad news is that in almost every other category of social welfare programs, we have, as a country, suffered a loss of both federal and state funds in health care, housing, services to children and families, and mental health programs.

Our social welfare system today illustrates a residual approach, reflective of the American values of individualism and hard work. The assumption is that the market, or democracy, the church and other mutual aid organizations, and the family should be able to meet the needs of U.S. families in the twenty-first century. But as we have seen in this book, they cannot.

The capitalist economy provides ownership and control of the means of production, distribution, and exchange to a minority of people. These resources are used to generate profit at the expense of the conservation of natural resources and the ill effects of production on laborers, consumers, and communities. Most people cannot own or control income-generating means of production, nor do they have a constitutional right to employment or adequate income. Capitalism's allowance of unemployment, income and opportunity gaps, alienating dominator hierarchical work environments, and the paucity of livable wages contributes to social welfare for the privileged few, lack of social welfare for the many, and social problems for all.

Political power, closely aligned with economic power in the United States, is curtailed for most; electoral politics, tied to the ability to access corporate wealth, make running for office almost impossible for those without money. Civic participation in community organizations is voluntary, nonmonetary, and not recognized as a critical part of the economy; people who can afford the time and money can donate their participation to civic life.

While it is a source of support for many families, the institution of religion, with faith-based organizations and groups that support spirituality, is fraught with controversy and marginalization in the broader society. With fundamentalists at one end and secularists at the other, many of those in between are fearful of the imposition of any belief system, and therefore prefer to limit talk of spirit, religion, values, and morality to the home. At the same time, people hunger for a sense of public and political morality in the affairs of the community, and on the global stage, conflict is pervasive. Fierce antagonisms such as those in the Middle East are driven, in part, by religious beliefs.

So, as a result, how is the institution of family faring these days, as a critical economic and social system for child rearing and emotional support?

A significant number of families feel the effects of institutional failings. Though the definition of *family* does not necessarily include children, most of us would agree that the functions of the modern family are to provide kinship and care, to socialize children to become productive citizens of our society, and to raise the future workers of tomorrow. Two social innovations linked to modernism have deeply affected the modern family: the rise in the material standard of living and the access to family planning services and technology. The good news is that, in the industrial world, affluence and birth control have made family size more a matter of choice than a biological or economic necessity (Garbarino, 1992). The bad news is that the third industrial revolution has brought with it stresses related to production and consumption that pose threats to the sustainability of the American family. At the global level, the economics of consumption and the oppression of women have influenced overpopulation of the planet, which, if unchanged, may threaten the carrying capacity of the planet.

What are some of the threats to the sustainability of the modern family? First, as we have already mentioned, is the threat to meaningful caring relationships as a result of the changes in time and space resulting from information technology. The time spent in front of a video-display terminal, whether a television or a computer monitor, is time away from face-to-face interaction with family members. In addition, though *community* may be an evolving term, it is questionable whether the virtual community is a substitute for the social sustenance that families and extended networks provide through face-to-face interactions.

Second, a question to ask ourselves here in the United States is, do we really experience a higher standard of living in terms of our quality of life, as a result of our GDP? Although our productivity is still leading the rest of the world, there are indicators that the family is not realizing the full benefit of this economic indicator. Job insecurity creates stress and poverty. Poverty is connected to child neglect and abuse, domestic violence, homelessness, and a host of other problems. When the economic system operates on market strategies for production and distribution, the result is overproduction of unnecessary goods with built-in obsolescence, which people with surplus (or perceived surplus) purchasing power are induced to buy through mindless advertising. It also creates underproduction and distribution of goods that people need (e.g., adequate affordable housing).

Of all the higher-income nations, families in the United States experience the greatest gap in terms of unequal distribution of incomes. Of the national income, 30% is in the hands of the top 10% of the population; 1.8% goes to the poorest 10% of the population (Worldwatch Institute, 2003). Among the sixteen countries for which data is available, the United States has the largest percentage of the population living in poverty; one of every six Americans lives below the poverty line. Americans work longer hours than citizens in any other industrial country. Most American workers receive two weeks of vacation; the average European receives six weeks of paid vacation. France recently adopted a thirty-five-hour workweek and, since its inception, has created more than 285,000 jobs as a result of this policy (Honore, 2002, qtd. in Rifkin 2004a).

Our consumption patterns are a problem for the world and for individual families. For example, globally, the two groups most vulnerable are at opposite ends of the consumption spectrum; they are dying of poverty and of affluence. Physical health is compromised most in Europeans and Americans by cardiovascular disease and cancers that primarily affect those who consume too many unhealthy foods, tobacco, alcohol, and drugs and who lead sedentary lifestyles (World Health Organization, 2000). Massive debt and spending toward the paying down of this debt threatens investment in the future of our children.

Shopping for experiences and commodities has become the great national pastime in the United States; it fills up our leisure time, and we don't even get physical exercise in the process, for now we can do it from home. Consumption patterns in the United States, while they reflect a high standard of living, as it is traditionally defined, are becoming obsolete in a world with limits to growth. As long as the richest 20% of the world continues to account for 86% of total personal consumption expenditures, worldwide tensions increase and natural resources are overexploited (UNEP, 2002).

While more and more countries scramble to enter the on-ramp to the information technology highway, here in the United States our families are barreling down the highway in their Hummers equipped with televisions, sound systems, global positioning systems, and cell phones. All of these distract them, of course, from the highway and from any possible human discourse—discourse that involves questions like, where are we going and why? What a metaphor! How does this conspicuous, often dangerous, and wasteful consumption enhance the quality of life for our families? How does it contribute to sustaining and improving the lives of community members in the global village?

Such modernization has had no simple effect on the overpopulation of the globe. In most respects, it seems to have resulted in a population boom followed by a lowering of the birthrate. In developing countries, most childlessness is involuntary, due to disease, while in industrial countries most childlessness is voluntary. It appears that in developing countries, affluence increases the birthrate, while in developed countries it decreases it (Garbarino,

1992). Overpopulation is the result of multiple factors; globally, it is related to poverty and the status of women and their access to family planning. Evidence indicates that the birthrate would decrease 25% to 50% worldwide if women who wish to limit their offspring were fully empowered to do so (Garbarino, 1992).

So, what can we do, as social workers, to help build systems that contribute to social welfare, not social problems? What is our vision?

## SOCIAL WELFARE: A NEW VISION

Today we are faced with a challenge that calls for a shift in our thinking, so that humanity stops threatening its life-support system. We are called to assist the Earth to heal her wounds and in the process heal our own—indeed to embrace the whole creation in all its diversity, beauty and wonder. This will happen if we see the need to revive our sense of belonging to a larger family of life, with which we have shared our evolutionary process.

In the course of history, there comes a time when humanity is called to shift to a new level of consciousness, to reach a higher moral ground. . . . That time is now.

—Wangari Maathai, *first African woman to win a Nobel Prize, 2004*

The vision we have can move us from an old world order, an empire society based on principles of domination, material excess, violence and warfare, profit over people, and global social injustice, to one of an earth community (Korten, 2006), based on partnership and participation, material sufficiency within our limits to growth, nonviolent processes of decision making and shared power, and an imperative for the global welfare of all species.

The vision and mission is to develop sustainable global, national, and local communities and social service organizations that support and enhance life through the following institutions:

- Communities and social structures that permit all species to flourish in an earth-centered system to replace the current anthropocentric ethic

- An ecological social democratic economy that provides meaningful work and fair distribution of resources (e.g., food, housing, health care) to ensure social justice

- Political and civic institutions that involve shared power, with avenues for citizen participation and leadership
- The incorporation of values, spiritual inquiry, and religion in education and other public arenas
- Greater inclusion of families in decision making in economic, political, and spiritual life of the community, through the connection of their private life with the future of the global commons
- Social welfare services that are developed in partnership with political, economic, spiritual, and family institutions, to ensure a broad array of social provisions from basic needs (e.g., housing, health care) to personal social services.
- Social service organizations that strive for social justice, create opportunities for empowerment of clients and staff, and achieve self-renewal through new innovative processes and structures to achieve these goals

Social policies are some necessary steps to realize this vision. Social policy is used broadly here; it goes beyond those policies we associate with the traditional arenas of social welfare (e.g., education). These could be guidelines, laws, and both formal and informal policies that affect individuals and groups in every arena of life. In previous chapters we saw some suggestions for sustainable policies and social work roles. Summarized here are some major recommendations in six arenas that might lead us to a more sustainable future. Recommendations regarding the environment are folded into the other systems, as the environment as the base of all life must be considered in every systemic change.

## KEY TRANSFORMATIONAL SHIFTS IN POLICY

### The Economy

1. The adaptation of a sustainability-first agenda for economic development, within ecological constraints, as recommended by the UNEP.
2. The adaptation of full employment and the elevation of the development of social capital to be included in remuneration as work to ensure economic justice.

3. The adoption of alternative measures of economic success or social indices (e.g., health, employment, education of citizenry) of progress to which governments are accountable.

4. Partnering of governments and community-based and/or nongovernmental organizations in collaborative economic development strategies to implement economic, political, and social goals.

5. Support of small-scale economic development enterprises that favor participant owners versus monopoly-scale absentee owners, through community development corporations, cooperatives, land trusts, and other such mechanisms.

6. The global adoption of the 1995 proposals of the UN Summit on Social Development in Copenhagen, including curbing of the global casino of insider trading, fraud, and capital flight; a new Bretton Woods conference to reform the IMF and other international monetary institutions; and a UN-controlled world financial authority to oversee global financial institutions and hold them accountable (Henderson, 1999).

7. Proposals and steps to shift ownership and control of the few to the many, from a capitalist system to a social democratic system.

## The Polity

1. The expansion of national priorities on human rights to include those in the Universal Declaration of Human Rights (e.g., a clean, healthy environment; universal access to food, housing, health care, and education; secure, nonviolent communities; meaningful work (full employment) and leisure opportunities).

2. The reformation of the electoral system to include such policies as public financing of elections; nonpartisan elections administration; open debate with equal airtime through public financing; an independent media; one person, one vote; and noninvolvement of corporate money (Korten, 2006).

3. Reformation of the powers of the UN toward legal authority over issues that affect the global commons (e.g., environmental threats, international trade, intra- or international conflicts).

4. Reformation of the UN's structure to equalize the power of large industrial countries and developing ones, and venues for both national and public participation in UN decision making.

## Religion and Spirituality

1. National and regional summits on ethics and meaning, with opportunities for citizens to participate via the Internet and learn from one another about religious beliefs, moral positions, and their implications for public policy, public behavior, and environmental sustainability.

2. Expansion of national and international service as a substitute for the armed forces via Peace Corps, AmeriCorps, or other avenues. Make benefits available similar to veterans' benefits for those who have served other communities in peace.

3. Infusion of spirituality and religion as a natural part of any public decision-making body whose decisions affect the quality of the life of the community and the protection of the natural environment (e.g., via debate, public forums, community panels of religious representatives, university involvement, inclusion of survey data).

## The Family

1. Harness the technological advances of the computer to reduce the workweek, and redistribute work so every family can spend some work time at home.

2. Build family support networks in every community to provide volunteer frameworks of assistance for families.

3. Reconnect the family and children to the natural environment through educational curricula, public and private service-learning initiatives, and family incentives (e.g., tax and educational credits for efforts in conservation, protection of natural resources).

4. Create councils of elders in each community and motivate social institutions to use the collective wisdom of these individuals.

5. Fight for flexible work hours and one year of paid family leave for parents-to-be with children in their first year of life.

6. Develop free and accessible family life education for all families, including conflict resolution and mediation services for estranged spouses.

7. Develop a partnership among public health, business, community members, and families, with compensation via a social wage so that the "village" can take care of children.

## Social Welfare

1. Develop preventive programs for children and families, collaboratively, via public health, education, employment development, and public social services, to reduce significantly the residual functions of child protective services.

2. Put in place collaborative planning rather than market-based strategies by public and private institutions in housing, environmental protection, food, health education, and employment sectors, so that services can be equitably developed and distributed over time; citizen input is a mandated part of this planning.

3. Develop personal social services for chronically vulnerable populations (e.g., disabled people, elderly, severely mentally ill people); these could be regional centers with case management delivered by bachelors of social work and development of new models and programs by masters of social work.

4. Propose a global definition of social welfare that sets social standards of basic human needs, such as those in the Universal Declaration of Human Rights, linked both with economic systems aimed at the protection and provision of these rights and with environmental preservation.

## The Organization

1. Work collaboratively with other organizations to serve the individual, family, and community in a holistic model; advocate for funding streams and structures that support this approach through service integration.

2. Strive to be learning organizations that embrace continual self-renewal and the empowerment of clients and staff.

3. Commit to maximum client participation in every possible aspect of the organization's governance, service delivery, and evaluation.

4. Operationalize the principles of cultural transformation theory in the management and leadership of the organization (e.g., shared power, value-based science).

5. Develop indicators of organizational success that reflect the social mission (e.g., social justice, enhancing quality of life in the community, capacity building of communities and families); involve consumers and key constituents in this development.

6. Embrace environmental sustainability in the decisions made regarding facility, technology, processes and procedures of service delivery, alliances, or contracts with other organizations.

The thrust of the previous proposals is the embedding of social welfare as the goal of all society's institutions to sustain and enhance all life, to develop needed resources and equitable opportunities, and to make human needs the centerpiece of both public and private policy agendas. Thus, the new definition of social welfare becomes the state of collective well-being toward a sustainable future for all species of a community, nation, or planet, brought about through collaborative efforts of the polity, economy, family, spiritual or mutual aid organizations, and social service organizations, in harmony with the natural environment. Where does this place the practice of social work?

## SOCIAL WORK: THE CURRENT PRACTICE PARADIGM

Let's look at what we call social work and then explore its relevance to sustainable social welfare. First of all, the mission of social work in the United States is twofold: to help meet the basic needs of all people and to promote social justice and social change (NASW, 1999). How do we do this? Do we have a paradigm or worldview of our practice? Malcolm Payne (2005) suggests that modern social work is a discourse between three perspectives.

Reflexive, or therapeutic, views are seen as therapeutic helping approaches (Dominelli, 2002). In this approach, social work promotes growth—self-enhancement of the individual, family, group, or community—through humanistic mutual influence between client and work. Through this interaction, clients gain an understanding of their world and are empowered to overcome or to rise above their suffering and situation. This approach expresses a social-democratic political perspective in its emphasis on self-determination and human potential for fulfillment and development. Some theories and models relevant to this approach are psychodynamism, humanism, existentialism, and crisis intervention. An example is a social worker helping an older single mother deal with the recent abandonment of the father and breadwinner to recognize her strengths and build on them through further mustering of her psychological and social supports.

Individualist-reformist views focus on meeting individual needs and improving services. These are seen as maintenance approaches (Dominelli, 2002), in that by helping individuals interface with society, they maintain the social order of society and social fabric of institutions. Politically, they stem from a liberal approach to society; basic social institutions function well but may need occasional tweaking or incremental change to better serve citizens. Theories and models relevant to this approach are systems, cognitive behavior, and task-centered practice. For example, a social worker helps interface between a senior center and an older isolated adult who is developmentally disabled to develop a fit between the older person's needs and what the center can provide.

The third view, socialist-collectivist approaches, sometimes called emancipatory (Dominelli, 2002) or transformational (Pease & Fook, 1999), assert, from a critical theory lens, that disadvantaged or oppressed people can gain empowerment only through social transformation. This view expresses socialist political philosophy and focuses on change in those institutions that impede social justice. Theories and models relevant to this approach are critical theory, feminist theory, and the empowerment model of practice. For example, a social worker helps educate and mobilize citizen groups in support of an upcoming state proposal to provide universal health care for all citizens through a public, private, and citizen partnership (Payne, 2005).

Payne argues that social work in the West uses all three of these, and social work in any one setting may use a mixture, depending on organizational and cultural expectations and societal expectations. However, the vast majority of our work uses the first two approaches, neither of which is very relevant to a new transformational vision of social welfare as global collective well-being. A broader approach that builds on Payne's (2005) socialist-collectivist approach is called for.

## THE NEW PARADIGM: WHAT MIGHT OUR PRACTICE LOOK LIKE?

There are many new ways we might become involved in changing the landscape of our fellow travelers. I will explore five that I believe are key in a new paradigm of sustainable practice: (1) prevention and long-term planning, (2) interdisciplinary social work, (3) sustainable social and economic development, (4) citizen and community empowerment, and (5) partnership education. After an exploration of these approaches, we will then look at their implications for social work education and research (Figure 3).

**Figure 3   A Model for Social Work in a Sustainable World**

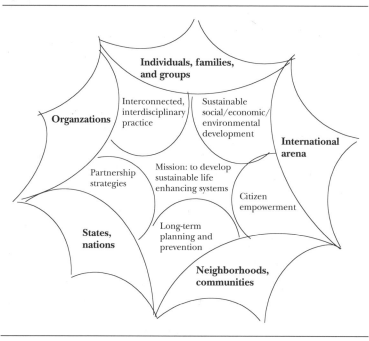

Because we are concerned with the conservation of resources and long-term sustainability, attention to basic causes versus presenting problems or prevention must be the order of the day (Boyer, 1984). The problems we are living with that threaten our future did not happen overnight; nor will their solutions occur overnight. We know that a quick fix is ineffective and has negative long-term consequences; we must consider the whole system and the whole problem, with a focus on preventing social problems. This means helping bring about a mandate for planning at every level. One role of the social worker is to advocate for these mandates. We can also gather together those with expertise on different aspects of the problem, bring them to the table, and begin to hammer out some shorter-term changes in the provision of preventive health care, jobs, and housing.

We must make these changes across disciplines. This is not new to us. Interagency collaboration, wraparound services, and service integration seem to be the buzzwords of social service delivery in the new millennium. They are attempts to work more collaboratively and to increase stakeholder participation, which may also lead to more effective and efficient services. They have also been a rational response to shrinking federal and state commitment to funding social services. We may see these, historically, as ways of coping with neoconservative, post–September 11 times, similar to the climate of the 1950s (Fischer, 2002). But this can be viewed as part of a shift from unsuccessful isolated, fragmented, and unilateral efforts of the past based on a singular worldview of the problem to a more multifaceted view and multiconstituent problem solving. Indeed, Gray (1989) suggests that the impetus for collaboration today is that many of the problems communities face are metaproblems that one entity or approach cannot solve.

As the literature on collaboration grows, examples of government and community partnerships evidence this collaboration. For example, many of the initiatives shared in Schorr's *Common Purpose* (1997), such as Baltimore's Sandtown-Winchester partnership or the South Bronx community development corporations, exemplify the interdisciplinary collaborative approach to community problem solving. Others, such as the aforementioned Neighborhood Action Initiative, evidence the power of citizen involvement in cross-agency teams in neighborhood planning (Potapchuk, 2002).

Across all levels of practice, the acceptance of approximate descriptions of reality impels us to a position beyond a multidisciplinary one, wherein we note stakeholder or professional worldviews. It requires us to move toward interdisciplinary practice, wherein we acknowledge each stakeholder worldview as having value in the process of coming to a workable intervention. This is fairly easy to see in environments, for example, like hospitals, wherein multiple professionals have expertise in the aspects of patient care. Where we are more likely to become myopic is in arenas where we are the dominant profession (e.g., child welfare), where the problem domain, combined with strict legal mandates, often pushes our specialized knowledge and values into one corner of a ring, with law enforcement, public opinion, or any number of adversaries in the other corner. These are some of the realities of day-to-day practice. The problem is, of course, that when professionals are busy fighting, there is only one winner and sometimes the client is lost in the melee.

Thus, an interdisciplinary approach is part of a sustainable agenda. It says that no one discipline or political party or authority has all the best answers. Rather, it values the different constructions of law enforcement officers, physicians, social workers, business people, churches, gang members, city planners, environmentalists, and concerned citizens in tackling the problems of, for example, gang violence in a community. Each of these groups has a stake, knowledge, and experience to bring to the table to attempt solutions. By inviting environmentalists to the table, for example, we may find other possible connections between youth and landscape beautification (e.g., community gardens, murals, art projects that use local talent). The danger in going it alone is that we may find ourselves opening the doors of our newly funded midnight basketball program only to find the court empty. For perhaps what youths in this particular community needed was not recreation but the preventive response—jobs—to compete with the drug economy on the street. But guess what! Youths weren't at the table when we defined our strengths and problems.

If the goal is to do more than catch people at the bottom of the waterfall, we need to move up to the top and, alongside our planning, begin to engage in some sustainable social and economic development. We can develop projects that preserve resources, consider the limits to growth, and operate on a scale at which people can be involved in their ownership and control.

For example, the Institute for Local Self Reliance in New York City developed a local planning and community capacity-building process to organize the Bronx Frontier Development Market. "After one year of operation it was producing 70 tons of finished compost a week. The compost was used to restore the soil for community gardens in the South Bronx" (Richardson, 1982). The Meadowcreek Project, working with Hendrix College in Conway, Arkansas, redirected its purchases toward local produce. "Within one year Hendrix increased its purchases of food within the state from 9% to 40%" (Daly & Cobb, 1989). Social workers could play a role in getting the right people to the table to develop some of these projects, ensuring community involvement in decision making.

There are two avenues to consider in this development. The first is to get ourselves involved in existing economic development arenas in our cities and counties. This means interjecting ourselves into discussions of, for example, how old military land will be used, whether wetlands should be converted, storage of toxic waste, or the development of a bike path. The second avenue is to create new alternative community-based projects to support people and their environments. Economic or social (caretaking) cooperatives, land trusts, community development corporations, community gardens, and farmers' markets are just a few of the many initiatives that social workers could involve themselves in. Examples of the development of social capital could involve building councils of elders (Garbarino, 1992) in communities to use the collective wisdom of older residents and to engage them in cross-generational activities or expanding family centers from social support to the creation of micro enterprises (e.g., home-based sewing).

Hand in hand with community development is citizen and community empowerment. If what is desired is a win-win solution within a shared-power paradigm, individuals must be equal partners with professionals in problem solving. The person-centered planning model in developmental disabilities (O'Brien & O'Brien, 1998), the recovery model in mental health (Jackson, 2001), and the family-to-family (Annie E. Casey Foundation, 2007) or wraparound initiatives in child welfare are examples of shared intervention strategies in social services.

A much larger shift needs to occur in the relationship of families to power in their communities. The job of the social worker should involve helping families gain access to the decision-making processes that occur in all the institutions that affect them. For example, we could develop consumer-advisory groups, citizen and youth commissions, school or neighborhood policy councils, or involve technology in the facilitation of citizen input into city council and planning meetings, countywide forums, or national elections. We could develop a local interfaith council, with the purpose of greater involvement of a community in its own development initiatives, or engage an existing one in sponsoring a communitywide forum on citizen involvement.

Every advisory group to government or the private sector, such as commissions, shareholder groups, and private boards of directors, should involve citizens in a meaningful way. This can range from formal membership to public forums, interorganizational planning groups, and other creative decision-making webs. The more citizens connect what they perceive as private problems to social problems, many of them global in nature, the more they will see the interconnectedness between their own behaviors and consumer patterns and those of the larger global commons.

In this same vein, if the desired model of society is of partnership rather than domination, we must begin to educate ourselves and others about this approach and start to consciously use it. This should not be difficult, as the ideas are already congruent with social work values. For example, one of my former students had an "aha" moment using Eisler's model. He realized that in his play therapy with the younger children at a clinic every game they played involved winners and losers. After one of our classes, he tried playing an ungame, cooperative play with a large nylon tent that all the kids could lift up and take turns crawling under and running through. He commented during the next class session that there were no losers, and he was able to recognize and reward each child's effort rather than spend time doing damage control to cajole the team members of the losing team.

Approaching every situation from a partnership mind-set, be it a family, a neighborhood, the city council, or the UN, means that as social workers we acknowledge a value base of life enhancement versus destruction and violence, a respect for conserving nature, open communication acknowledging different worldviews of a problem, and a holistic approach to assessment and problem solving. Thus, conflict resolution within a client system, an agency situation, or on the world stage involves nonviolent win-win strategies. It is not a social service or mental health agenda that is pushed; it is a child and family agenda that is promoted. Rather than advocate for a pro-Israel or pro-Palestinian position, we take a position for peace.

In a sustainable model of practice, the approach must change institutions, not just individuals. We spend less time diagnosing problems of homelessness and more time working on universal housing. We spend less time delivering treatment programs for adolescent offenders. We turn our attention to advocacy to attain equitable funding for schools, to develop high school curricula that support conflict resolution, and to community service and job exploration for all students. We can choose to continue school-based counseling with disenfranchised students who have been tracked in the dead-end vocational path and see no real option but the armed services, or we can assist in the creation of meaningful

work in an array of employment opportunities, work that can provide monetary or social wages for products or services that contribute to enhancing the lives of the community and the country.
If our vision is to move toward sustainable systems, these alternative approaches move us to the top of the waterfall to begin to
change the landscape and the futures of our families.

## IMPLICATIONS FOR SOCIAL WORK EDUCATION

Evolving toward partnership and a sustainable world has implications for both classroom curricula and field practice of social work
programs. In social work curricula, we should first look to broaden
of our view of person-in-environment to include a more holistic
view of human behavior and the inclusion of the natural world.
Second, we should place greater emphasis on a global perspective
of social welfare. Third, we should use more knowledge and skill
development in conflict resolution and conflict management.
Fourth, we should consider additional coursework in interdisciplinary and interagency collaboration.

I am hopeful that a case has been made that new systems theories such as the web of life; the connections among mind, body,
and spirit; the imperative of sustainability; and the evolution of
models of shared power are important to our understanding of
ourselves in the world. This next comment is for faculty, in response to the perennial whine, "But we already have so many theories of human behavior to cover, how can we possibly cover all of
this stuff, too? And in other countries! You want us to look at new-
systems theory, sustainability, and economics!" Well, isn't that sort
of like saying, "We have one class that covers social welfare history
and policy, and we've always taught it that way. The more history
we get, the more impossible it is to cover it, so we'll just start with
the New Deal"?

My response is that we must reexamine our frameworks. We
have the information highway as a tool for students to explore
these connections and theories. We have the expectation that, indeed, students are motivated and empowered to determine what
they can learn. The role of faculty is to make available to them
what is relevant and to help them help others make a difference
in their lives and in the future social welfare of their communities
and the planet. It behooves us to fashion curricula to do this.

Clearly, social workers are committed to nonviolence across systems. Although an attempt to use nonadversary approaches is desirable, whenever possible, it would be dishonest and irresponsible to teach collaboration as the only viable community practice strategy. Having said that, I suggest that if we are committed to putting our heads together to problem solve, then perhaps more attention should be paid in the curriculum, across all levels of practice, on the skills of conflict resolution and conflict management. There are materials to help us in this area as well (Barsky, 2000; Weinhold & Weinhold, 2000). Because Riane Eisler's work is so congruent with social work and has been developed for educational settings, it could be seriously considered in any or all of social work's policy and practice classes.

Coursework on interdisciplinary and interagency practice is relevant to today's social service arenas. Research on why we need to collaborate and what makes a good collaboration is growing (Winer & Ray, 2000). For example, the Annie E. Casey Foundation (1998), in its report on preparing human service workers for interprofessional practice, has begun to explore many of the issues involved in implementing effective social, educational, and health services across disciplines and social service systems. In response to the increased need for interagency partnerships, the social work department at California State University, San Bernardino, has recently revamped its curriculum with emphases, in the advanced year, on empowerment, leadership, and interdisciplinary and interagency collaboration. If many of today's problems are metaproblems and we are committed to a more holistic approach, we may need to somehow reach out to other practitioners in other disciplines and professions to get a more complete view of the elephant.

Field placements should be developed in nontraditional field settings such as the planning, economic development, housing, and related departments of city hall, similar county departments, or with county supervisors, community development corporations, and industries such as utility companies, environmental oversight agencies, and businesses. Students, especially if placed with students from other disciplines, could form teams in program development, planning, or neighborhood revitalization, and could educate these arenas regarding a more holistic problem-solving approach. Service-learning classes across disciplines could be another route to more holistic problem solving.

At a larger systems level, I recommend university reform. Before World War II, liberal arts colleges, with learning ordered toward more humanist ends, provided the major image of education. Disciplines did not dominate colleges. Specialized knowledge is important to advance our understanding of the world; however, academic disciplines tend to isolate some aspect for study in separation from the rest, treating it as if it were self-contained and related only to the external areas it was abstracted from. This works against a discipline's contribution to a broad human need of understanding the interconnectedness of phenomena (Daly & Cobb, 1989). Some of the following initiatives from the Annie E. Casey Foundation (1998) could assist in promoting a more relevant interdisciplinary university:

- A department or center for the study of social and global crises. This could encourage cross-disciplinary research on the urgent needs of the time. If combined with a requirement for service learning, this center could spearhead local and global problem-solving strategies.

- Interdisciplinary centers, similar to women's studies or peace studies, could be developed.

- Social work departments, by nature interdisciplinary, need not wait for top-down initiatives for cross-discipline initiatives (e.g., a master's-degree concentration could be developed in sustainable development involving economics, environmental studies, geography, and other relevant departments).

- Foundations and government could be engaged in the funding of projects that address the study of interprofessional education issues.

## IMPLICATIONS FOR SOCIAL WORK RESEARCH

Social work is committed to the core values of promoting social justice and social change, through practice, education, and research (NASW, 1999). How do we see, understand, and study the world around us? Perhaps the most obvious implication of a sustainable approach to social work is the profession's acceptance of alternative paradigms in the conduct of social work research. New systems theory and a partnership approach acknowledge intuition, spirituality, and a science of empathy. We cannot separate our research from our value base.

It is therefore quite appropriate for social workers to consider using any of the four paradigms that Morris (2006) suggests in the pursuit of these aims. If research is framed in an ideological commitment to social justice and has social or political action as an agenda, then a systematically applied critical theory paradigm can bring enlightenment and action to a social issue. If the purpose of the research is to gather various stakeholder perceptions in the attempt to define the issues and the solutions, then a constructivist paradigm is useful. The assumption in this approach is that these constructions or worldviews vary from one time and place to another; stakeholders are allowed to influence one another's worldviews in this process, and the end result may be a commitment to a longer-term problem-solving effort.

Indeed, accepting approximate descriptions of reality or theological statements is part of the new systems paradigm and requires of us an openness to various ways of exploring the world as an always-changing, dynamic system. This does not mean we embrace sloppy research. Each of the four paradigms that Morris (2006) offers are applied in a systematic fashion. Rather, we can acknowledge that there are various ways of knowing, that reality can never be separated from context, and that we are challenged to examine these realities in a value-based, thoughtful, and methodical way.

This brings us to research that should be done to help further our understanding of our interconnectedness, the relationships and tensions between science and religion, and the myriad concepts we have explored in sustainability. This book has shared some examples of social workers who are engaged in efforts focused on new-paradigm thinking. Direct practitioners are using a holistic approach to healing; community practitioners are attempting to bridge the gap and bring peace between Hispanic and Asian gangs; local and international social workers are trying to influence community development strategies toward sustainable environmental and economic solutions. Such interdisciplinary initiatives should include a range of research designs, including value-based or critical theory and constructivism, as components of their studies.

Currently, it is not known to what extent social workers are aware of or embrace, for example, the theory of interconnectedness or the web of life, the mind-body-spirit connection, an ecological credo, or many of the other notions of sustainability we have explored in politics, economics, technology, or family life.

In other words, I have asserted that scholars across many disciplines and cultural creatives are experiencing a shift in thinking about themselves and their place in the universe. But to what extent are social workers experiencing this shift in their own thinking? If some have, how has the shift affected their personal worldviews? The way they perceive science and religion? The way they see themselves and the natural world? The way they practice? Work by groups such as the Institute for Noetic Sciences and the Center for Integral Studies can assist researchers in formulating research questions relevant to social work and new-paradigm thinking.

## ADDITIONAL THINGS TO THINK ABOUT

1. Using the narrow lens, define a problem such that the unit of analysis is the individual. Then, widen the lens, reframe the problem, and define it.

2. If social workers shift their work in mental health from individual treatment to the larger context of prevention and planning, what could they do to alleviate conditions that lead to mental illness?

3. What social, political, or economic theories are you learning about in your courses in human behavior and the social environment that widen the lens on social problems?

4. Consider a population or social problem that is of great interest to you. How might you use the strategies for practice outlined in this chapter to plan for or to develop effective responses that would promote a sustainable future?

5. In cooperative day care, family members give some of their time to work with children. What are some other social and community needs that cooperatives could meet? How might fiscal and social policy better support them? Tax incentives? Public assistance?

6. Theoretically, if social workers help develop more preventive programs (versus protective programs) for at-risk children, families, or elders, what might the employment of social workers be? Sites? Job titles?

# MAIN POINTS

1. We have arrived at our current understanding via a narrow lens, with focus on the individual and emphasis on biological and psychological theories of individual behavior.

2. Sustainable social work uses a broader lens to identify the social, political, cultural, and environmental factors that influence social problems.

3. The themes of this book expand our values to include values-based science, a new identity with the environment, interconnectedness, a collective economic model, and principles of transformational politics.

4. The vision of social work in a sustainable world is to develop global, national, and local communities through institutions that are sustainable and support all life.

5. A new paradigm of sustainable social work involves the following five strategies: (1) prevention and long-term planning, (2) interdisciplinary social work, (3) sustainable social and economic development, (4) citizen and community empowerment, and (5) partnership education.

6. Implications of this paradigm for social work education involve broadening our view of person-in-environment, a global perspective of social welfare, greater emphasis on conflict resolution, interdisciplinary collaboration, and university reform.

7. Social work research needs to be values based and should incorporate critical theory and constructivist designs to research social problems and sustainable responses.

## For Further Reading

Gil, D. (1992). *Unravelling social policy.* Rochester, VT: Schenkman Books.

Korten, D. C. (2006). *The great turning: From empire to earth community.* San Francisco: Kumarian Press.

Payne, M. (2005). *Modern social work theory.* Chicago: Lyceum Books.

Specht, H. & Courtney, M. E. *Unfaithful angels: How social work has abandoned its mission.* New York: The Free Press.

# CHAPTER 8

# Evolving Toward Partnership

My Mother's Garden

> my mother sits at the window staring
> at the place her garden
> used to be. the birdbath is empty
> and dry like the flowerbeds, she
> contemplates the grass,
> how brown it has become,
> and the pale hostas trouble her.
>
> i look out the window too, but
> at the city instead. I am ten
> and want to change the world
> and become president
> and travel to third-world countries.
> "somalia is starving," I say.
> and she says
>
> "my garden is dying."
> i am ten and angry with her
> for her lack of concern. I recite
> facts about poverty, name
> the wars that I've heard of.
>
> my mother smiles as she always has
> and turns back to the small universe
> of her garden. "sasha, we have to start
> somewhere," she says, and on her grocery list
> writes *flower seeds.*

—Olivia Cole,
*2007 poetry award winner, Nuclear Age Peace Foundation*

Let ours be a time remembered for the awakening of a new reverence
for life, the firm resolve to achieve sustainability, the quickening of the
struggle for justice and peace, and the joyful celebration of life.

—Earth Charter Commission, *The Earth Charter*

The world we live in is not a partnership world. It is not, totally, a dominator world. It is changing. However, if you look at current trends and rely on mainstream media to convey and interpret them, you can easily conclude that, as my grandmother used to say, we are going to hell in a handbasket.

Scientists tell us that the human race is living beyond its means as we continue to use fuel, water, and food beyond the carrying capacity of the planet. We continue to lose species every day, the earth is growing warmer, there is ongoing violence in the Middle East, and the gap is widening between the world's richest and poorest people. The United States has initiated a war on terror and will have spent $450 billion this year on the military, while about one-thirtieth of that could seriously address the needs of the world's poorest people (Sachs, 2005). The richest country in the world has no universal health care, and we rank second to last among developed countries in childhood poverty (Rifkin, 2004a).

So, how do we get from where we are to where we want to be? This book will not provide you with a road map. What I do know is that we will not get there overnight. Some of the destructive paradigms, such as Eisler's dominator model of society, have been embraced for centuries. What I would suggest, however, are three things. First, each of us needs to reexamine where we get our information about the world. Second, each of us, as social workers, should commit to some kind of action within the context of a sustainable world. This action needs to be headed toward systems change, not business as usual. Third, we should not despair but have faith that we are an evolving species capable of changing the world and preserving it for future generations.

With respect to our sources of information, Federal Communications Commission Commissioner Michael Copps asserts that "democracy is premised on giving people sufficient depth and breadth of information that they'll generally make intelligent decisions for the good of the country" (Goetzman, 2007, p. 53). It is dangerous to rely on the message of mainstream media, as five media conglomerates control 80% of the media in this country (Goetzman, 2007). If we rely on such media alone to gauge our overall daily welfare, it is quite likely we will perceive ourselves and our neighbors as living in a fearful, greedy society. We fear terrorists, wiretapping, credit-card fraud, sexual predators, drive-by shootings, computer viruses, airplane hijackers, and people who hate freedom. The newspaper menu, on those pages not bought by Macy's or some other corporate conglomerate, features political intrigue and corruption, street crime, international finance, and weekend movie profits. Unless you read, for example, the *Christian Science Monitor* or other alternative news, or perhaps listen to public radio, you will seldom hear about any groups or individuals in public or private life that are making a positive difference for themselves and their neighbors. People feel disenfranchised by the government, immersed in consumer frenzy, and valued primarily as consumers not citizens. Perhaps the world is going to hell in a handbasket.

We must avail ourselves of alternative media and read from disciplines other than our own. For example, *Scientific American* or *National Geographic* are not just important for natural scientists, nature lovers, or photographers. Given our access to the information highway, each of us can learn a bit about how physicists, philosophers, religious leaders, or business owners have a slightly different take on the world. If you are plugged into the information highway, you can receive any number of daily updates from sources such as the Worldwatch Institute or UN programs, and perhaps you will develop a more complex picture of human evolution. So what is reality? Wherein lies the real truth? Are we to feel comforted that the market, our invincible entrepreneurial spirit, and technology will ensure our long-term survival? Or are we teetering on the brink? Have we already passed the time when we could have saved the planet? Or do we just all hold hands and pray, or sing "Kumbaya"?

I prefer the following approximate description of reality put forth by David Korten, the founder of *Yes! The Journal of Positive Futures*: As a species we humans are at a critical moment in time. For the first time in our history, we have the opportunity and the challenge to assume the collective responsibility for creating our own future (Korten, 2006). But we must begin to change things. Paradigm change happens at all levels, so I would like to share with you some thoughts about systems change.

## SYSTEMS CHANGE

Though the situation is stark, the destructive environmental threats we are facing are all of our own making (Brown, 2006). If we have the will, as humans working with our own ingenuity within the institutions and the technology we have created, we can rapidly mobilize changes. Consider this startling reality. One month after the bombing of Pearl Harbor, our country embarked on the greatest industrial conversion in modern times. A ban on sales and production of cars went into effect, a rationing program for fuel, oil, sugar, and other products was instigated, and we began to produce the greatest increase in industrial output in the nation's history— for military use (Goodwin, 1994). When there is a will there is the way to restructure an entire economy in record time, and with an event, not a slowly evolving threat. If we mobilized for war, we can mobilize for energy and the future of a dying planet. We might consider three fronts to this effort: public education, money, and politics (Brown, 2006).

A massive public education campaign would raise public awareness about the gravity of the situation. Books such as *Collapse* (2005), by Jared Diamond, and movies like Al Gore's *An Inconvenient Truth* are helpful. Articles in the *New York Times* also help get the word out; this newspaper devoted the majority of its op-ed page to Diamond's book and the lessons we can learn from civilizations that had moved to an environmentally deteriorating path similar to ours. There are also many publications that we can avail ourselves of and contribute to in an effort to understand the threat and the positive steps that are being taken to give us some hope and to help us join in the movement.

For myself, I depend on Internet updates from the UN and a regular dose of Web sites that keep me plugged into a panoply of activities all over the globe that are moving in the direction of a more sustainable society. For example, the previously mentioned quarterly journal *Yes! The Journal of Positive Futures*, in its recent spring 2006 issue, highlighted the ten most hopeful trends of the past ten years. Among these are global movements of nonviolence, including groups such as the International Fellowship of Reconciliation and Peace Brigades International; efforts to clean up the environment from recycling garbage in the South Bronx to a youth movement in Montreal to push the extension of the Kyoto Protocol; and challenges to consumerism, such as that of Bhutan, a small country that sits between India and China, and its adoption of a gross national happiness index that promotes sustainable socioeconomic development. Let me be candid. This magazine gives me hope with every issue.

On the science and spiritual front, the Network of Spiritual Progressives, cochaired by Cornel West, Michael Lerner, and Sister Joan Chittister, hosted a conference in May 2006 on spiritual activism. Workshops were held on topics such as spiritual economics, nonviolence training, ecology and spirituality, and spirituality as a bottom line in professions. This conference and network hopes to energize efforts toward creating a society that promotes caring relationships and families, social responsibility for economic and political life, and a separation of church and state that does not alienate values from the public sphere.

On the partnership front, the Center for Partnership Studies in Pacific Grove California, founded by Riane Eisler and David Loye in 1989, is involved in conferences, research, and educational curricula to develop a partnership way of problem solving. In Pakistan, the Urdu edition of *Tomorrow's Children*, was adopted in 2004 as part of the Lahore Government College in its masters in education curriculum, a breakthrough for partnership education in the Muslim world. A recent initiative of this center is the Spiritual Alliance to Stop Intimate Violence (2007) "to break cycles of violence in families and the family of nations" (Spiritual Alliance to Stop Intimate Violence, 2007). This is a program of the Center for Partnership Studies, founded by Riane Eisler, in Pacific Grove, California.

Of course, it will take more than education. It will take major shifts in our economic system to sustain us as a species on this planet, and we have talked about some of these. One immediate shift needed is in the monies allocated by the United States and globally for sustainability. In *Plan B 2.0* (Brown, 2006) the author suggests a budget that shifts $161 billion from military spending in response to terrorist threats toward expenditures to meet social goals and restore the earth. This budget, roughly one-third of the current U.S. military budget and one-sixth of the global military budget, spends money on the following:

## Basic Social Goals

- Universal primary education
- Adult literacy
- School lunch programs for the world's forty-four poorest countries
- Assistance to preschool children and pregnant women in world's forty-four poorest countries
- Universal basic health care

- Reproductive health and family planning
- Closing the condom gap

## Earth Restoration Goals

- Reforesting the earth
- Protecting topsoil on cropland
- Restoring rangelands
- Stabilizing water tables
- Restoring fisheries
- Protecting biological diversity

How do we influence this shift? Politics, of course! But we can't rely on the old power at the top. Frustrations with Washington's lack of leadership in ignoring the Kyoto Protocol has led people to act. For example, mayors of more than 180 cities decided to come together to honor the protocol's goal of cutting carbon emissions 7% below the 1990 level over the upcoming decade (Brown, 2006). The same kinds of things are happening at the state level. You and I can become a part of this politics by, for example, voting with our pocketbook for sustainable products, writing to or meeting with local representatives around fiscal priorities and restructuring tax systems, and educating ourselves on the issues to present them in our own professional, civic, and personal arenas of power. We have the power if we choose to use it.

Let me share an example of using this kind of power. In spring 2007, my foundation masters of social work students were completing their policy practice projects. Their assignment was to pitch a policy proposal to a single person or group of decision makers. Some chose to attend the state's legislative days, wherein they met with their own elected representatives. The students completed the assignment, but more important, they came back to class with a new sense of empowerment. They have come to view themselves as power holders, as experts and change agents, and they are committed to attend lobby days next year, as did the cohort before them.

Another group in the class was completely taken with the idea of community land trusts as a more sustainable approach to affordable housing. I was concerned that venturing into the complex policy arena of housing, which was fairly foreign to the group members, was quite ambitious in ten weeks. But by the end of the fall quarter they had put a decent, though brief, proposal together. By early spring, they were ready to pitch their idea to a neighborhood-housing group. None of us could have predicted what occurred as a result of their perseverance. In the end, having researched the topic through scholarship and interviews with housing officials and attending a conference on the topic, the students delivered a PowerPoint presentation and packet of materials to not one group, but to three housing stakeholders in their local community: representatives from the Department of Housing and Urban Development, the nonprofit neighborhood-housing corporation, and the Fair Housing Authority. The other organizations were brought into the pitch by invitation of the neighborhood-housing group, which was so impressed with the quality of the research the students had done that they felt a broader audience was needed. The results were twofold: first, the interagency group is committed to pursuing the idea; second, this group of housing experts has been educated that social workers can and should operate in the housing arena. They demonstrated skills as catalysts, and they brought people together at the table to confer about more sustainable solutions to the housing crisis. In my eyes, this is transformative.

These are some actions we can take. But, as you know, we may have to leave our comfort zone and change the way we think. The problems we face today cannot be met with the same kind of values and constructs that gave rise to them. "We are fighting terrorism, poverty, criminality, cultural conflict, environmental degradation, ill health, even obesity and other 'sicknesses of civilization' with the same kind of thinking—the same means and methods—that produced them in the first place" (Laszlo, 2006, p. 3). How do we affect the evolution of our thinking?

## CULTURAL CHANGE: EVOLUTION TO SPIRITUAL CONSCIOUSNESS

There are many theories of how innovations become adopted and move into the mainstream. Relevant to our focus, for example, Elgin, in *Voluntary Simplicity* (1993), suggests four stages in the transformation from the world "problematique," or crucial problems like material excess, poverty, and alienation from nature, to one of physical and spiritual harmony with the natural world. First is the stage of denial and feeling powerless to get involved. Second, a growing number of people cross a threshold of awakening and become involved in grassroots activities or innovation. Third is the point of initiation, where forces of adversity (e.g., resource shortages, increasing civil wars) and forces of opportunity (e.g., increasing alternative energy production, citizen engagement) push us to make a choice. Do we go backward or forward? Fourth is a bounce upward to corrective measures and to a new level or a crash into an evolutionary wall.

Ken Wilber (2000) offers a complex and fascinating theory of the evolution of consciousness on a more psychological level. However, I believe David Korten's path from empire to earth community is quite relevant to what we now face in the challenges to our societal and cultural views of the world.

## FROM EMPIRE TO EARTH COMMUNITY

Drawing on the work of scholars such as Carol Gilligan, Erik Erikson, Abraham Maslow, and Lawrence Kohlberg, Korten (2006) devises a fivefold path to spiritual consciousness. This may prove useful and relevant to us as social workers, as it can be applied to the development of individuals as well as to whole cultures and societies. The following is a summary of Korten's five-stage path in a cultural evolution from empire to earth community.

We have an opportunity to evolve into a more mature human society that can move us from a dominator model to more of a partnership model. The first of five stages is magical consciousness, and occurs among young children from about two to six years of age. In this stage, children have the rudimentary ability to relate cause and effect and to distinguish fantasy and reality. Magical consciousness depends on others to make things right, as individuals in this stage are unable to understand the consequences of their own actions.

Imperial consciousness, stage two, occurs around age seven. The learning agenda is to understand that actions have consequences. It also involves learning that you can get what you need by complying with authority figures. A desire to please others to improve your own standing or to avoid being caught, rather than selfless concern for the needs of others, motivates good behavior.

Around the age of eleven or twelve, children begin to see themselves through the eyes of others and to develop empathy. In the third stage, socialized consciousness, an individual constructs identity through his or her primary reference groups. Very attuned to the expectations of peer groups, people in this stage know the importance of playing within rules. Korten (2006) says the good news is that people at this level have a foundation for good citizenship. The bad news is that they are quite susceptible to manipulation by propagandists, and their strong sense of identity makes them willing to demand rights for their own identity group that they would deny others; thus, they may have a strong distrust of the "other."

Adulthood may usher in the fourth critical consciousness stage. If a person stays in the third stage, then his or her philosophy remains, "The way of my people is the only way." However, critical consciousness involves seeing that there are different cultures with different cultural truths. This stage is the beginning of a true moral consciousness concerned with order and protection of one's own interests as well as the interest of others, or social justice. This stage is critical for developing a worldview that is inclusive and understands the possibility of life-affirming societies for all. However, Korten (2006) believes that people rarely achieve this stage before the age of thirty and that most people in today's modern industrial societies are unable to achieve it. Why? Most political, economic, religious, and even educational institutions discourage it. However, people who achieve this state can be considered cultural creatives, like we talked about in chapter 1.

Spiritual consciousness, the highest expression of what it means to be a human, involves relating to diverse people and situations with a goal of understanding life's possibilities. According to Korten (2006), people who have achieved this stage are sages, religious leaders, tribal leaders, valued elders, and wise people who have an integral worldview and find themselves as cocreators and partners with others to understand the whole and their place in it. People in this stage have let go of narcissism and embraced a larger identity. They do not alienate themselves from or rise above the world; rather they transcend exclusive conventional group loyalties and live "in creative service to the whole" (Korten, 2006, p. 48).

It is not difficult to translate the characteristics of a state of spiritual consciousness into the values and principles of a sustainable future, as we have defined it: the recognition that we are all interconnected and connecting with a larger wholeness; the need to marry the material and the spiritual; and the principles of long-term sustainability, such as the value of all life, respect for the environment that sustains us, equality and social justice, and a partnership model of society instead of a dominator model. These are all congruent with spiritual consciousness.

As individuals, we can and should explore our own consciousness and meaning in the world. But it is important for us to understand that these are not just individual stages of development. They are also collective in nature, for humans are social animals. The values and societal norms that we decide to adopt as life enhancing involve a balance between individual needs and desires and those of the collective. The collective, in our view of a sustainable future, is the planet. So, is there hope for developing such a collective consciousness that allows for individuality, embraces diversity, and strives for the good of all?

Again, let's remind ourselves that changes in paradigms occur slowly, over time, and we must not despair. Consider the journey of African Americans in the United States. It has taken centuries for our country to shift its thinking about humanity, slavery, the economics of cotton, and slaves and laborers as property. We are still shifting. Social and economic justice for people of color, women, people with disabilities, gays and lesbians, and other oppressed groups are still battles to be won, a vision for the future. It takes dialogue, education, social action, policy changes, and belief and faith.

So are we heading in the right direction? Will we get there? Is there hope? These are not questions for scientists alone. These are questions for parents, pastors, teachers, citizens, neighbors, and professionals like us. These should be the questions for our developing children, as they take on the roles of adulthood. But we are social workers, and we have no choice but to face these questions head-on. Our calling and our code of ethics challenge us to "enhance human well-being and help meet the basic needs of all people." Our mission is not psychotherapy. Our mission, in the past 150 years, has been to assist the most vulnerable in our society to cope with the ill effects of industrialization. Today the industrial world has made us all sick. All of us, humans, our plant and animal species, the planet itself, may die if we do not intervene at the river, and not from the bottom of the waterfall. We are not individual lifeboats. We are connected on one big boat called planet Earth.

## PERSONAL CHANGE

As social workers, we are the only helping profession that is specifically charged and trained to intervene across all systems, from the individual to the planet. Are we willing to engage others in taking up this calling?

If so, our lens needs shifting. Since the inception of our profession, the focus on individual casework versus larger social change has waxed and waned. But now we know, thanks to our planet's image from space, that we're all on the same boat. We must, for ourselves and the families, communities, and countries we work with, connect the fate of the family with the fate of the earth. Whether that means looking at fashion, or the foods we buy or grow, or the newspapers we throw away, or the car we drive, or the number of children we have, or a host of other personal choices, we should be ever mindful that the choices of hundreds of individuals are connected to the choices of the corporation, the government, and other civic institutions—all of which we can influence. Some of us may not think beyond our own future or our children's future. As professionals, it is difficult for many of us to look beyond our daily responsibilities to the immediate needs of our clients, with so many suffering on this day, now, when we are so aware that government is disengaging in its support for social welfare. But some of us are. And more of us must.

I am not currently in the trenches. I work primarily in academia. But for me, this profession, this challenge, means that every day I wake up with the glass half full. It is an attitude, not a scientific truth. It is faith. Faith that people can change their situation for the better, which is, of course, one of our beliefs. Faith, combined with knowledge, gives me hope for a sustainable future.

It is important that I am informed by science. However, I know in my heart that science and technology alone do not have the answers to keep us from destroying our home—this "fragile blue and white Christmas tree ornament in the sky," as seen by our astronauts. I must also believe that I can make a difference, and use knowledge and belief and faith to frame my approach. Perhaps we'll see it when we believe it, and not vice versa. I am hopeful that you too have decided to pursue this profession with some sense that affecting the bigger picture may result in greater benefits to individuals and families. Enough with the bottom of the waterfall—let's start taking those steps to the top.

## ADDITIONAL THINGS TO THINK ABOUT

1. What do you think about the supposition that social workers should be involved in large systems change rather than psychotherapy?
2. Why did you choose social work over an advanced degree in psychology or another field? How does your choice relate to the calling of the profession of social work?
3. What is your reaction to Korten's stages of evolution from empire to earth community?
4. You are granted one wish for a sustainable future. What is it?
5. What are you doing now to make that wish a reality?

## MAIN POINTS

1. To have hope in the future we cannot solely rely on the worldview or constructions of mainstream media; we must supplement our diet with stories of hope.
2. There are immediate steps we can take to advocate for funding and for policies that ensure a sustainable future.
3. Social change takes time. If we recognize the need for a paradigm shift, and we aspire to attain a level of spiritual consciousness, we can and should explore our individual place in the world.
4. Our profession is unique, in that it teaches us to intervene across systems. Our systems need changing. Are we willing to take up the challenge for change?

### For Further Reading
Korten, D. (2006). *The great turning: From empire to earth community.* San Francisco: Kumarian Press.
Laszlo, Ervin (2006). *The chaos point: The world at the crossroads.* Charlottesville, VA: Hampton Roads Publishing.

# References

Abels, S. (Ed.). (2000). *Spirituality in social work practice.* Denver, CO: Love Publishing Company.

Affigne, A. (1995, August/September). Transforming the American political landscape. Paper presented at the Annual Meeting of the American Political Science Association, Chicago.

Al-Krenawi, A. (2000). Reconciling western treatment and traditional healing: A social worker walks with the wind. In S. Abels (Ed.), *Spirituality in social work practice* (pp. 5–30). Denver, CO: Love Publishing Company.

Annie E. Casey Foundation. (1998). *Myths and opportunities: An examination of the impact of discipline accreditation on interprofessional education.* Baltimore: Annie E. Casey Foundation, in collaboration with CSWE, University of California School of Social Work and Department of Nursing, and California State Fullerton Center for Collaboration for Children.

Annie E. Casey Foundation. (2007). *Family to family.* Retrieved October 10, 2007, from http://www.aecf.org/majorinitiatives/Family%20to%20Family.aspx

Argyris, C. (1964). *Integrating the individual and the organization.* Hoboken, NJ: John Wiley and Sons.

Ashford, J., LeCroy, C., & Lortie, K. (2001). *Human behavior and the social environment: A multi-dimensional approach.* Belmont, CA: Thompson.

Atkisson, A. (1991, Fall/Winter). *Citizens and politics: The Kettering report* [Electronic version]. *In Context,* 30, 2. Retrieved October 9, 2007, from http://www.context.org/ICLIB/IC30/moyer.htm#Atkisson

Austin, J., & Peter Drucker Foundation for Non-Profit Management. (2000). *The collaboration challenge.* New York: Jossey-Bass.

Bache, C. (2000). *Dark night, early dawn: Steps to a deep ecology of mind.* Albany: State University of New York Press.

Barsky, A. (2000). *Conflict resolution for the helping professions.* Belmont, CA: Thompson Learning.

Baum, M., & Twiss, P. (Eds.). (1996). *Social work intervention in an economic crisis: The Rivers Community Project.* New York: Haworth Press.

Beck, B. (1980). Social work and the future. In K. Dea (Ed.), *Perspectives for the future: Social work practice in the '80s* (pp. 35-43). Silver Spring, MD: NASW Press.

Bell, D. (1973). *The coming of the post-industrial society.* New York: Basic Books.

Berger, R., & Kelly, J. (1993). Social work in the ecological crisis. *Social Work, 38*(5), 521–526.

Besthorn, F. (2001). *Is it time for a deeper ecological approach to social work: What is the earth telling us?* Retrieved October 8, 2007, from http://www.ecosocialwork.or/essays.html

Beyond War. (1985). *Beyond war: A new way of thinking—communicator's guide.* Palo Alto, CA: Beyond War.

Bodaken, M. (2000). Saving America's rental housing stock: The crisis and the appropriate financial services role. *Community Development* (Orange County, CA). Retrieved October 9, 2007, from http://www.occ.treas.gov/cdd/Spring2000.pdf

Boulding, E. (1978). Las mujeres y la violencia social. *Revista Internacional de Ciencias Sociales, 30*(4), 30–46.

Boulding, K. (1992). *Towards a new economics: Critical essays on ecology, distribution, and other themes.* Northampton, MA: Edward Elgar.

Boyer, W. (1984). *America's future: Transition to the 21st century.* Sisters, OR: Praeger & Greenwood.

Brooklyn College, English Department. (2006). General characteristics of the Renaissance adapted from *A guide to the study of literature: A companion text for core studies 6, landmarks of literature.* Retrieved June 26, 2006, from http://academic.brooklyn.cuny.edu/english/melanie/cs6/ren.html

Brown, L. (2006). *Plan B 2.0: Rescuing a planet under stress and a civilization in trouble.* New York: Earth Policy Institute and W. W. Norton.

*BusinessWeek.* (1993, May 10). Technology is fueling retail productivity, but slowing job gains, 16.

Campbell, C. (1997, December 29). Depletion patterns show change due for production of conventional oil. *Oil and Gas Journal,* 37.

Canda, E., & Smith, E. (Eds.). (2001) Transpersonal perspectives on spirituality in social work [Special issue]. *Social Thought Journal of Religion in the Social Services, 20*(1/2).

Capra, F. (1982). *The turning point: Science, society, and the rising culture.* New York: Bantam Books.

Capra, F. (1996). *The web of life.* New York: Bantam, Doubleday, Dell.

Capra, F., & Steindl-Rast, D. (1991). *Belonging to the universe: Explorations on the frontiers of science and spirituality.* San Francisco: Harper.

Carson, R. (1962). *Silent spring.* Boston: Houghton Mifflin.

Cass, W. (1984). Homosexual identity formation: Testing a theoretical model. *Journal of Sex Research, 20*(2), 143–167.

Center for Economic Conversion and Henry George School for Social Science. (1995). Exercise: A Royal Meeting in *Sustainable economics: A supplementary curriculum for high school economics courses*. Mountain View, CA: Author.

Cheung, F., & Tsui, M. (2000). A wake-up call to the social work profession. *Families in Society: Journal of Contemporary Human Services, 83*(2), 123–124.

Closson, M. (1992, August). *Success stories of economic conversion*. Presentation at the town meeting of Long Beach Area Task Force on Economic Conversion, Long Beach, CA.

Cnaan, R., Sinha, J., & McGrew, C. (2004). Congregations as social service providers: Service, capacity, culture and organizational behavior. *Journal of Administration in Social Work, 28*(3/4), 47–68.

Coates, J. (2003). *Ecology and social work: Toward a new paradigm*. Halifax, Nova Scotia: Fernwood Publishing.

Coleman, D. (1994). *Ecopolitics: Building a green society*. New Brunswick, NJ: Rutgers University Press.

Congress, E. (1999). *Social work values and ethics*. Chicago: Nelson-Hall.

Conservers battle achievers in futurist scenarios. (1979, October). *NASW News, 24*, 4–5.

Cowley, A. (1993). Transpersonal social work: A theory for the 1990s. *Social Work, 38*(5), 527–534.

Cowley, A. (1996). Transpersonal social work. In F. Turner (Ed.), *Social work treatment* (pp. 663–698). New York: Free Press.

Crosby, J., & Van Soest, D. (1997). *Challenges of violence worldwide: An educational resource*. Silver Spring, MD: NASW Press.

Cross, W. (1971). The negro to black experience: Toward a psychology of black liberation. *Black World, 20*(9), 13–27.

CSWE. (2004). *Educational policy and accreditation standards*. Retrieved October 9, 2007, from http://www.cswe.org

Daly, H. (2005, September). Economics in a full world. *Scientific American*, 100–107.

Daly, H., & Cobb, J. (1989). *For the common good: Redirecting the economy toward community, the environment and a sustainable future*. Boston: Beacon Press.

Day, P. (2000). *A new history of social welfare*. Boston: Allyn and Bacon.

De Quincey, C. (2001). A theory of everything? *Noetic Sciences Review, 55*, 9–21.

Derezotes, D. (2005). *Revaluing social work: Implications of emerging science and technology*. Denver, CO: Love Publishing.

Devaney, R. L. (1989). *An introduction to chaotic dynamical systems* (2nd ed.). Reading, MA: Addison-Wesley.

Diamond, J. (2005). *Collapse: How societies choose to fail or succeed*. New York: Viking Penguin.

Dodda, C. (2004). *Economics for international students.* Retrieved June 10, 2006, from http://www.cr1.dircon.co.uk/chrisdodda.htm

Dominelli, L. (2002) Anti-oppressive practice in context. In R. Adams, L. Dominelli, & M. Payne (Eds.), *Social work: Themes, issues and critical debates* (2nd ed., pp. 3–19). Basingstoke, UK: Palgrave Macmillan.

Dudley Street Neighborhood Initiative. (2007). *Fact sheet.* Retrieved April 24, 2007, from http://www.dsni.org/For%20the%20Press.htm

Durkheim, E. (1972). *Selected writings.* Cambridge, MA: Cambridge University Press.

Durning, A. (1990). Ending poverty. In Brown et al. (Eds.), *State of the world.* New York: Worldwatch Institute.

Dye, T. (1998). *Understanding public policy* (9th ed.). Saddle River, NJ: Prentice Hall.

Ehrlich, P. (1968). *Population bomb.* New York: Ballantine Books.

Eisler, R. (1995). *The chalice and the blade: Our history, our future.* New York: Harper Collins.

Eisler, R. (2000). *Tomorrow's children: A blueprint for partnership education in the 21st century.* Cambridge, MA: Perseus Books.

Eisler, R. (2002). *The power of partnership.* Novato, CA: New World Library.

Eisler, R. (2005, Winter). Spare the rod. *Yes! A Journal of Positive Futures, 32,* 30–36.

Eisler, R., & Loye, D. (1990). *The partnership way.* San Francisco: Harper.

Eisner, A. (2006, February 8). Evangelicals urge action on global warming. Retrieved February 27, 2006, from http://www.news.com/evangelicals-urge-action-on-global-warming

Elgin, D. (1993). *Voluntary simplicity.* New York: William Morrow.

Elgin, D. (2000). *Promise ahead: A vision of hope and action for humanity's future.* New York: Harper Collins.

Elgin, D., & LeDrew, C. (1997). *Global consciousness change: Indicators of an emerging paradigm.* San Anselmo, CA: Millennium Project.

Elias, R. (1993). *Victims still: The political manipulation of crime victims.* Newbury Park, CA: Sage.

Elias, R. (1997). A culture of violent solutions. In J. Turpin & L. Kurtz (Eds.), *The web of violence: From interpersonal to global.* Chicago: University of Illinois Press.

Estes, R. (1984). *The social progress of nations.* New York: Praeger.

Estes, R. (2005). Global change and indicators of social development. In M. Weil (Ed.), *Handbook of community practice.* Thousand Oaks, CA: Sage.

Falk, R. (1995). *On humane governance: Toward a new global politics, the world order models project report of the Global Civilization Initiative.* University Park, PA: Penn State University Press.

Farvar, M., & Glaeser, B. (1979). *The politics of ecodevelopment.* Berlin: International Institute for Environment and Society.

Fischer, R. (2002). Beyond September 11: Justice through outreach. *Families in Society: The Journal of Contemporary Human Services, 83*(2), 118.

Ford, J. (1988, April 28). This little pig rushed to market. *New Scientist,* 27.

Forest, L. (1991). Discovering public life. *In Context, 30,* 2-42.

Forum Vauban. (2002). *Sustainable urban district Freiburg-Vauban.* Retrieved October 10, 2007, from http://www.forum-vauban./de/overview.shtml

Freire, P. (2000). *Pedagogy of the oppressed.* New York: Continuum.

Garbarino, J. (1992). *Toward a sustainable society: An economic, social and environmental agenda for our children's future.* Chicago: Noble Press.

Gardner, G., & Sampat, P. (1998). *Mind over matter: Recasting the roles of materials on our lives* (Worldwatch Paper No. 144). Washington, DC: Worldwatch Institute.

Gellis, Z., & Reid, W. (2004). Strengthening evidence based practice. *Brief Treatment and Crisis Intervention, 4*(2), 155–165.

Germain, C. (Ed.). (1979). *Social work practice: People and environments—An ecological perspective.* New York: Columbia University Press.

Germain, C., & Gitterman, A. (1980). *The life model of social work practice.* New York: Columbia University Press.

Gandhi, M. (1948). *Mohandas K. Gandhi autobiography: The story of my experiments with truth.* New York: Dover Publications.

Giddens, A. (1984). *The constitution of society.* Berkeley: University of California Press.

Gilbert, R. (1998) Transformational political leadership: Insights from the example of Václav Havel. In S. Woolpert, C. Slaton, & E. Schwerin (Eds.), *Transformational politics* (pp. 201–214). Albany: State University of New York Press.

Glaeser, B. (Ed.). (1984). *Ecodevelopment: Concepts, projects, strategies.* Oxford: Pergamon Press.

Goetzman, K. (2007, July/August). Big media meets its match. *Utne Reader,* 52–58.

Goodwin, D. (1994). *No ordinary time: Franklin and Eleanor Roosevelt, the home front in World War II.* New York: Simon and Schuster.

Grant, P., Starr, C., & Overbye, T. (2006, June). A power grid for the hydrogen economy. *Scientific American,* 78–84.

Gray, B. (1989). *Collaborating.* San Francisco: Jossey-Bass.

Grumet, J. (2006, May). *Testimony at U.S. Senate Committee on Foreign Relations hearing on energy security and oil dependence.* Retrieved October 9, 2007, from http://www.energycommission.org/site/pge.php?tesimony=17

Gurr, T. (1993). *Minorities at risk: A global view of ethnopolitical conflicts.* Washington, DC: United States Institute of Peace Press.

Hawaíi Alliance for Community-Based Economic Development. *About HACBED.* Retrieved April 24, 2007, from http://www.hacbed.org/article.php?story=20050730184754883&mode=print

Hardina, D. (2002). *Analytic skills for community organization practice.* New York: Columbia University Press.

Harman, W. (1994). A re-examination of the metaphysical foundations in modern science: Why is it necessary? In W. Harmon & J. Clark (Eds.), *New metaphysical foundations of modern science* (pp. 1–14). Sausalito, CA: Institute of Noetic Sciences.

Harman, W. (1977, February) The coming transformation. *The Futurist,* 5–11.

Harris, S. (1994). *Reclaiming democracy: Healing the break between people and government.* Philadelphia: Camino Books.

Hatfield, C. (2001). How long can oil supply grow? *Hubbert Center Newsletter, 97*(4). Retrieved February 6, 2005, from http://www.hubbert/mines.edu/news/v97n4/mkh-news.htm

Havel, V. (1994, August 1). Post-modernism: The search for universal laws. *Vital Speeches, 60*(20), 613.

Henderson, H. (1988). *The politics of the solar age: Alternatives to economics.* Indianapolis: Knowledge Systems.

Henderson, H. (1989, November 3). Beyond economism: New indicators for sustainable development. Unpublished paper presented at Globescope Pacific Conference, Los Angeles.

Henderson, H. (1996). *Building a win-win world: Life beyond global economic warfare.* San Francisco: Berrett-Koehler.

Henderson, H. (1999). *Beyond globalization: Shaping a sustainable global economy.* West Hartford, CT: Kumarian Press.

Heywood, A. (2002). *Politics.* New York: Palgrave Macmillan.

Hokenstad, M., & Midgley, J. (1997). *Issues in international social work: Global challenges for a new century.* Washington, DC: NASW Press.

Hoff, M., & McNutt, J. (Eds.). (1994). *The global environmental crisis.* Brookfield, VT: Ashgate.

Hubbard, B. (1998). *Conscious evolution: Awakening the power of our social potential.* Novato, CA: New World Library.

Hudson, C. (2000). At the edge of chaos: A new paradigm for social work? *Journal of Social Work Education, 36*(2), 215–230.

Hurdle, D. (1998). The health of Alaska native women: Significant problems, emerging solutions. *Journal of Poverty, 2*(4), 4–61.

Hutchison, W. (1998). The role of religious auspiced agencies in the postmodern era, *Social Thought, Journal of Religion in the Social Services, 18*(3), 55–69.

Huxley, A. (1945). *The perennial philosophy.* New York: Harper and Brothers.

International Federation of Social Workers (2005). *Ethics in social work: Statement of principles.* Retrieved October 7, 2007, from http://www.ifsw.org/en/p38000324.html

Jackson, R. (2001). *The clubhouse model: Empowering applications of theory to generalist practice.* Belmont, CA: Wadsworth.

Jacksonville Community Council. (1994). *Life in Jacksonville: Quality indicators for progress.* Jacksonville, FL: Author.

Jones, A. (2000). Social work: An enterprising profession in a competitive environment. In I. O'Connor, P. Smith, & J. Warburton (Eds.), *Contemporary perspectives on social work and the human services* (pp. 150–163). Melbourne: Longman.

Kahn, H. (1976). *The next 2000 years.* New York: William Morrow.

Karenga, M. (2000). Making the past meaningful: Kwanzaa and the concept of sankofa. In S. Abels (Ed.), *Spirituality in social work practice* (pp. 51–68). Denver, CO: Love Publishing Company.

Kent, G. (2003). Blaming the victim globally, *UN Chronicle, 40*(3), 59–60.

Kerka, S. (1995). The learning organization: Myths and realities. Retrieved June 22, 2006, from http://www.cete.org/acve/docgen.asp?tbl=archivedID=a028

Knight, B. (1998). A theory for transforming political community: Applying chaos and feminist theory. In S. Woolpert, C. Slaton, & E. Schwerin (Eds.), *Transformational politics* (pp. 57–72). Albany: State University of New York Press.

Kondrat, M. (2002) Actor-centered social work: Revisioning "person-in-environment" through a critical theory lens. *Social Work, 47*(4), 435–448.

Korten, D. (2006). *The great turning from empire to community.* Bloomfield, CT: Kumarian Press.

Kreutziger, S. (2000). Spirituality in faith. In S. Abels (Ed.), *Spirituality in Social Work Practice* (pp. 69–80). Denver, CO: Love Publishing Company

Kuhn, T. (1996). *The structure of scientific revolutions.* Chicago: University of Chicago Press.

Kurtz, P. (Ed.) (2003). *Science and religion: Are they compatible?* New York: Prometheus Books.

Laird, J. (1993) Introduction. *Journal of Teaching in Social Work, 8*(2), 1–10.

Lang, P. (2005). *Evidence based social work: Towards a new professionalism?* Bern, Switzerland: Academic Publishers.

Larson, E., & Witham, L. (1997). Scientists are still keeping the faith. *Nature, 386,* 435–436.

Laszlo, E. (2006). *The chaos point: The world at the crossroads.* Charlottesville, VA: Hampton Roads.

Lerner, M. (1997). *The politics of meaning: Restoring hope and possibility in an age of cynicism.* Reading, MA: Addison-Wesley.

Lorenz, C. (1972). *Predictability: Does the flap of a butterfly's wings in Brazil set off a tornado in Texas?* Presentation at the December meeting of the American Association for the Advancement of Science, Washington, DC. Retrieved October 9, 2007, from http://www.cmp.caltech.edu/mcc/chaos

Louv, R. (2005). *Last child in the woods: Saving our children from nature-deficit disorder.* Chapel Hill, NC: Algonquin Books.

Lovejoy, A. (1936). *The great chain of being.* Cambridge: Harvard University Press.

Lovelock, J. (1979). *Gaia.* New York: Oxford University Press.

Lovins, A. (1977). *Soft energy paths: Toward a durable peace.* San Francisco: Friends of the Earth International.

Lowery, C. (2000). American Indian narratives: "My spirit is starting to come back." In S. Abels (Ed.), *Spirituality in social work practice* (pp. 81–96). Denver, CO: Love Publishing Company.

Lum, D. (1996). *Social work practice and people of color: A process stage approach* (3rd ed.). Pacific Grove, CA: Brooks Cole.

Lyon, D. (1994). *Postmodernity: Concepts in social thought.* Minneapolis: University of Minnesota Press.

Macarov, D. (1991). *Certain change: Social work practice in the future.* Silver Spring, MD: NASW Press.

Mack, J. (2003, June–August). Deeper causes: Exploring the role of consciousness in terrorism. *Noetic Sciences Review, 64,* 11–17.

Marquand, R. (1997, September 15). "Globerati" try to find "common values." *Christian Science Monitor.*

Mary, N. (2001). Political activism of social work educators. *Journal of Community Practice, 9*(4), 1–20.

Mary, N. (1994). Social work, economic conversion, and community practice: Where are the social workers? *Journal of Community Practice, 1*(4), 7–25.

Mary, N. (1996, Fall). Swords to ploughshares. *Reflections, 49*–54.

Mary, N. (1997). Linking social welfare policy and global problems: Lessons learned from an advanced seminar. *Journal of Social Work Education, 33*(3), 587–597.

Mary, N., & Morris, T. (1994). The future and social work: A global perspective. *Journal of Multicultural Social Work, 3*(4), 89–101.

Mattessich, P., Murray-Close, M., & Monsey, B. (2001). *Collaboration: What makes it work?* (2nd ed.). St. Paul, MN: Wilder Publishing Center.

McCartan, B. (2005, December 16). Some good news on Planet Earth [Opinion], *Seattle Post Intelligencer,* December 16.

McDevitt, S. (2002). Catching up to the rest of the world. *Families in Society: The Journal of Contemporary Human Services, 83*(2), 119–120.

McDonald, C. (2003). Forward via the past? Evidence based practice as strategy in social work. *The Drawing Board, An Australian Review of Public Affairs, 3*(3), 123–142.

McHale, J. (1969). *The future of the future.* New York: Ballantine.

McLaughlin, C., & Davidson, G. (1994). *Spiritual politics: Changing the world from the inside out.* New York: Ballantine Books.

Meadows, D. (1972). *The limits to growth.* New York: New American Library.

Meenaghan, T., Kilty, K., & McNutt, J. (2004). *Social policy analysis and practice.* Chicago: Lyceum Books.

Meinert, R., Pardeck, J., & Murphy, J. (1998). Introduction to postmodernism, religion and the future of social work. *Social Thought, 18*(3), 1–19.

Mesarovic, M., & Pestel, E. (1974). *Mankind at the turning point.* New York: Dutton.

Metzner, R. (1993). The split between spirit and nature in western consciousness. *Noetic Science Review, 25,* 4–9.

Midgley, J. (1995). *Social development: The developmental perspective in social welfare.* Thousand Oaks, CA: Sage.

Mills, C. (1957). *The power elite.* Oxford: Oxford University Press.

Mirabella, R., & Wish, N. (2000). The 'Best Place' debate: A comparison of graduate education programs for non-profit managers. *Public Administration Review, 60*(3) 219–229.

Mishra, R. (1999). *Globalization and the welfare state.* Northampton, MA: Edward Elgar.

*Monthly Labor Review.* (1993, February). 1992: Job market in doldrums. *116*(2), 3–14.

Morris, T. (2006). *Social work research methods: Four alternative paradigms.* Thousand Oaks, CA: Sage.

Morrison, R. (1995). *Ecological democracy.* Boston: South End Press.

Moyers, B. (1991, Fall/Winter). Yearning for democracy, reclaiming politics. *In Context, 30,* 1–9. Retrieved October 9, 2007, from http://www.context.org/ICLIB/IC30/moyer.htm#Atkisson

Mullaly, B. (1997). *Structural social work: Ideology, theory and practice.* Ontario: Oxford University Press.

Mullen, E., & Streiner, D. (2004). The evidence for and against evidence based practice. *Brief Treatment and Crisis Intervention, 4*(2), 111–121.

NASW. (1999). Code of ethics, revised 1999. Retrieved October 6, 2007, from http://www.socialworker.org/pubs/code/code.asp

NASW. (2000). *Social work speaks: NASW policy statements—Environmental policy statement, 2000–2003.* Silver Spring, MD: NASW Press.

NASW & the Center for Workforce Studies. (2006). *Assuring the sufficiency of a frontline workforce: A national study of licensed social workers.* Retrieved June 3, 2006, from http://workforce.socialworkers.org/studies

Nathan, O., & Norden, H. (Eds.). (1981). *Einstein on peace.* New York: Avnel Books.

Neighborhood Reconciliation Services. (2007). *Repairing the harm caused by conflict.* Retrieved October 9, 2006, from http://www.nrsinc.org

Newcomb, P. (2002). 9/11: Our cultural, political and psychological response. *Families in Society: The Journal of Contemporary Human Services, 83*(2), 119–120.

Northouse, P. (2007). *Leadership: Theory and practice* (5th ed.). Thousand Oaks, CA: Sage.

Novotny, P. (1999, Fall). The post–cold war era, the Persian Gulf War, and the peace and justice movement in the 1990s. *Social Justice, 26*(3), 190–203.

O'Brien, C., & O'Brien, J. (1998). *Person-centered planning.* Toronto: Inclusion Press International.

Ornstein, R., & Ehrlich, P. (1989). *New world, new mind: Moving toward conscious evolution.* New York: Simon and Schuster.

Park, K. (1996). The personal is ecological: Environmentalism of social work. *Social Work, 41*(4), 320–323.

Parsons, T. (1951). *The social system.* New York: Free Press.

Parton, N. (2000). Some thoughts on the relationship between theory and practice in and for social work. *British Journal of Social Work, 30,* 449–463.

Payne, M. (2005). *Modern social work theory.* Chicago: Lyceum Books.

Pease, B., & Fook, J. (1999). *Transforming social work practice: Postmodern critical perspectives.* New York: Routledge.

Pedler, M., Bergoyne, J., & Boydell, T. (1991). *The learning company: A strategy for sustainable development.* London: McGraw-Hill.

Pew Center on Global Climate Change. (2007). *Global warming and the arctic—FAQ.* Retrieved October 7, 2000, from http://www.pewclimate.org/arctic-qa.cfm

Pew Research Center for the People and the Press. (2000, September 20). *Religion and politics: The ambivalent majority.* Retrieved October 9, 2007, from www.peoplepressorg/reports/display.php3?ReportID=32

Piaget, J. (1952). *The origins of intelligence in children.* New York: International University Press.

Popple, P., & Leighninger, L. (2005). *Social work, social welfare, and American society.* Boston: Allyn and Bacon.

Potapchuk, W. (2002). Neighborhood action initiative. In D. Chrislip (Ed.), *The collaborative leadership fieldbook* (pp. 170–186). San Francisco: Jossey Bass.

Prison Fellowship International, Restorative Justice Online. (n.d.). Retrieved October 9, 2007, from http://www.pfi.org

Proctor, E. (2002). Social work, school violence, work mental health, and drug abuse: A call for evidence-based practice. *Social Work Research, 26*(2), 65–69.

Prugh, T., & Assadourian, E. (2003, September/October). What is sustainability, anyway? *Worldwatch Magazine,* 10–21.

Putnam, R. (2000). *Bowling alone: The collapse and revival of American community.* New York: Simon and Schuster.

Raffoul, P., & McNeece, C. (Eds.). (1996). *Future issues for social work practice.* Needham Heights, MA: Allyn and Bacon.

Ramanathan, S., & Link, R. (1999). *All our futures: Principles and resources for social work practice in a global era.* Belmont, CA: Wadsworth.

Ray, P. (1996). *The integral culture study: A survey of the emergence of transformational values in America.* Sausalito, CA: Institute of Noetic Sciences.

Raymo, C. (2003). Celebrating creation. In P. Kurtz (Ed.), *Science and religion: Are they compatible?* New York: Prometheus Books.

Reid, W., & Fortune, A. (2003). Empirical foundations for practice guidelines in current social work knowledge. In A. Rosen & E. Proctor (Eds.), *Developing practice guidelines for social work intervention: Issues, methods and research agenda* (pp. 59–87). New York: Columbia University Press.

Reisch, M., & Gambrill, E. (Eds.). (1997). *Social work in the 21st century.* Thousand Oaks, CA: Pine Forge Press.

Renner, M. (1999) *Ending violent conflict* (Worldwatch Paper No. 146). Washington, DC: Worldwatch Institute.

Rensenbrink, J. (1988). *What Marx forgot, liberals have never known, and conservatives find frightening: The ecology of democracy.* Paper presented at the Annual Meeting of the American Political Science Association, Washington, DC.

Richardson, J. (1982). *Making it happen: A positive guide to the future.* Washington, DC: U.S. Association for the Club of Rome.

Rifkin, J. (1995). *The end of work.* New York: J. P. Putnam's Sons.

Rifkin, J. (1998). *The biotech century.* New York: Penguin Putnam.

Rifkin, J. (2000). *The age of access: The new culture of hypercapitalism where all of life is a paid-for experience.* New York: Jeremy P. Tarcher/Putnam

Rifkin, J. (2002). *The hydrogen economy.* New York: Jeremy P. Tarcher/Pergamon.

Rifkin, J. (2004a). *The European dream: How Europe's vision of the future is quietly eclipsing the American dream.* New York: Penguin Group.

Rifkin, J. (2004b, February 27). Presentation at plenary session of Annual Program Meeting of CSWE, Anaheim, CA.

Rioux, D. (1996). Shamanic healing techniques: Toward holistic addiction counseling. *Alcoholism Treatment Quarterly, 14*(1), 59–69.

Robbins, S., Chaterjee, P., & Canda, E. (1998). *Contemporary human behavior theory: A critical perspective for social work.* Boston: Allyn and Bacon.

Rodriguez, N. (2007). Restorative justice at work: Examining the impact of restorative justice resolutions on juvenile recidivism. *Crime and Delinquency, 53*(3), 355–379.

Rohter, I. (1992). *A green Hawaii.* Honolulu: Na Kane O Ka Malo.

Sachs, J. (2005). *The end of poverty: Economic possibilities for our time.* New York: Penguin Group.

Schiele, J. (1996, May 1). Afrocentricity: An emerging paradigm in social work practice. *Social Work, 41*(3), 284–294.

Schmidt, L. (2005, December 16). In the lab with the Dalai Lama. *Chronicle of Higher Education,* B10–B11.

Schorr, L. (1997). *Common purpose: Strengthening families and neighborhoods to rebuild America*. New York: Anchor Books.

Schriver, J. (2004). *Human behavior and the social environment: Shifting paradigms in essential knowledge for social work practice*. Boston: Pearson.

Schumacher, F. (1973). *Small is beautiful*. Vancouver: Harper-Collins.

Schweickart, R. (1983). No frames, no boundaries. In V. Hall (adaptor), Rediscovering the North American vision. *In Context, 13* (Summer), 16. Retrieved October 13, 2007, from http://www.context.org/ICLIB/IC03/schweik.htm

Shulman S. (1990, February 1). Sagan appeals to world religions' leaders. *Nature, 343*, 398.

*Scientific American.* (2005, September). *Crossroads for Planet Earth* [Special issue].

Scott, E. (2003). The science and religion movement: An opportunity for an approved pubic understanding of science. In P. Kurtz (Ed.), *Science and religion* (pp. 111–116). Amherst, NY: Prometheus Books.

Senge, P. (1990). *The fifth discipline: The act and practice of the learning organization*. London: Random House.

Senge, P., Kleiner, A., Roberts, C., Ross, R., Roth, G., & Smith, B. (1999). *The dance of change: The challenges to sustaining momentum in learning organizations*. New York: Doubleday.

Sheldrake, R. (1994). *The rebirth of nature: The greening of science and god*. Rochester, VT: Park Street Press.

Sheridan, M. (2000). Honoring angels in my path: Spiritually sensitive group work with persons who are incarcerated. In S. Abels (Ed.), *Spirituality in social work practice*. Denver, CO: Love Publishing Company.

Siporin, M. (1975). *Introduction to social work practice*. New York: MacMillan.

Sivard, R. (1996). *World military and social expenditures*. Washington, DC: Priorities Inc. Publishing.

Slaton, C., & Becker, T. (1990) A tale of two movements: ADR and the greens. In J. Burton & F. Dukes (Eds.), *Conflict: Readings in management and resolution*. New York: St. Martin's Press.

Slaton, C., Woolpert, S., & Schwerin, E. (1998). Introduction: What is transformational politics? In S. Woolpert, C. Slaton, & E. Schwerin (Eds.), *Transformational politics* (pp. xix–xxx), Albany: State University of New York Press.

Spayde, J. (1998, January–February). The new Renaissance. *Utne Reader, 42–47.*

Steinberg, S. (1995) *Ethnic cleansing, diversity, and education*. (Student paper available from Nancy L. Mary, California State University, San Bernardino)

Straus, M. (1994). *Beating the devil out of them: Corporal punishment in American families and its effects on children*. Boston: Lexington Books.

Stone, S. (2004). Reflecting on the social environment dimensions of HB and SE: An HB and SE faculty member as discussant. *Journal of Human Behavior and the Social Environment, 10*(3), 111–118.

Strahl, B. (2006). Nevada program uses mediation to assist the home-coming of released prisoners. *Voma Connections, 23*, 1–10.

Suzuki, D. (2006, January 27). *Climate change has unexpected effects—A guest commentary.* Retrieved February 6, 2007, from http://www.enn.com/today.html?id=9756

Taylor, S., Mulroy, E., & Austin, M. (2004). Social work textbooks on human behavior and the social environment: An analysis of the social environment component. *Journal of Human Behavior and the Social Environment, 10*(3), 85–110.

Thoreau, H. (1893). *Walden.* New York: Houghton Mifflin.

Turpin, J., & Kurtz, L. (1997). *The web of violence: From interpersonal to global.* Chicago: University of Illinois Press.

Umbreit, M., Vos, B., & Coates, R. (2005). *Opportunities and pitfalls facing the restorative justice movement.* Center for Restorative Justice and Peacemaking, University of Minnesota. Retrieved February 2, 2006, from http://www.rjp.umn.edu

Union of Concerned Scientists. (1992). *World scientists' warning to humanity.* Retrieved February 6, 2006, from http://www.ucsusa.org/ucs/about/1992-world-scientists-warning-to-humanity.htm

UN. (2002). *The Millennium Project report: A practical plan to achieving the millennium development goals 2002–2006.* Retrieved February 6, 2005, from http://www.unmellianprojects.org/reports

UN Chronicle. (1995). Giving peace a chance: Recognizing the achievement. *32*, 7–14. Retrieved October 21, 2004, from http://vnweb.hwwilsonweb.com/hww/results/results_single.jhtml?nn=65

UNEP. (2002). *Global environmental outlook 3: Past, present and future perspectives.* London: Earthscan Publications.

U.S. Department of Labor. (1990, September) Technology and labor in three service industries. *Bulletin 2367,* 19.

Van Den Bergh, N., & Cooper, L. (Eds.). (1986). *Feminist visions for social work.* Washington, DC: NASW Press.

Van Soest, D. (1992). *Incorporating peace and social justice into the social work curriculum.* Washington, DC: NASW Press.

Van Wormer, K. (2006). *Introduction to social welfare and social work: The U.S. in global perspective.* Belmont, CA: Thompson.

Van Wormer, K., Besthorn, F., & Keefe, T. (2007a). *Human behavior and the social environment: Macro level.* New York: Oxford University Press.

Van Wormer, K., Besthorn, F., & Keefe, T. (2007b). *Human behavior and the social environment: Micro level.* New York: Oxford University Press.

Vest, G., & Ronnau, J. (1997). Alternative health practices in ethnically diverse rural areas: A collaborative research project. *Health and Social Work, 22*(2), 95–103.

Waldrop, M. (1992) *Complexity: The emerging science at the edge of order and chaos.* New York: Touchstone (Simon and Schuster).

Walker, L. (2000, November/December). A Hawaii public housing community implements conferencing: A restorative approach to conflict resolution. *Journal of Housing and Community Development.* Retrieved October 9, 2007, from http://www.restoratvejustice.org/articlesdb/articles/5404

Watkins, K., & Marsick, V. (1992). Building the learning organization: A new role for human resource developers. *Studies in Continuing Education, 14*(2), 115–129.

Webber, A. (1999). Learning for a change. *Fast Company, 24,* 178. Retrieved October 9, 2007, from http://www.fastcompany.com/magune/24/singr.html

Weber, M. (1946). *Essays in sociology.* New York: Oxford University Press.

Weick, A. (1987). Beyond empiricism: Toward a holistic conception of social work. *Social Thought, 13*(4), 36–46.

Weiner, J. (1990). *The next one hundred years: Shaping the fate of our living earth.* New York: Bantam Books.

Weinhold, B., & Weinhold, J. (2000). *Conflict resolution: The partnership way.* Denver CO: Love Publishing.

Wheatley, M. (1999). *Leadership and the new science.* San Francisco: Berrett-Koehler.

Wheatley, M., & Kellner-Rogers, M. (1996). *A simpler way.* San Francisco: Berrett-Koehler.

Wilber, K. (2000). *The collected works of Ken Wilber.* Boston: Shambhala.

Wilkinson, R. (1997, December). A shifting paradigm: Modern restorative justice principles have their roots in ancient cultures [Editorial]. *Corrections Today.* Retrieved June 26, 2007, from http://www.drc.state.oh.us/web/Articles/article28.htm

Wilson, E. (1992). *The diversity of life.* Cambridge, MA: Harvard University Press.

Wilson, R., Prinzo, M., McWhinnie, A., Picheca, J., & Cortoni, F. (2007). Circles of support and accountability: Engaging community volunteers in the management of high-risk sexual offenders. *Howard Journal of Criminal Justice, 46*(1), 1–15.

Wilson, W. J. (1987). *The truly disadvantaged, the inner city, the underclass and public policy.* Chicago: University of Chicago Press.

Winer, M., & Ray, K. (2000). *Collaboration handbook.* St. Paul, MN: Amherst H. Wilder Foundation.

Wink, W. (Ed.). (2000). *Peace is the way: Writings on nonviolence from the Fellowship of Reconciliation.* Maryknoll, NY: Orbis Books & the Fellowship for Reconciliation.

Witkin, S., & Harrison W. (2001). Whose evidence and for what purpose? *Social Work, 46*(4), 293–296.

Woolpert, S., Slaton, C., & Schwerin, E. (1998). *Transformational politics: Theory, study, and practice.* Albany: State University of New York Press.

World Commission on Environment and Development. (1987). *Our common future.* London: Oxford University Press.

World Health Organization. (2000). Global mortality by cause, in World-watch Institute, *Vital Signs 2003* (p. 109). New York: W.W. Norton and Company.

Worldwatch Institute. (2003). *Vital signs: The trends that are shaping our future.* New York: W. W. Norton.

Zeitlin, M., Megawangi, R., Kramer, E., Colletta, N., Babatunde, E., & Garman, D. (1995). *Strengthening the family: Implications for international development.* New York: UN University Press.

Zoroya, G. (1993, July). Violence grows at county jails. *OC Register, 13,* 1–2.

# About the Author

Nancy L. Mary is a professor emerita at California State University, San Bernardino. She earned her MSW and DSW degrees from UCLA and an undergraduate degree from Pitzer College in Claremont, California. Working in Southern California in the field of developmental disabilities, she joined Cal State in 1989 to help develop a new MSW program. In June 2007, she retired from a rewarding career teaching students of social work to be with her garden, her Rhodesian Ridgebacks, her cats, her music, and her pursuit of writing. She may write a best-selling novel, or she may sit in a tree and learn to really play the ukulele. It's hard to say at this point.

# Index

Access to goods and services, age of, 113–115
  fairness and, 114
Accountability, in evaluating social service programs, 6–7
Accountability movement, social welfare and, 5
Addams, Jane, 150
Afrocentrism, 79, 81, 147
Agenda 21, UN, 101
Al-Krenawi, Alean, 83–84
Alternative health care, need for new paradigm for, 81–84
Alternative media, 185–186
Annie E. Casey Foundation, 179, 180
Aquinas, Thomas. *See* Thomas Aquinas
Arctic, warming of, 107
Arctic Council, 107
Aristotle, 16
Attractors, 54

Bacon, Francis, 16
Bateson, Gregory, 38
Beck, Bertram, 18
*Belonging to the Universe: Explorations on the Frontiers of Science and Spirituality* (Capra and Steindl-Rast), 72
Berry, Thomas, 1
Besthorn, Fred, 9
Biotechnology, challenges of, 108–110. *See also* Technology
Boiled frog syndrome, 34
Boundaries, 51–52
Bronx Frontier Development Market, 175
Brown, Lester, 35
Brundtland Report, 32–33
Butterfly effect, 53

Capitalism, 91, 157, 163
Capra, Fritjof, 15, 21, 49–50, 72
Caring communities, getting to, 150–151
Carson, Rachel, 24, 35
Center for Partnership Studies, 188
Change, personal, 194–195
Chaos theory, 52–56, 139
Charity Organization Society, 67
Chittister, Sister Joan, 187
Citizen empowerment, 176
Citizen involvement, 136
Climate change, 34
Closed systems, 51–52
Club of Rome, 93
Coates, John, 21–22, 43
Code of ethics, NASW, 6, 160
Cole, Olivia, 184
Collaboration
  government/community partnerships and, 174–175
  leadership and, 63–65
Collective learning, 62
Communities of caring, creating, 141
Community, 164
Community-based initiatives, 42
Community development, 176
  case study of, 60–61
  new systems thinking and, 58–59
Community empowerment, 176
Conflict perspective, of social work, 155–156
Consciousness, 75
  evolution to spiritual, 190–191
  Wilber and, 75–76
Constructivism, 78
Consumption, in U.S., 165
Copernicus, 16